Speaking Effectively

Speaking Effectively

JAMES WOOD

University of Texas—El Paso

RANDOM HOUSE   NEW YORK

First Edition

987654321

Copyright © 1988 by Random House, Inc.

Library of Congress Cataloging-in-Publication Data

Wood, James A. (James Allen)
  Speaking effectively / James A. Wood.
    p.   cm.
  Bibliography: p.
  Includes index.
  ISBN 0-394-32779-9
  1. Public speaking.   I. Title.
PN4121.W57 1988
808.5'1—dc19   87-22935
                            CIP

Book Development: Domenig and Henry; Executive Editor: Roth Wilkofsky

Manuscript Editor: Tom Holton; Production Manager: David Saylor

Text design: Leon Bolognese

Cover design: David Lindroth

Cover Art: Theodore Roszak
        Construction In White 1937
        National Museum of American Art, Smithsonian Institution;
        Gift of the Sara Roby Foundation

Manufactured in the United States of America

Preface

This book is guided by the assumption that students will use a public speaking textbook primarily for one highly pragmatic reason: to become more confident and effective speakers. The value of a textbook and course in public speaking is proved later, outside the course when students face a variety of speaking situations. In those situations the speaker's needs will be best served by a sound sense of method in preparation, by insight into what works to achieve intended purposes with each particular audience, and by recognition of speechmaking as a creative extension of the speaker's individual personality.

This view of student needs governs the orientation and structural strategy of *Speaking Effectively*.

Orientation of the Book

Four general aims define the orientation of the book.

First, I have sought to emphasize a rational, audience-centered method for preparation of a speech which, flexibly applied, will serve the speaker in virtually any situation. This method, most of it familiar to speech professors, is a process that is broken down into six major steps:

1. Decide on a specific purpose for the speech.
2. Obtain material for the speech.
3. Plan the basic structure.
4. Fill in basic structure with supporting materials.
5. Do final planning, including introduction, transitions, and conclusion.
6. Practice and present the speech.

This six-step process is introduced in Chapter 1, enabling students to apply the process in preparing their first speeches. More detailed development of the process occurs in Chapters 4 through 9, and special applications to persuasion appear in Chapter 10. Such explicit emphasis on process provides the student speaker a clearly charted path through efficient preparation and a framework within which to organize and remember detailed techniques and strategies in speech preparation.

For this emphasis on step-by-step process to be viable it must be realistic in terms of what actually happens in speech preparation. Adaptation to audience is essential in speechmaking. Therefore discussions of audience analysis and other situational factors occur frequently and are developed appropriately for each step in speech preparation where such analysis is applied, rather than being covered as one separate step in preparation. In selecting a topic to fit the situation a speaker thinks of the audience in a somewhat different way, for example, than when selecting and shaping supporting materials.

The text not only recognizes that various applications of theory overlap among steps in preparation, but also helps the student to understand and take advantage of such overlapping. For example, choice of language is discussed, in different aspects, in relation both to outline planning and to rehearsal, because effective speakers frequently work on phrasing key headings and major transitions at the outline stage and work on additional polishing of language during rehearsal. Similarly, a speaker is well advised to reevaluate specific purpose after initial gathering of ideas and research.

The second general aim is to provide the student at each step with detailed guidance that can be readily understood and applied. To ensure student speakers practical help at every point in preparation I have drawn from sources as diverse as Aristotle and Chaim Perelman, as well as from my own teachers and colleagues. I have also frequently learned from my students' comments, problems, and strokes of inspired genius. Material is selected according to its value in meeting students' practical needs. Some matters, such as planning basic structure and using rehearsal are given detailed treatment. On the other hand, less useful theory and research findings are given less space or are entirely avoided.

To make instructional concepts clear and more readily applicable, examples and sample outlines are used extensively. Checklists, such as tests for a good specific purpose and possible places to use transitions, provide quick, convenient ways for a student to discover how to add strength or avoid weakness at different points in planning. Abbreviated case studies are frequently used to develop insight into how choices in speech planning are actually made.

My third aim is to encourage understanding of speechmaking as a creative expression of the speaker's personality. In such matters as organizational strategy and selection of supporting material, the student speaker is in control and makes creative choices to achieve a specific purpose. To foster this sense of personal decision making, instructional guidance is frequently offered in the form of options, guidelines, or suggestions rather than rules. In gathering and shaping material for the speech considerable emphasis is placed on the speaker's use of personal resources, such as background knowledge and imaginative adaptation to the particular audience, and on use of other sources in addition to library research. The student speaker who regards speechmaking as creative and personal expression, rather than as mechanically processing information or fulfilling formulas, seems more likely to enjoy a public speaking course and to be prepared for later speaking experiences that rely largely on creative use of personal resources.

The fourth general aim is to provide insight into *why* speakers use particular methods and techniques. Why does a speaker use an outline to plan the organization of a speech? What functions are performed by different sorts of supporting materials? Under what circumstances would a persuasive speaker use one organizational strategy rather than another? The speaker is encouraged to understand that many suggestions are worth following because they increase efficiency in preparation or they contribute to the basic qualities—clarity, interest, credibility, and appropriateness—which characterize effective speaking. Insight into the purposes and appropriate circumstances for applying suggestions encourages students to try the suggestions. More important, it also enables them to adapt and exercise choice more skillfully in new situations they will encounter outside the speech course.

Structure of the Book

The overall structure of the book reflects the notion that growth in skill takes place largely as an expanding understanding of a limited number of basic principles. Part I provides basic principles of method and an understanding of communication activity. Part II provides more detailed resources for skill in each step in the method for speech preparation. Method does not occur in the abstract; therefore, the description in Part II is mainly in terms of informative speeches. Early in Part II the distinction between informative and other sorts of speeches is explained as an aspect of adaptation to the situation in which the speech occurs. Part III expands and adapts application of the method of preparation to persuasive speeches, special occasion speeches, and group discussion.

Part I Since the primary aim of students is to learn how to give speeches, Chapter 1 immediately explains what a speech is and provides a basic understanding of six steps by which a speaker prepares and presents one. The student is shown a process for moving from specific purpose and raw material through basic structure and addition of detail to final outline plan. For the last step, presentation of the speech, Chapter 1 deals with important needs of the inexperienced speaker: seeing a speech as communication rather than performance, dealing with nervous tension, and using rehearsal. By the end of Chapter 1 students should be able to handle speeches of some substance requiring out-of-class preparation.

The next two chapters reflect on public speaking in a broader perspective. Chapter 2 discusses the relation of public speaking both to the broader range of communication activity and to the needs and character of the student. Chapter 3 deals with listening skills, particularly as these are applied in obtaining information, in evaluating persuasion, and in critiquing speeches.

Part II Each of the six steps in the method for preparing a speech treated briefly in Chapter 1 is now elaborated on in a separate chapter.

Chapter 4 explains how speech preparation begins with analysis of the speaker's resources, the occasion, and the audience. These three aspects of situation guide the speaker in discovering a topic area and shaping a specific purpose.

In Chapter 5 the process of gathering material is separated into an initial survey of the speaker's own mind and possible sources for material, a detailed research stage which may draw on library and other print materials, observation, interviewing, and chance sources, as well as personal resources, and finally a stage (used only occasionally) when the speaker must return to fill in gaps which do not become apparent until later stages of preparation.

Chapters 6, 7, and 8 carry the student through the process of planning organization from research and initial ideas to final outline and speaking notes.

Chapter 6 introduces the student to functions of organization for speaker and audience and to the rationale for an outline in planning. It provides method for discovering and selecting the structure of mainheads and major subheads and for checking basic structure. Common patterns for informative speeches are explained and illustrated.

Chapter 7 explains how verbal and visual supporting materials are added to the basic structure in order to accomplish certain functions for the particular audience and purpose.

Chapter 8 begins by suggesting that the student review the structure of the body planned so far. This review helps to guide the student in forming an introduction, transitions, and a conclusion adapted to the particular purpose and audience and in revising the phrasing of major idea headings on the outline. The last section in Chapter 8 provides a model and guidelines for the detailed outline which most commonly culminates written planning of a major speech. Possible reasons and forms for alternative levels of detail on a final outline as well as use of speaking notes are explained.

Chapter 9 explains the attitudes underlying effective and confident presentation of a speech. Detailed attention is given to use of rehearsal to expand and improve both choice of language and techniques of vocal and physical delivery. Other modes of delivery, such as speaking impromptu or from a manuscript, are discussed in detail.

Sense of method is reinforced by exercises in which a student works step by step on a major informative speech as the class goes through the chapters in Part II. In addition, short classroom presentations focus on the major concern of each chapter.

Part III   These chapters provide a variety of opportunities for extending skills in public speaking.

In Chapter 10 a treatment of audience analysis specifically for persuasion lays the foundation for a pragmatic explanation of modes of appeal and organizational strategy. The chapter ends with a brief treatment of the six-step process adapted to the uses of the persuasive public speaker.

Chapter 11 extends speech preparation skills to common ceremonial occasions and to occasions calling for conflict reduction speeches.

Chapter 12 deals with the aims, structures, and participation skills in both private and public group discussion.

Resources for Instruction

In the Appendix, an essay on "Sources for Further Reading" directs the interested student or class to eleven significant, commonly available works in classical and contemporary rhetorical theory. The essay introduces major theorists who provided much of the foundation for this book.

The *Instructor's Manual* outlines alternative course structures, contains critique sheets and checklists that can be photocopied, and provides suggestions for increasing instructional effectiveness in meeting particular challenges of public speaking courses. Exercises in the *Instructor's Manual* help provide thorough in-class practice on each step as well as broader application of theory through observation and discussion.

Acknowledgments

Three people have my special gratitude for support far beyond professional assistance: Tom Treat, for initiating my interest in this project and for encouragement at crucial moments; Rosalind Federman, heroic worker of miracles as a typist; and above all, Kathleen Domenig, for her unfailing friendship and humor and for persistently applying her remarkable editorial expertise to my stubborn notions of what an introductory speech text should be. I am also permanently grateful to Roth Wilkofsky for his benign patience in allowing this project to run its course to completion. Among the many other people who helped this book along the way, I'd like especially to note Tom Holton at Random House, Philip Metcalf and Kirsten Olson previously at Random House, and Judy Gill and Helen Bell in El Paso.

The professors who offered comments at various stages in this project should know that I read and reread their reviews with care and profit. In some places their influence will be obvious; in others it is less direct. In all cases I appreciate the thoughtful assistance. These reviewers include: Clifton Cornwell, University of Missouri, Columbia; Jeanne W. Creech, DeKalb College; Jack W. Deskin, Central State University, Oklahoma; L. Patrick Devlin, University of Rhode Island; Thurston E. Doler, Oregon State University; Thurmon Garner, The University of Georgia; Nancy Goulden, Kansas State University; Michael T. Hayes, Wichita State University; Wayne E. Hensley, Virginia Polytechnic Institute and State University; Richard W. Massa, Missouri Southern State College; Fred McMahon, California State University, Northridge; Paul J. Kaufman, Iowa State University; Mary H. Pelias, Southern Illinois University, Carbondale; Janice Peterson, Santa Barbara City College; Lonnie Polson, Bob Jones University; John H. Powers, Texas A & M University; J. Dan Rothwell, Western Washington University; John Kares Smith, State University of New York at Oswego; Larry G. Schnoor, Mankato State University; Jack Stokes, Belleville Area College; W. F. Strong, Oregon State University; William E. Wiethoff, Indiana University.

Contents

PART II
Techniques for
Speech Preparation and Presentation 47

Chapter 4 Analyzing Situation and Deciding on a Specific Purpose 48

Chapter 5 Obtaining Material for the Speech 67

Chapter 6 Planning Basic Structure 84

PART III
Further Development of
Speech-Communication Skills   199

PART I

Understanding What Happens in Effective Public Speaking

PART I

CHAPTER ONE

Aims and Method in Preparation: Your First Speeches

A person gives a speech to achieve an effect on an audience. The effects that speakers seek range widely in type and importance. A student wants his audience to know more about the challenges of a job delivering phone-ordered pizzas. An engineer needs to explain to his technical staff the results of some recent research in laser technology. A sales manager wants to persuade her clerks to be more alert and polite in serving customers. A taxpayer wants to convince others at a public meeting to support higher county taxes to maintain needed social services. A student wants to persuade a faculty-student committee not to abandon funding for an activity she considers important.

True, the initial intent of most students beginning a speech course is to learn and practice some techniques of public speaking, or at least to survive the course with some composure and a satisfactory grade. But remember also that in this class, as elsewhere, you are an individual with personal information, ideas, and opinions, and you have listeners willing to hear what you have to say. Even in a speech class you gain confidence and skill faster when you think of your speeches as informing or persuading your classmates—achieving an effect—rather than just as exercises to fulfill an instructor's requirements or as ordeals to be survived.

Your speeches can be highly effective even though you may be nervous when you give them. As a matter of fact, the great majority of speakers, professionals as well as beginners, are nervous when they rise to speak. Experienced speakers triumph over the nervousness of the moment, however, because they have a deep-seated confidence that they know how to handle the task. They are confident because they understand what is involved in public speaking and have developed specific skills and techniques to cope successfully with the situation.

This chapter will provide a beginning understanding of what a public speech is and how you go about efficiently preparing a good one. Practical experience does much to build confidence, and having this information will enable you to begin immediately developing your first speeches in the course.

A Speech as Response of Speaker to Occasion and Audience

With surprisingly few exceptions, such as soapbox orators in the park, the occasion calls for the speech rather than the speaker creating the occasion. In a speech course it may seem artificial for you to be assigned to give a certain sort of speech on a certain day. In your later career, however, most of your speaking will be in response to similar "assignments"—from your boss or the company, from the role you have taken as an officer in an organization, as a spokesperson for a group, or in a variety of other ways. A lawyer does not design brilliant defense speeches and then try to find cases and clients to fit the speeches.

The Situation and the Speaker

The situation—the particular occasion that has brought these listeners together—will always place some limits on the speaker. If you are asked to present an award to someone for a particular achievement and you are expected to do it in two minutes, you do not have much freedom of choice in what you will talk about. Neither does the swimming instructor in front of a class or the salesperson addressing a group of prospective customers. On the other hand, if a local civic organization asks you to talk about your travels in the Himalaya Mountains, or your high school wants a speech telling the seniors what they can expect in college, you have a good deal of freedom within a broad topic area. You have even more freedom if your speech instructor assigns you to give an eight-minute informative speech, with no specification as to topic. But even here, your freedom may be less than you expect, if you adapt successfully to the situation. A speech on how you trained your dog to do tricks may suffice for a warm-up speech early in the course, but on later rounds your audience may expect somewhat more complex or significant topics. Some occasions call for you to try to persuade the listeners to your point of view, others call for you to provide objective information.

Virtually any situation will limit the speaker, whether rigidly or informally, to a certain amount of time for the presentation. The speaker adapts the breadth of her topic and the level of detail to fit this time frame.

A skillful or ambitious speaker uses adaptation to situation as a positive stimulus, rather than merely as a restriction. During preparation she thinks about such questions as these: In what aspects of the topic are my listeners likely to be most interested? What kinds of information do they hope for or expect me to provide on the occasion? What examples or other supporting detail can I use to make this idea clearer or more interesting to this particular audience?

This emphasis on adapting to audience and occasion may suggest that the speaker's own inclinations and opinions are not important. On the contrary, when preparing and presenting a speech you make a multitude of creative choices, choices that reflect your own personality. You may select the topic; and even if the general topic is assigned, you usually may decide what slant to take on it. For example, if you are a movie buff who accepts an invitation to speak on old movies to the classic car club, your topic—old movies—is assigned. However, you decide that in this speech your slant will be to show with film clips how the silent film comedians Keaton and Chaplin deserve special appreciation just as do classic cars. You also decide what main ideas to emphasize, how to develop those ideas, and how to handle yourself vocally and physically in giving the speech. Your most satisfying speeches are likely to be ones that skillfully adapt your own ideas and creativity to the requirements of the occasion and the nature of the audience. This will be true both in speech class and after.

The Basic Qualities of an Effective Speech

What makes one speech more effective than another? We are more likely to judge a speech a good one, or to be affected by it as the speaker intends, if the speech seems *appropriate*, if it seems reliable or *credible*, if it is *clear*, and if it is *interesting*. Is this not true of your own reactions to speakers, even instructors in other courses? We have already considered the first quality in terms of appropriateness to situation and speaker. In a sense, appropriateness is the broadest of all the qualities, because when we judge if a speech is clear, credible, and interesting, we are asking if it is clear, credible, and interesting to the specific audience for that speech.

The relative importance of these qualities varies according to different situations. For a speech on UFOs to a high school assembly or a civic organization, interest is likely to be most important. For a sales manager explaining to new clerks how to operate cash registers, clarity is most important. For a speech urging a new tax policy, credibility may be most important.

Often, listeners' judgments about these qualities are made subconsciously. A listener does not usually decide, for example, whether his interest in the speech is caused by the novel examples, or by the speaker's energetic delivery, or by the fact that the speaker is drawing on her unusual experiences. Nor is a listener likely to decide consciously whether the credibility of the speech is caused by the speaker's control over her material so that it comes out in a fluent and well-organized way, by her citation of factual information from several sources, or by her personal experience with the topic. Clarity, likewise, is the result of a great variety of techniques, ranging from an easily audible voice and a carefully planned organization to the liberal use of examples, visual aids, or other specific detail to give distinct meaning to major ideas.

Perfection in all four qualities, as with most undertakings in life, is rarely achieved. Do, however, keep appropriateness, clarity, interest, and credibility

Effective speakers adapt their own ideas and interests to the audience and the occasion. (Susan Lapides/Design Conceptions)

in mind as you plan a speech. These qualities, as aims, help guide your choice and application of the techniques you will learn in this course. And they, together with a sense of purpose, are far more important as guides in preparing and presenting a speech than are any "rules" you could learn. Realize also that you already have some ability to achieve these qualities—the ability to use an interesting example from your personal experience, for instance.

How does one produce an effective speech? Creativity and effort play a big part, but you can use your energy much more efficiently if you add method. First understand the product you are aiming to create—that is, learn the anatomy of a speech—then you can more skillfully apply a method for preparing that product. We will look first at product and then at method.

Anatomy of a Typical Speech

There are two basic ways of thinking about what a speech is. One way is to think of it as so many minutes of talking. The other is to think of it as a unified strategy aimed to achieve a specific effect within a given time limit. The latter view is more likely to produce satisfying results for the speaker and for the audience.

It isn't really stretching the point to think of a good speech as akin to a work of art such as a painting or a play. In both, all the parts contribute to a central purpose, and thus the work is unified. The speaker calculates what will be used in the speech, where, and why. Like plays and short stories, most speeches unfold in a sequence that carries the audience through a planned progression of ideas in order to produce the intended effect.

The Parts of a Speech

Normally a speech has three main parts: introduction, body, and conclusion. Each of these parts has its own functions in the speech. (You will get a clearer notion of the anatomy of a speech if you turn to the sample speech, "A Sport for the Electronic Age," pages 8–10, and spot the items on the outline as you read about them in the next few pages.)

The Introduction   One necessary task of the introduction is to tell your audience what your speech is about. You do this with a *statement of focus* early in the speech. At this stage in a speech course it is usually best to state the focus bluntly and directly, and be sure it stands out clearly in the presented speech: "Today I want to explain how you can use dead-bolt locks to make your home more secure."

In almost all situations, a polished speaker will lead up to her statement of focus with at least a few sentences of other introductory material. This introductory material may be used to make the listeners more interested in the speech, perhaps with a striking example that relates to the topic or with a brief explanation of the speaker's special qualifications on the topic.

The Body   In the statement of focus you tell your audience what you are going to do. In the body of the speech you do it. An audience is more interested in a speech if they can see some key ideas and if the speech appears to be going somewhere rather than just rambling around a general topic. Thus even a speech that is only a few minutes long is almost always clearer and more satisfying for the audience if some planned structure is imposed on material in the speech.

The body is divided into a few main sections. For each main section, a *mainhead* is used by the speaker to tell the audience the central point of that main section. For example, in a speech on cooking in a wok pan, the specific slant is how to prepare a chicken and vegetable dish. The body of the speech is divided into three main sections: preparing the ingredients, actual cooking, and serving. The statement of focus plus mainheads could appear like this:

Statement of focus: I will show how to use a wok in preparing a chicken and vegetable dish.

I. The first step is to prepare three sorts of ingredients for the wok.
II. The next step is to do the actual cooking in the wok, which takes place in stages.
III. The third step is to serve the chicken and vegetables.

Each of the mainheads in the speech in some way develops or supports the statement of focus.

In most speeches, each main section in the body is divided into subsections. Each subsection develops some more limited aspect of the mainhead under which it falls. A *subhead* is used to state the central idea of a subsection. In speeches that are intended to convey a fairly complex pattern of ideas, you may have two or more levels of these subheads.

Supporting material is used to make the ideas in the mainheads and subheads clear and credible, and to make the speech interesting. Common types of supporting material that you are likely to use in early speeches include specific examples from your present knowledge and personal experience, explanations of processes, and visual aids in the form of charts or objects. Other types that you are likely to use as you go on to do library research include quoting or citing the opinions of experts on your topic, and using statistics and factual examples you encounter in your reading.

Transitions—phrases and sentences in addition to the idea headings and the supporting materials—are planned specifically to lead the audience clearly from one section to the next and to emphasize key ideas. At the end of the first main section of the body, the speaker on wok cooking could use as a transition (in parentheses):

(Now that you have your meat, vegetables, and sauce all laid out, you are ready for the next step.)
II. The next step is to do the actual cooking in the wok, which takes place in stages.

The body, then, is an interweaving of three elements: ideas in mainheads and subheads, supporting materials, and transitions.

The Conclusion The audience should feel that a speaker is ending his speech smoothly and in control of the situation, rather than just running out of something to say and sitting down. A planned conclusion enables the speaker to end with that sense of control and polish. The most common sort of conclusion is a summary of main ideas from the body of the speech. Other sorts include a remark or two that ties back into the introduction or that suggests how the audience can apply the content of the speech. The conclusion should avoid raising new ideas that actually belong in the body of the speech.

We see that the core of the speech is the body. The introduction paves the way for the body, and the conclusion wraps the speech up smoothly.

A Sample Outline

This anatomy of a typical speech is illustrated by the following outline for a speech about seven minutes long. Developing an outline is usually your best way to prepare the content of a speech, so this sample outline may also give you an idea of what to aim for in your own written planning. (The left column is only to clarify the anatomy of the outline. Ordinarily you would not do this on your own outlines.)

Title (for person who introduces you)	**A SPORT FOR THE ELECTRONIC AGE**
	Introduction
Linking of topic to audience	I. Have you noticed how many different places downtown or in shopping centers you are likely to see people playing video games? A. In arcades, but also in restaurants, bowling alleys, theater lobbies, even grocery stores. B. Twenty-two billion quarters last year.
Linking of topic to speaker	II. I confess to being hooked on them enough to play three or four times a week.
Statement of focus	III. Today, I'm going to explain why, I think, people play arcade video games.
Transition preoutlining mainheads in body	(There seem to be two main reasons: to meet and be with other people, and to practice a skill.)
	Body
Mainhead: first main idea	I. Meeting other people is one reason a video game addict spends money in an arcade rather than playing on his home TV set.
Subhead: idea	A. You share something with strangers, as well as friends, who have the same interests as you.

Supporting material	1. Example of playing Gorf against restaurant waitress.
Supporting material	2. Example of showing stranger how to get through mine field in Moon Patrol.
Subhead: idea	B. You can meet different sorts of people at different arcades.
Supporting material	1. Family atmosphere at some; pro players, teen-agers, hoods, or a mixture at others.
Supporting material	2. Example: why I usually go to "Magic Land" rather than "Detour."
Transition to help audience move from section I to section II	(So, arcade video game players do meet people, and they can even pick the sorts of people they meet by where they go to play. But that's only part of why they go to arcades.)
Mainhead: second main idea	II. The second reason people play arcade video games is that practicing their skills produces some real satisfactions.
Subhead: idea	A. Good players have concentrated eye-hand coordination to adapt to a shifting visual field.
Supporting material	1. Chart-sketch of Defender screen.
Supporting material	2. Coping while thinking ahead, as in basketball or boxing.
Supporting material	3. Quote Professor Hall on reacting to configurational field as part of life in electronic age.
Transition to show shift from A to B and C	(Using these skills leads to some personal satisfactions.)
Subhead: idea	B. You are always challenging yourself to improve strategies and skills.
Supporting material	1. Variety of types of strategies, as in Pac Man, Rally X, Star Gate, and Donkey Kong.

Supporting material

2. Example of my breakthrough from second to fifth level in Super Cobra.

Subhead: idea.

C. Other people watch and respect good players.

Supporting material.

1. Similar to performance in music or athletics.

Supporting material

2. Example of group following guy around as he set day's record on four machines.

Conclusion

Link back to audience

I. When you are near a video game room and have some time, why not drop in and see if you agree with my reasons why people play the arcades?

Summary of main points from body of speech in A and B

A. You will probably discover mostly pleasant people who feel comfortable in each other's company.

B. You could also spot a good player and watch concentration and coordination as he challenges himself to run up a top score.

Link back to introduction

II. If you are not careful, though, you may start with a few quarters and end up being another contributor to a multi-billion dollar industry.

Note that in this outline, the phrasing of key headings and transitions is planned carefully in an oral style that could actually be used in the presented speech. Items of supporting material, however, are often only indicated by short sentences or phrases. Although this is just one method of doing an outline, it is often a good one because it draws your close attention to wording those key headings and transitions that convey your main ideas and enable the audience to follow the organization of the speech. Precise phrasing of supporting material is usually not so important. Later in this chapter we will recognize situations that might call for less detail in outline form.

Using Method to Prepare a Speech

The ability to use a step-by-step method, however flexibly, is itself an important skill for a speaker (and a writer) to develop, for several reasons.

First, a method helps you avoid mental blocks that sometimes paralyze writers or speakers. Method provides a relatively painless way to get preparation started, and it tells you what you can do next at each step along the way. A second advantage of method is efficiency. For example, if you know how to select a good topic in the first place, you avoid wasting time by jumping from topic to topic; and if you know the steps to take before library research, you can avoid gathering piles of notes you will never be able to use. A third advantage is that a sound method provides you with the techniques that can be used and the points to be checked at each stage in preparation, and thus increases the likelihood that you will make the shrewdest and most creative decisions at each point in preparation.

Beginning with your first speeches, then, consciously apply method in your preparation. It will usually pay off in the speeches you give in class, and skill in using a method is itself an important part of what you should get out of the course.

The great majority of speeches given in speech classes and in personal and professional life afterward use the *extemporaneous method*. In this method the speaker plans the structure and supporting material of the speech, often over a period of several days or weeks, rehearses the speech a few times, and presents it relying on some combination of this advance planning and the conversational spontaneity of the moment for phrasing in delivery. He has a plan he can rely on, but he avoids a word-for-word manuscript or memorization.

This last point is worth emphasizing. For inexperienced speakers especially, word-for-word preparation usually produces monotonous delivery and a lack of adequate attention to clear organization. True, your instructor may not be able to assign speeches longer than seven or eight minutes. You could write these out and you could perhaps even memorize them. But will you be able to do so when you have to give a half-hour speech on relatively short notice? Or would you even want to? In speech preparation there are usually much better ways to spend your time than laboriously writing out speeches word for word. The opposite extreme, a speech plan that consists of only a few brief headings, often produces a rambling and not very effective speech, but at least its delivery is usually more listenable than is that of the manuscript speech. (Later in the course, your instructor may have you do manuscript speeches to develop some special skills with language choice and manuscript delivery, but right now we are concerned with basic, all-purpose skills.)

Six Steps in Speech Preparation

In this book, the method for speech preparation is divided into six steps. Explanation in this and later chapters is intended to help develop your ability to use the method flexibly as a sequential process that makes sense and to expand your understanding of what can be done at each step in the process.

Step 1: Decide on a Specific Purpose for the Speech   Search your own interests, concerns, experiences, and beliefs to discover a topic about which you have at least some feeling or knowledge. Better yet, discover two or three such topics, so that you can choose the one that is most comfortable for you, is most likely to interest the audience, and best fits the assignment.

It is often advisable to reshape your initial idea into a more distinct and narrower specific purpose. A student began by intending to tell his audience about "My job in a grocery store last summer." He realized, however, that this purpose was too broad and vague. After some thought about what he had actually learned on his job, he focused on a narrower aspect of the topic that would be more manageable for him and more interesting to his audience. He can now define the specific purpose for his speech: To inform the audience how merchandise is arranged to tempt customers. He concludes step 1 by phrasing his statement of focus for the audience: "This morning I will explain how stock in a grocery store is arranged to encourage impulse buying of unneeded items."

At this point, be just a bit tentative in your commitment to the purpose and the statement of focus as they stand. As you move through the next two steps, you may discover that you want to modify somewhat your specific purpose for the speech, and then you will change your statement to the audience.

Step 2: Discover Ideas and Other Material   Gather a supply of general points that could be made about your topic, as well as examples and other specific detail from which to develop the speech. The more of this material you have to choose from as you go through the later steps of preparation, the better your speech will probably be. Most of this raw material comes from three sorts of places: your own mind, what you run across more or less by chance while you are preparing the speech, and deliberate research in print material and by interview.

The best way to begin gathering ideas and other material is to ransack your own mind. If you want your listeners to obey legal speed limits what reasons can you give them? What examples of close-call driving can you draw from your own or friends' experience? Why do you or other people speed? What is wrong with these reasons for speeding? Have any accidents caused by speeding been reported recently in the news? What other crimes can speeding be compared with? Such questions about your own topic may help you discover main points, examples, and other material already in your mind.

After you start this process of searching your own mind, you may also decide to do some research in the library or in other sources. Take notes on both what you think of and what you encounter in other sources, even in conversation.

Step 3: Plan Basic Structure   There comes a time when you decide on your basic plan for the speech. This basic structure is the statement of focus plus the mainheads in the body of the speech. How can you divide your topic into a few main sections or main points? If no such division seems obvious in the material, don't be afraid to take charge—to say, "These are the *main* points *I* want to make about this topic." Your plan may also include the major subheads under each mainhead.

Keep the basic plan simple, usually no more than three or four mainheads. Sometimes only two will do. Similarly, if you plan subheads, divide material under each mainhead into as few subheads as you logically can. You cannot expect an audience to understand a large number or a complicated pattern of ideas in a short speech.

Step 4: Fill in Basic Structure with Detail   Draw on material you gathered in step 2 to fill in specific examples and other detail under each of the headings in your basic structure. You may also want to do some further creative thinking or research.

The speaker on "A Sport for the Electronic Age," outlined earlier in this chapter, drew on his notes for two personal examples to support his first major subhead, that "You share something with strangers, as well as friends, who have the same interests as you." For a later subhead, that "Good players have concentrated eye-hand coordination to adapt to a shifting visual field," he used a wider variety of material: a visual aid, a comparison of video games to basketball and boxing, and a quote from his philosophy professor.

Step 5: Complete the Written Planning   In this step the speaker looks over his planning so far to see if he can make any final improvements in organization or selection of material for the body of the speech. He also adds an introduction and a conclusion to his plan, either by creating them at this point or by drawing on ideas that have already occurred to him. For example, as he moved through the preceding steps in preparation, he may have thought of ways to link the topic to the audience or to himself in the introduction and to summarize or otherwise wrap up the speech in the conclusion. He also adds to the plan any transitional material he intends to use in the body of the speech.

As you make these final decisions in your own planning you will probably have several different sheets of paper—an overview outline of main ideas on one sheet, some sheets of idea notes, a sheet with one main section planned in considerable detail, an example to arouse interest in the introduction on another sheet, and so forth. That is fine. Scattered through this mess of notes is your plan. However, this is not a very handy set of notes from which to practice and deliver the speech.

Therefore, use the notes to prepare a neat, coherent outline of your speech. The outline is a visual picture of your plan. Run through the speech aloud from beginning to end once or twice before doing the final version of the outline. This permits you to check the length of the speech against the time limit. You may also make improvements—a clearer way to state a main idea, for instance, or a better example—that don't occur to you until you hear yourself give the speech aloud.

How detailed should your outline be? For major speeches, the sample on pages 8–10 provides a good level of detail: Writing out idea headings and major transitions as they could be stated in the presented speech will give you confidence that you have the organization under control and can make it clear to the audience. Such a detailed outline may contain as much as 30 percent to 50 percent as many words as the presented speech. For short speeches in less demanding situations, however, your instructor may suggest a somewhat simpler sort of planning.

Let's follow the planning for a speech that might be given early in a public speaking course. We will go back to begin with the first steps of finding a topic and specific purpose and discovering ideas and materials.

The speaker is assigned to speak on some personal experience, gripe, or belief. When looking for a topic, she remembers dropping out of an art class because of some rather vicious criticism of her work by her teacher and a few fellow students. So in beginning her preparation she decides to use her speech as a chance to complain against hostile criticism. She thinks of an English composition teacher she had in the tenth grade who put nothing but red marks and negative criticism on her papers. This reminds her of how her composition teacher the next year restored some of her confidence by pointing out what she did successfully, as well as what wasn't so good, in her writing. A friend tells her about his basketball coach who not only urged him to play more aggressively but also explained how. As she ransacks her mind and talks to friends and accumulates more notes, her specific purpose in the speech shifts somewhat. She decides to be more positive and explain what good criticism is.

She decides to make three points about good criticism: it's balanced, it's honest, and it's constructive. She had put down a fourth point—good criticism is accurate—but later discarded it because that idea seemed to overlap somewhat with her other points and because three main points seemed plenty to develop in a four- or five-minute speech. She groups the examples in her notes under the three main points, and then she selects in each group the one or two examples that seem most likely to clarify the point and interest her audience.

She adds an introduction that links the topic to both herself and the class, plans a conclusion, and times her rough draft by saying the speech aloud as best she can. She is now ready to prepare her final outline.

Because she is comfortably familiar with the material and because the structure of the speech is simple enough for the audience to follow easily, she decides to show the pattern of ideas by just brief topic headings. Her outline looks like this:

Introduction

I. Dropped art course because of criticism.
II. Will all be criticizing each other in speech class.
III. (Focus) This morning I'm going to describe three qualities of good criticism.

Body

I. First quality: balanced between positive and negative.
    A. Tenth-grade English teacher, all bad; hurt confidence.
    B. Eleventh grade teacher, some good and some bad; raised confidence.
II. Second quality: honest.
    A. My comment on friend's dress for party.
    B. Would want from family critic when practicing a speech.
III. Third quality: constructive.
    A. Shows how to improve.
    B. History teacher who looked at my class notes and exams.
    C. Joe's basketball coach on aggressive play.

Conclusion

I. Three qualities: cover both the good and the bad; be honest; show how to improve.
II. I hope to keep in mind as speech critic this semester.

Whether, for this speech, the speaker would be better off with this relatively informal outline or with a more complete version modeled after that on pages 8–10 is debatable. Such a choice varies according to speaker and situation. Notice, however, that even in this sketchy outline, the speaker did several things to help ensure an effective speech—things you also can do as a minimum for written planning that will work for you.

She has a separate introduction and conclusion, each of which performs its special functions distinct from the body of the speech.

She has marked her focus statement so that she knows where it is and that it will be stated clearly in the presented speech.

She has decided on main ideas for the body of the speech, and has shown these as roman numeral headings.

She has selected and placed the examples and other items of detail to support each main idea.

She has even gone beyond minimum planning of structure by putting in some transitional phrasing to help ensure that each main point will stand out clearly in her presentation: She has numbered each main point and repeated the key word "quality" in each mainhead.

Careful preparation is vital to effective speaking. (Susan Lapides/Design Conceptions)

Her outline provides her with a good visual picture of a simple but well-organized speech plan. She can practice the speech, following this same basic plan each time, until she is comfortable and confident with it. She can time the speech again as she becomes more fluent, and if she has to shorten, expand, or otherwise modify it, the outline gives her a convenient way to make the changes without having to start over.

Step 6: Rehearse and Deliver the Speech   These rehearsals are used to develop a comfortable sense of the pattern of ideas and materials in your speech. Keep this sense of the *ideas* alive in your mind. You may even have to ask yourself such questions as, "What are my main ideas?" or "How do I get that second point across?" to remind yourself of what you intend to do in the speech. As you rehearse you will probably unconsciously memorize some phrasing of key ideas, transitions, details in description, or other items. That is fine, but avoid deliberately trying to memorize the speech; reliance on deliberate memorization is, for most speakers, the very opposite of a comfortable grasp of the plan of the speech. Do, however, become familiar enough with the pattern of your ideas so you can move through the speech reasonably fluently and without depending on your notes for every point.

The final rehearsals are also used to develop a comfortable "feel" for the physical and vocal act of delivering the particular speech. For this reason, it is very important that these final rehearsals be done aloud, standing up, using a lectern if you will use one in the actual presentation, using the outline or briefer speaking notes you will speak from, going through the speech as a unit from beginning to end and with the sort of vocal projection and physical movement you are likely to use when presenting the speech. In sum, duplicate the actual speaking situation as closely as possible. For at least one or two rehearsals, it may be useful to have a friend or two as audience. If this trial audience can also function as honest, competent, and gentle critic, that is a bonus. However, even if it is your mother or a girlfriend utterly blind to your defects, such an audience is better than none because you develop the feel of really talking to someone.

How many times should you rehearse the speech? Obviously, rehearse at least until you get a comfortable sense of the pattern of ideas and a comfortable feel for the act of delivery. The amount of rehearsal varies according to the speaker, and even for one speaker it will vary a great deal according to the particular speech and situation. For the first speeches given in your class, three rehearsals will be adequate for some speakers and a dozen rehearsals will be barely enough for others. For most speakers it is better to spread out the rehearsals. A half-dozen rehearsals over two or three days are usually worth more than a dozen back-to-back the morning of the speech. Spreading out the rehearsals lets the ideas sink in and lets you test yourself, thus building more confidence.

Almost everyone is nervous before a speech—and that "everyone" includes the experienced, the highly successful, the famous, and the professional speakers. Being nervous is not necessarily pleasant, even for a professional speaker, but it is useful because it provides the energy to do a fully effective job. In order to use this nervous energy to advantage, and especially if you are worried about being nervous (and most speakers are), a couple of suggestions will help—if you act on them. First, think of the speech not as a performance or a personal ordeal but rather as an occasion for getting your ideas across to your audience. That audience is far more interested in what you have to say than they are in how you feel or whether you give a perfect performance while saying it. Thinking in terms of getting ideas across begins in the first steps of your preparation, when you select a topic and supporting materials with your specific audience in mind. Second, be really prepared. Know what you intend to cover in the speech, and use the outline to help you with this planning. Perhaps the most important part of this preparation, at least for producing confidence, is rehearsal. Those rehearsals aloud and standing up may feel awkward at first. Do them anyway. It is better to feel any initial awkwardness in the privacy of your room than in front of twenty people.

To handle this nervousness to advantage in the long run there is probably no substitute for experience, and even in a single introductory speech course you will get enough of that to do you considerable good.

Your first speeches will probably not be very demanding, so concentrate on the task of communicating rather than on how you feel about it. Later, after only one or two experiences, you will be able to take more complex speeches in stride.

In the actual delivery of your first speeches, talk with your audience, much as you would in conversation. Don't worry about "mistakes" in delivery. Just say what you have to say as well as you can. If you forget where you are in your outline, stop and look at your notes, or pick up whatever you can remember and go on, or at worst just conclude the speech. Don't apologize; the audience does not know whether you are following your outline or have forgotten it and are just ad-libbing.

About the only technical quality in delivery that must be achieved from the beginning is that you speak loudly enough to be heard easily by all members of your audience. In at least some of your final rehearsals, be sure you achieve this level of volume and projection, and continue it when you give the speech. You are also ahead if you can begin immediately to have some genuine eye contact with the audience, keep a firm but not rigid posture, and have some freedom to move around and gesture.

Additional Suggestions for Using Method

If you follow a process at least roughly like this six-step method, you are likely to get the best results and make the most efficient use of your time and energy. Four further suggestions will increase your chances of success.

First, *start early*. The sooner you can arrive at a specific focus, or at least a topic area for a speech, the more time you have for the remaining steps in preparation. The point here is not so much the total hours you put into preparing a speech as the value of spreading that preparation time over a period of several days or even weeks. This allows time for ideas to bubble up from the subconscious, for sparks of inspiration to occur, for rethinking decisions about organization, and for spreading rehearsals over time in order to gain greater confidence in delivery.

The second suggestion is that you *think* about your speech over a period of time. Jot down ideas that occur to you even when you are not deliberately working on the speech. Be receptive to useful material you run across in conversation, on television, or in other chance ways. Use small bits of time to rethink basic structure or your choice of supporting material. It is a lot easier to make good use of this thinking time and these chance sources if you keep all your working notes and other material for a particular speech together and separate from your other work. A file folder or large clasp envelope is a handy way to keep material together. As you make notes, develop rough drafts of the outline, and so forth, just drop them in the folder or envelope.

Third, *pace* yourself. There comes a point at which it is necessary to stop gathering ideas and go on to organizing the speech, and another point at which you must decide that the plan of the speech is good enough and you will now move into rehearsal. The pace for one speaker or one speech will be different from that of another. The important point here is to avoid getting so hung up on one stage of preparation that you are forced to neglect later stages.

Finally, *consciously apply theory* you learn from the textbook and from your instructor's remarks. To improve in any skill, we have to change; and the theory provides sound directions for improvement. This suggestion includes applying what you learn by observing other students' speeches.

Summary

A speech is intended to achieve an informative, persuasive, or other effect with a specific audience on a specific occasion. The speech is effective to the extent that it is clear, interesting, credible, and appropriate for that audience.

A speech is composed of introduction, body, and conclusion. Each of these parts has its special functions. The body is a pattern of idea headings, supporting materials to develop each idea, and transitions to enable the listeners to follow the pattern.

For a better speech, making more efficient use of time and effort, you can use the six-step method offered in this chapter:

1. Decide on a specific focus for the speech, usually by narrowing and shaping a broader topic idea.
2. Discover ideas and other materials, from your own mind as well as from research.
3. Plan the basic structure—the main ideas or divisions of your topic, stated as mainheads and perhaps as subheads.
4. Fill in the basic structure by planning examples, comparisons, and other supporting material for each idea heading.
5. Complete the written planning with an introduction and conclusion, and with a final draft of your outline.
6. Rehearse the speech to become comfortable with your plan, and deliver it with a sense of simply telling your ideas to your listeners.

In addition, to use your time to best effect, start early, think about your topic over time, pace yourself through each stage in preparation, and consciously apply the theory you learn.

Chapters 4 through 9 offer more suggestions, options, and techniques to improve your skill at each step. Each chapter deals with one step in the sequence.

Exercises

1. Prepare and present a three- to five-minute speech drawn from your own experience and observation. Do *not* use the library or any resource other than your own background, imagination, and encounters with other people. Areas to search for possible topics include these: your hobbies or jobs, beliefs and values you hold, organizations to which you belong, unusual experiences you have had from which you can draw general points, or anything else in your background or current situation that might produce a specific topic you would want to talk about and your audience might want to hear about.

Since this may be your first formal speech, some suggestions may help you achieve the best results for a beginning speech. Know what you intend to accomplish in the speech, and have a clear statement of focus in the introduction. Even though the topic is familiar to you, use some form of outline to plan what you are going to say, so you don't just ramble on hoping something will occur to you on the subject while you are speaking. Include personal examples or other supporting material you will enjoy telling the audience. Time the speech as early as possible in its preparation to be sure of being within the time limit. Rehearse the speech aloud and standing up.

2. Introduce yourself to the audience in a two- to three-minute speech. Cover these points: where you are from, what year you are in school, your major, your professional aims, what you hope to get out of this speech course, and your hobbies, other activities or any special experiences you have had. Go into some detail on at least one aspect of this biographical material, such as a description of your home town or how you came to be interested in your major field. (One purpose of this assignment is to provide you as a future speaker in the class with some sense of your audience as you listen to the speeches of your classmates.) Even though your job as a speaker may appear easy, at least plan what you are going to say and run through it aloud a couple of times to be sure you will be within the time limit and can move through the material smoothly.

Developing Yourself as a Speaker

I n Chapter 1 you gained enough technical understanding of what a speech is and how to put one together to begin gaining experience making speeches. In this chapter we will take a broader view of speech skills as part of one's personal equipment for leading a satisfying and productive life. We will also consider how to develop those skills most efficiently in a speech course.

Public Speaking as a Form of Communication

You may already have realized that public speaking has much in common with conversation, writing papers, and other familiar sorts of communication. In fact, if you combine the planning you might do before writing a term paper with the energetic delivery you would probably use in a heated discussion, you have a good start toward an effective speech. You can learn public speaking more easily if you apply what you already know and do in other forms of communication. It works the other way also: Many of the skills and techniques you develop in this course can make you more effective in other forms of speaking and writing. Some students, for example, find that a public speaking course increases their confidence in class discussion or helps them organize and support their ideas in written reports for other courses.

Both the ease and the value of a public speaking course are increased when you see how public speaking is related to other forms of communication you engage in every day. A standard model of the communication process will help explain how public speaking is a part of this broader range of communication.

A Standard Model of the Communication Process

Let's begin with an ordinary sort of occurrence. On a late Friday afternoon, after a hard week's school, you and a friend are relaxing in his apartment. You are trying to persuade him that he would enjoy seeing a rerun of the movie *The Empire Strikes Back*. First, you praise the multiple matte effects in the movie, but he doesn't seem to know what you mean by multiple matte effects, and he doesn't seem much interested in seeing a movie just to admire special effects technique anyway. So you change your tack and praise the plot and continuous action, and you even become physically animated when describing some of the action. Finally he agrees to go to the movie.

In this exchange we can isolate the seven components of the communication process. You as (1) the *source* had (2) a *message*, "You should see this movie," to convey to (3) a *receiver*, your friend. You used language and vocal inflection presented orally and facial expression and gestures presented visually as (4) the *channels* through which to convey your message. When your friend didn't understand what you meant by "multiple matte effects" there was (5) an *obstacle* in the flow of communication. By his confused or bored facial expression or perhaps by his asking a question (his choice of channels), he got across to you the fact that your praise of special effects was not working. You adapted to this (6) *feedback* from him by shifting to different arguments for the movie, and finally you got positive feedback to your whole message when he agreed to go to the movie. The whole conversation took place in the relaxed (7) *situation* of your friend's apartment on a Friday afternoon.

A MODEL OF THE SPEECH COMMUNICATION PROCESS

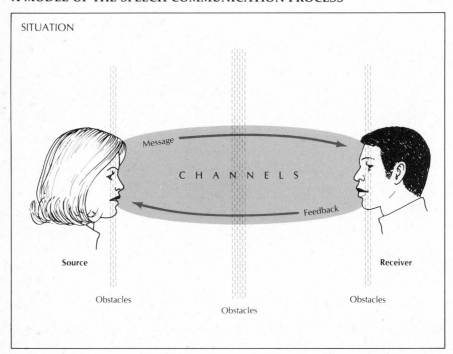

SITUATION

Message

C H A N N E L S

Feedback

Source

Receiver

Obstacles

Obstacles

Obstacles

The relationships between public speaking and other sorts of communication will be clearer if we look more closely at the components in this model. By applying the model we can also get at what happens in an attempt to get a message across and what causes the communication to succeed or fail.

The core of any act of communication is a source attempting to get a message across to a receiver. When you are operating as a *source* you are usually trying through the message to create some understanding or some attitude in the person who is receiving the message. As source, for example, you might seek to inform your listener objectively about what parking regulations exist on campus, or you might seek to persuade her that these regulations are unfair and perhaps even arouse her anger toward the regulations. The *message* you actually send is a product not only of what you intend it to be but also of your skills in expressing ideas and the accuracy with which you adapt to your listener. The message the *receiver*, in turn, understands is a product of the words, gestures, and other cues you send interacting with (1) what she associates with those cues and (2) other factors, such as her attitude toward you and the way she interprets the situation in which the communication takes place.

As a *channel* for conveying meaning, language, whether oral or written, is not as precise as one might expect. Language is essentially a system of symbols, or words, and almost any given word means something at least a little different to each different person. Frequently, our own meanings for words reflect our personal feelings about things as much as they reflect objective reality. Your understanding of a word—"car," "police," "mother," "college"—is the product of all the uses and experiences you associate with the word. But those uses and experiences are at least a little different from the ones someone else associates with the word. The speaker or listener has additional channels—vocal inflection, facial expression, and gestures—through which to help clarify the meaning, and both oral and written communication can use visual aids. Use of these additional channels, however, cannot fully substitute for choosing the most appropriate words.

The sending of a message from source to receiver occurs in a larger physical and psychological *situation*. Such aspects of situation as the physical surroundings, emotional climate, and purpose of the occasion influence the effects of public speeches and other sorts of communication. Do you not have an easier time understanding a teacher in a classroom that is neither tense nor apathetically relaxed? An exciting basketball game would not seem a very appropriate situation in which to approach a faculty adviser for serious career counseling. Even the physical distance between people in a conversation can either help or hinder their communication. The skillful communicator not only senses and adapts to the situation, but also realizes that sometimes he can control the situation in order to improve the chances of effective communication. Some teachers work best when they sit among their students as a group, others are more effective controlling the class from behind a lectern. Land promoters and other salespersons will sometimes treat a potential customer to a good dinner as a way of softening him or her up for the pitch.

An *obstacle* is anything that interferes with the successful transmission of a message from source to receiver. The information theorists who first developed this model of the communication process called such interference "noise." Noise may be literally the noise that drowns out a conversation or distracts a reader, or it may be other interference in the channel, such as a dead microphone. More common obstacles, however, are those that occur in the minds of sources and receivers—that is, in the minds of people like you and me when we communicate. When as receivers we distrust the source, or are bored with the subject, or are confused because we are not familiar with words and concepts used in the message, or are simply pessimistic about ever understanding what is being said, then we have some strong obstacles preventing us from understanding the message clearly. Similarly, if as sources we have no real interest in getting our message across to the receiver or we lack the knowledge or skills needed to form and adapt the message for the receiver, then we have other obstacles.

Such obstacles in either source or receiver, or both, occur when communicating through letters, reports, conversations, discussions, essay exam answers, lectures, and alas, textbooks. Occasionally, you can see obstacles operating on both sides in attempts at communication between a teacher and a student. A student, for example, does not understand the terms a teacher is using, and the teacher does not see any need to provide examples or other details that might help the student understand the concepts. Each blames the other for the lack of understanding, and the frustration felt by both raises additional obstacles, thus further reducing the chances of effective communication.

One way to approach much of what we do in communication is to think of skills as ways of overcoming the obstacles in the other person's mind or even in our own. The student signals his particular point of confusion to the teacher. The teacher adds explanatory detail or examples. Listening to a lecture on which he will be tested, the shrewd student eliminates, at least for the moment, his negative attitudes toward the course or the instructor. Such negative attitudes are obstacles that only reduce his own efficiency in comprehending the lecture. The public speaker consciously plans clear organization and familiar examples to avoid confusing her listeners. Two particularly useful ways to reduce obstacles in communication are to use language carefully and to use feedback constructively.

A speaker or writer tries to select and combine words on the basis of what they will mean to the listener or reader. The listener or reader, in turn, should be willing to try to interpret the words as the source intended them. We intuitively adapt choices of language to our listeners in conversation—though we do not always make the best choices, especially when emotions run high. Public speaking, however, permits advance preparation during which a speaker can take time to sharpen her choice of language, especially for certain key parts of the speech.

As a receiver, you can use *feedback* constructively to warn the source about the parts of the message you find confusing or unconvincing. You can also encourage a source by signaling agreement and other positive responses. In conversation and group discussion, feedback can be stated. When you listen to a speech, however, you usually provide feedback by your facial expression and other body language and, less frequently, by shouts of approval or applause. When a public speaker, discussant, or other source can interpret feedback accurately and adapt to it flexibly, he or she has a significant advantage in getting messages across effectively. It is useful to think of instructors' comments on your papers and oral presentations as feedback from a receiver—feedback calling for interpretation and adaptation in future messages from you as a source.

We do not always or automatically communicate well with one another, but certain conditions increase the chances that we will do so. Successful communication is most often a cooperative act that requires at least some degree of willingness by each person to communicate with the other. It also requires words or other cues for which both source and receiver have at least roughly the same meanings. One evidence of a generation gap occurs when parents and children use the same words but do not have the same meanings for the words. Effective communication also often profits from special skills—as training programs for business managers, teachers, public relations experts, journalists, and others suggest. Your public speaking course is one such training program.

Public Speaking and the Communication Process

The communication model helps to remind a speaker that he is not simply reciting a string of words to a passive audience. Rather, his listeners will interact with his message in terms of what is already in their minds. As the speaker becomes more experienced, he can seek to build on relevant points of interest, knowledge, and belief already existing in the listeners' minds. He can also ask what possible obstacles in their minds might block them from being interested in, understanding, and accepting his message, and then can plan ways in his speech to overcome these obstacles. He can seek feedback in post-speech discussions, and he can begin to sense and adapt to less obvious feedback while giving the speech. He is aware that not just his words but also his vocal inflections, his physical cues, and his visual aids (if he uses them) all convey meaning through important channels to which the audience will respond. He is aware that he can increase his effectiveness by adapting to the total situation: What does the audience expect from him on this occasion? For example, is the emotional climate serious or relaxed?

While it is useful to see how public speaking is like other sorts of communication, it is also necessary to see that a public speech is a distinct form. In a conversation or discussion we have much more opportunity to listen to feedback from other people and adapt what we say next on the basis of this feedback. Time limits, if there at all, are usually loose. In a speech, on the other hand, we have to plan in advance a strategy for achieving our purpose with the particular audience in what is usually a limited amount of speaking time. Effective speeches by skillful speakers often have an aura of spontaneous conversation, but speeches that are really done as off-the-cuff, rambling conversations are usually poor.

Nor is a speech exactly like a written paper. The listener, unlike the reader, cannot stop and ponder an idea or look back. So a good speaker makes each idea clear as he covers it in the speech. He not only uses vocal emphasis and gesture but also may need repetition and supporting detail that would be excessive in an essay.

The Value of Special Training in Speech

Most of us would like to feel we have some influence over what happens around us and to us. Citizens speak out to influence policy on abortion, use of nuclear power, conserving the environment and endangered animals, registration of guns, the draft, local and state taxes, the appropriate use of funds by organizations of which they are members, proper land use and rehabilitation of urban areas, the nature of education in the public schools, and a host of other issues. Some of these affect the speakers' immediate self-interest, others are attempts to make the social environment conform more closely to their own ideals. To speak on such matters effectively enough to influence the opinions and actions of others is to exercise power.

Even in jobs relying on technical specialization, the opportunities and demands for public speaking skills remain more common than many college students realize. The engineer finds that if his career is to advance he must be willing to accept management duties that include speaking to groups of employees, or he must serve as spokesperson for consultant teams presenting results to agencies outside the company. The certified public accountant finds an opportunity to teach classes in her area of specialization. The dentist has to give speeches as an officer of his dental association, or he must speak as a lobbyist before regulatory agencies.

Sometimes you may have speech-making thrust on you as part of your duties in your job or organization. Perhaps more frequently you will have opportunities where you speak voluntarily, as when you speak out in a meeting or join the speakers' bureau of the company for which you work. Some of these speaking situations will be of little consequence; you will feel better if you do the speech well, but it will not really make much difference. In other situations, the stakes may be significant for you, for groups you represent, or for the audience. In any of these situations, it is comforting to know that you can do at least an adequate job. And you may not be content merely to get through the task adequately. To be able to increase listeners' understanding or to persuade them is one of the most civilized ways we as individuals have for affecting our environment.

Some beginning speech students are surprised to discover that they

Many jobs include opportunities or requirements for public speaking. (Judy S. Gelles/Stock, Boston)

can give a public speech at all, much less the skillful and effective ones they will be producing by the end of the course. However, anyone reading this book has *now* the ability to give a public speech of some sort. The primary purposes of a speech course are to expand your understanding of techniques and strategies in public speaking, and to give you some practice so that you will be more confident and effective in more situations. With skill and confidence you develop a power to benefit both yourself and the society around you.

How to Improve Speech Skills

Some 2,400 years ago people began to think systematically about what caused some speakers to be more effective than others. For the ancient Greeks and Romans political advancement, protection of friends and property—sometimes even of life itself—often depended on their skills as speakers in the courts and assemblies. Understandably, they were interested in how to improve their speech skills. The means of improvement they discovered, and most of the means developed from then until now, fall into three general categories: learning theory, practicing by preparing speeches and other exercises, and observing other speakers as models.

The most efficient approaches to improvement usually combine these three sorts of means, and that is what your course will do. Let's consider each in turn.

Three Means for Improvement

Theory   Although studying theory may not by itself make you a better speaker, theory does contribute one big advantage: efficiency. You profit from what practitioners and observers of successful speaking have discovered over centuries. You can in several weeks achieve a greater understanding of sound method than if you had to learn everything by your own trial and error over a period of years. Also, speech theory—beginning with Aristotle's great work on persuasive speaking, the *Rhetoric*—has drawn on psychology. Thus you not only learn what works in particular situations, you get some notion of *why* it works. You learn in which sorts of situations to apply particular techniques.

You should keep in mind that these theories are only generalizations about what works. They are usually valid, but they are not necessarily right in every case. When, for example, a teacher or a textbook tells you that considerable rehearsal for a speech will improve your confidence and the effect of the speech, your own experience will very likely prove the advice to be valid. However, you might in a particular situation give a hastily prepared and largely ad-libbed speech and have brilliant results. Take seriously the theories presented in this book and by your teacher. But treat them as guidelines and general insights rather than as rigid rules.

Practice   Even the best theory is not very useful until it is absorbed into your own ways of doing things. This requires that you practice. The first advice here is that you consciously use theory when you prepare and rehearse a speech. Otherwise, you are back to muddling along by trial and error. Often it takes only a few minutes to apply the theory covered in this course—for example, to check your topic against standards for a good speech topic, to remind yourself of the different types of supporting detail that can be used, to check for sound organization. Such applications of theory can markedly increase the success of your speeches and can fix the theory in your mind for later use.

As part of your practice you will receive criticism from your instructor and classmates. Ideally, such criticism tells you what you are doing right as well as what you are doing wrong, and it gets beneath surface reactions to say *why* your speech is interesting or unclear or otherwise effective or not. The value of criticism—even good criticism—is largely determined by how you react to it. On the one hand, don't accept criticism blindly, especially if it comes from only one person. Try to figure out why comments, either positive or negative, are made, and see if they really make sense. Also, a critic may choose to comment on the two things you did poorly and ignore the eight things you did very well. So don't be overwhelmed by criticism, particularly negative comments. On the other hand, don't ignore criticism or be so concerned about defending your ego that you miss the point of the criticism. On even a serious weakness, you can usually improve in the next speech. Try to understand the comments and to apply them the next time, both by building on strengths and by correcting weaknesses.

Observation Your speech class provides an unusual opportunity for critically observing and learning from other speakers as models. You can begin by evaluating the qualities of appropriateness, clarity, interest, and credibility as you respond to a speech. Try to determine why the speech has, or fails to have, each of these qualities. Is the speech interesting, for example, because of the delivery or because of the vivid supporting material? Why does the delivery hold interest? What in the early part of the speech aroused interest in the rest of the speech?

You can gain a great deal by trying yourself to do what other effective speakers do—in delivery, in use of supporting material and transitions, in introductions and conclusions, and in other areas of technical skill. Observation can especially provide practical illustrations of ways to correct weaknesses that are pointed out in criticism of your own speeches. Even excellent speakers have defects and make mistakes, so be sure that what you are pinpointing to try yourself are really the speaker's strong features. Be sure also that what works well for him or her will work well for you in your particular situation.

The Importance of Attitude

Attitudes also do much to determine a student's degree of success in a speech course. The students who ultimately will be successful are the ones who realize that they really can improve. Speeches can be made more interesting. Delivery can become more confident. Organization can become clearer. You will probably see some classmates improve dramatically. This leads to a second attitude. An athlete on the way to success does not have practice sessions just for the sake of getting through practice sessions. Rather, he or she uses practice sessions to develop the skills that will produce success in real competition. Similarly, the successful speech student does not learn theory just to get through the next exam or prepare a speech just to get through the next round. He or she is consciously pulling together the theory, practice, and observation in order both to improve during the course and to master skills for later use.

As your skills increase, so does your ability to inform and influence audiences. This raises questions as to how you will use that ability.

Public Speaking and Personal Ethics

Admittedly, ethics are a very personal matter, and about all a textbook or instructor can do is point out some choices. Let us also admit, however, that even in the modest opportunities for public speaking most of us are likely to encounter, we do often choose how closely we will heed the ideal of the great Roman orator-statesman Cato: to be a good person skilled in speech.

It does not seem very helpful to draw up a list of unethical practices in speaking and urge you to avoid them. A few techniques—such as falsifying information or deliberately misleading an audience as to the consequences of an action you are advocating—are clearly unethical in almost any conceivable situation. And one thing is worth pointing out: You cannot neatly separate what you say to an audience from what you really are. It is hypocritical to yourself to think, "I'm a very honest person. I just happened to lie to twenty people this morning."

The morality of most techniques, however, depends more on the situation and the speaker's intention than on the techniques themselves. Students of speech are sometimes told, for example, that it is unethical to arouse an emotional state such as anger or pity because this warps the audience member's rational judgment. Perhaps so in some situations, but as one of the more idealistic modern rhetorical theorists, Richard Weaver, suggests, it is often necessary to arouse an audience's emotions to get them actually to do what they know they should do. Members of a neighborhood association may know that their state legislator does not work in their best interests, but they do nothing about it. Only when a speaker makes them angry or fearful enough of the legislator's corrupt behavior will they give their time and money to campaign against his reelection.

Questions of ethics in regard to aims become somewhat complicated in an age when large segments of society make a living as paid persuaders—in politics, law, advertising, public relations, and other fields (and many of these people receive a good deal of their training in advanced speech courses). Even in these situations, the speaker does make choices, and these choices reflect character. Political campaigners, for example, do refuse to use certain techniques; they even abandon the campaigns of candidates with whom they become disenchanted.

Unethical speakers are often marked by their attitudes toward audiences. They seem to think of their listeners only as objects to be manipulated. Or they are irresponsible toward their task, feeling that neither purpose nor audience justifies real effort on their part. Their speeches are filled with vague ideas, unsupported assertions, outdated or irrelevant information, and general nonsense. Often, their offense is not so much misleading the audience as it is wasting the listeners' time.

We have yet to consider what for many people is the greatest ethical challenge. That is, the willingness to speak. The nurse who volunteers time from a busy schedule to speak on life-saving techniques to a high school class, the woman who volunteers to serve as spokesperson for a group petitioning the city council, the college teacher who gives noncredit lectures on study skills, the man who undertakes to lead a fund-raising drive, the person in a business or civic organization who rises to challenge the established ways of doing things—all of these people have taken the initiative to give information or make positions known or support worthy causes. Often, it would be more comfortable to remain silent; but with such silence important tasks go undone. The heart attack victim dies unnecessarily. The needed playground does not get built. The business continues its unfair treatment of employees. We may admire the speaker who avoids questionable techniques. We usually admire much more the person who volunteers effort and skill in public speaking for the social good.

Summary

Similarities between public speaking and other forms of communication are revealed by a standard model of the communication process: A *source* sends a *message* through one or more *channels* to a *receiver*. This act is influenced by the *situation* in which it occurs. For the source to affect the receiver in the intended way, *obstacles* in the minds of source or receiver or in the channel or situation must be overcome. The source's success can be judged by *feedback* returned from the receiver. Because of these similarities, many skills and techniques that improve your public speaking can also help you be more effective in other forms of communication.

Yet public speaking is a specialized form of communication that meets needs of both speakers and audiences in a great range of situations. A person increases in speaking ability by learning theory, by practicing, and by observing other speakers. Positive intention to improve also increases the value of speech training. Being able to speak in public confers satisfactions, and being able to do it well confers power.

With the ability to speak effectively in public, go some ethical considerations and responsibilities, such as willingness to prepare sufficiently to meet the demands of the situation. Probably the greatest ethical challenge is to accept, rather than evade, opportunities to do good for others through public speaking.

Exercises

1. Describe an oral communication occurrence in terms of the seven-part model explained in this chapter. Cover each part of the model explicitly in your description.

If the communication was less than successful, try to explain why it failed—for example, in terms of obstacles that were present. You may be a participant or just an observer. Among possible sorts of occurrences to analyze are a purposeful conversation among family or friends, an exchange between a teacher and a student, a salesperson's attempts to sell something to a customer, or an exchange between a boss and an employee. Present your description in a two-minute oral report.

2. For two or three days, watch critically every instance of public speaking you have a chance to observe, such as a speaker on campus or in an organization of which you are a member, or your teachers in other courses. Think about your own responses to each presentation. What for you as a listener helps or hinders appropriateness, clarity, interest, and credibility? From your observations, arrive at a list of a half-dozen or so "do's and don'ts" for a public speaker. Be prepared to explain one or two of these in a class discussion of what effective public speaking is.

Listening Effectively

Two students take a course based largely on material covered in class. One gets an A, the other gets a D. What causes the difference? Both students attended class regularly. But one student profited a great deal more from the lectures and oral instructions for assignments than did the other. As this case reminds us, we are often the listeners rather than the speakers in public speaking and other oral communication. And often our skill as listeners can significantly affect our self interest.

This is likely to be equally true in your career and other activities outside the classroom. Instructions, updated training, and other important information are given to employees orally, sometimes in workshops with speakers. Managers function by making decisions based on processing information, much of which they receive by listening. Costly mistakes can result if employees and managers don't absorb and comprehend the information accurately. In order to make prudent decisions, listeners can use special skills to evaluate salespersons' persuasive appeals, the flow of debate in a committee meeting, or the attempts of national leaders on television to influence opinion on public issues.

We don't all have equal skills as listeners. Our skills can, however, be markedly improved. This chapter will first suggest ways to improve the skills common to most kinds of listening and then consider the special skills used in three different sorts of listening.

Basic Ways to Improve Listening

A basic distinction that you should make is between *functional listening* and *consumer listening*. Usually when we watch television, go to a movie or play, or engage in casual conversation, we have no aim beyond "consuming" the experience itself. However, when we are being urged toward a decision or being given information for future use, our listening performs a function beyond enjoyment. The distinction is important: The person who approaches all listening situations as sources of passive enjoyment is not likely to accomplish serious functions in listening very effectively. Functional listening, as in some lecture classes, may be enjoyable, but beneath the fun it also takes some effort and skill. And sometimes functional listening is just plain hard work, justified only by the benefits it produces later on.

You can improve your effectiveness in virtually any kind of functional listening if you increase your sense of purpose and if you remove obstacles to efficient listening that are largely in your own mind.

Be Aware of Your Purpose   You are more likely to listen effectively if you have a clearly defined purpose. A person lost in an unfamiliar and perhaps dangerous part of a city will probably listen very attentively to directions for reaching his destination. Remind yourself of what sort of purpose you have in listening to the material. Are you listening for information? If so, an open-minded receptivity will usually be appropriate. When listening to persuasion, however, you will need to listen more cautiously to evaluate arguments and appeals to your emotions.

Eliminate or Overcome Obstacles to Effective Listening   A listener's understanding of a speaker is rarely if ever perfect. As explained in Chapter 2, no two people are likely to have precisely the same meanings for the words used. In addition, although vocal inflection, gesture, facial expression, and other nonverbal cues enrich meaning, all these cues also can be misread by listeners. Finally, each listener filters the speaker's message through his or her own "mental set": sense of purpose, expectations, and attitudes toward speaker, topic, and occasion. In this filtering we tend subconsciously to ignore or misperceive that which does not fit our expectations or which seriously threatens our beliefs or values. With this many difficulties built into the very nature of oral communication, accurate conveyance of understanding from speaker to listener is risky enough even when both have the best intentions. As listeners, we can increase our chances of overcoming these difficulties by taking the following three steps:

1. *Avoid using an irrelevant aspect of the situation as an excuse to tune out the speaker.* Sometimes these aspects can be as trivial as the speaker's accent, mode of dress, or physical mannerisms. Sometimes they can be real impediments that must be overcome, such as an uncomfortable seat, a room that is too hot or too cold, or a boorishly whispering neighbor. We may use the fact that our attendance is required as sufficient reason to refuse to listen even when we know that being attentive would make the time more profitable. These irrelevant excuses can be especially tempting if we have personal problems or fantasies we would rather think about. Remember, however, that you have your own purposes in listening, and you can't always rely on the speaker to make it easy for you.

2. *Perceive accurately the speaker's purpose and attitudes toward listeners and topic.* Though we want to give a persuasive speaker a full and fair hearing, we don't want to forget that his purpose is to persuade rather than give objective information. Persuasive messages, ranging from political speeches to con games, frequently rely on the listener's failure to interpret and evaluate the message as persuasive. Somewhat the opposite occurs when students or employees either ignore or misinterpret messages by a "tough" teacher or manager: The listeners feel, usually wrongly, that the speaker is personally hostile toward them, and they resent or fear even messages that are intended to be helpful. We are more likely to interpret a message accurately and respond intelligently if we "see behind the message" to the speaker's intentions and attitudes in the situation.

3. *Avoid letting your personal bias unduly distort your response to a speaker.* A trial lawyer speaking to a civic organization mentions that he once defended a notorious criminal, and many listeners refuse to listen fairly to his later plea for more humane treatment of first offenders. An art teacher illustrates a point by referring to a movie that happened to be X-rated, and that is the last favorable attention she gets from some listeners. Listeners are often too quick to seize on some affront to their values, perhaps in only a minor supporting point of a speech, and see this affront as reason to listen with a hostile attitude that distorts the rest of the speech.

The rest of this chapter provides suggestions for three especially important sorts of functional listening. The first two—listening for information and evaluating persuasion—are dealt with mainly in terms of public speeches, although much of what is said also applies to listening in one-to-one and other less formal situations. The third sort is listening to speeches as models of speechmaking techniques in order to critique and learn from them.

Listening for Information

You can most immediately apply the special skill involved in listening for information to the lectures, discussions, and oral reports in your classes, where it has a significant effect on learning and grades. Listening in class should also be viewed as practice in developing skill for later use— for example, in a business or professional career. Although explained mainly in terms of college situations, the following suggestions also apply to on-the-job training, learning from conferences, and other career situations. To obtain useful information through listening, you need to pay attention, comprehend the material, and retain the material.

Improving Attention

As you know, it's not always easy to pay attention. But there are ways to make it easier. By nature we almost automatically pay attention to what we need and to what we expect to find more pleasant than painful. *Remind yourself of what*

Listening for information is important in many parts of your life. (Sandra Johnson/The Picture Cube)

you stand to gain by effective listening to a particular lecture or class discussion more confidence in the course, more success in the next exam, clarification of particular points in the course, future uses after the course is over, even being able to impress a friend with your understanding of the material. Often, getting the material in class sessions is easier than digging it out of books or other sources later—and you are sitting in class anyway. In some courses effective listening in class sessions is the only way you can get much of the material.

You will also find it easier to pay attention if you *become a more active participant in the situation.* Contribute and ask questions in discussion sessions. Use smiles, nods, shifting forward in your seat, and other nonverbal positive feedback; but avoid the mindless, monotonous head nodding mastered by some students. Think about what you are hearing. Do you understand what is being said? If you don't understand a point, ask the speaker about it, if that is permitted; otherwise, make a note to check in a textbook or ask a friend. The act of taking notes itself can keep you more actively tuned in to the scene, and some successful students are actually uncomfortable if they can't take notes.

Improving Comprehension

A listener's active skill in understanding is important because, unfortunately, the importance of what speakers have to say is not always in direct proportion to their ability to say it clearly. Like most skills, our ability to understand information we receive orally can be improved—dramatically for many people—with some insight and practice.

Understand accurately what you are supposed to get out of the particular session. How will the instructor's material in this class session fit into the larger purposes and structure of the course? What is the specific emphasis of the session and what sorts of learning are you expected to derive? A history teacher may lecture because he expects you to *learn* masses of detail under some overall pattern of main points, whereas a philosophy or math teacher may use more class interaction because she expects you to *understand* a few key insights from the class session.

Listen to spot key terms, main ideas, and structural plan. In much informative speaking, even when it is not well organized, important material is clustered around key terms that you should be able to recognize from reading or earlier lectures. In more tightly organized lectures, if you can detect the speaker's overall organizational strategy, it is much easier to spot major ideas and fit the various points together in a logical way. A lecture on an American novelist, for example, may appear to be leaping chaotically back and forth among various novels unless the listener realizes that the lecturer's overall plan is to cover the novelist's major themes one by one. Relate the supporting ideas and detail to the larger, more important ideas. Be alert to spot a speaker's verbal and nonverbal cues to structure and to the relative importance of ideas: restatement and vocal emphasis, transitions such as listing in advance the points to be covered, and writing terms or brief outlines on the blackboard.

Relate the discussion or lecture to a broader context. Even a well organized lecture is not likely to be clear or very interesting if the listener does not understand technical terminology or allusions to other information the speaker is using. A rambling lecture or class discussion may seem a meaningless chaos if the listener doesn't have the framework of theory to make sense of the examples being developed or the issues being argued. As a listener, you will find each class session easier to comprehend if you recall and review earlier sessions, read assigned material in advance, and otherwise go into each class session with a frame of reference from what has gone before. You can also often increase comprehension (and interest) by relating points made in class to your own experience or uses outside the course. What examples from your own experience, for example, would further illustrate points made in a psychology or sociology class?

Improving Retention

There are two places to retain the material you will need for exams and other assignments or job performance: in your notes and in your memory. Ideally, it would all be in your memory, ready for instant application. Very few people's memories are able to handle the load, however, so we develop a combination of notes and memory.

Take notes you can use effectively later. Close analysis of a group of freshman students' notes on relatively well organized lectures revealed a very high correlation between quality of notes and exam grades. You get the good notes that lead to good exam grades by building structure into your notes and by getting enough notes.

The most obvious way to build structure into your notes is to try to take notes in outline form—showing examples, lists of subpoints, and other detail as subordinate under a small number of major headings. Some lecturers help you do this. Some don't. Sometimes you have to spend time after class looking over the notes and using outline enumeration in the margin plus underlining to impose some sense of structure on the notes.

How many notes are "enough"? Enough notes will give you the detail you need months later. If the lecturer spends several minutes on a key point or concept, you need more than a couple of words to jog your memory. Note definitions and examples and copy diagrams an instructor uses. For a discussion that focuses on illustrating a few key ideas, you might spend ten minutes listening in gradually decreasing puzzlement until insight strikes, then write furiously for a couple of minutes, then go back to another several minutes of attentive listening. On the other hand, for some rapidly moving lecturers giving condensed information you must almost risk writer's cramp to get a good set of notes.

Use your memory. You are more likely to know material reasonably well even before you start cramming for an exam if you can become interested in the material and can comprehend it fully during class. Also, it is much easier to remember material in the organized frameworks or outlines recommended for notetaking: You can begin by remembering only a few key notions; then you can associate each key notion with the subpoints under it, and so on down to the most detailed levels you need to remember.

You can remember class material more easily if you review and tinker around with the material after the session in which you receive it. Some students routinely recopy their own class notes. Though usually effective, this may not always be the most efficient use of time. You can, however, often fill in some detail here and there, improve the organization, spot links between lecture and textbook, and otherwise improve the notes. You can also review earlier notes from time to time, testing yourself, for example, by covering up subheadings and trying to fill in detail under main headings. Just as with a speech, you get a more solid grasp of the material if you fix it in mind over a period of time rather than all at the last minute.

Evaluating Persuasion

It is one thing to admire and analyze a persuasive speaker's skill. It is quite another thing to be conned out of our savings by that speaker. The aim of this section is to enable you to evaluate persuasive appeals and techniques so that when faced with persuasion you can make decisions that are really in your own interest.

Attitudes Toward Persuasion

Attempts to persuade us may be open and rational. Often, however, persuasion is not obvious in its attempts to manipulate our feelings, beliefs, and behavior in ways other than by rational appeals. Thus in evaluating persuasion we need to begin by striking a balance between being on guard against manipulative persuasion and being open-minded to give the messages a fair hearing.

Detecting Fallacies   Being able to detect fallacies will help put you on guard. The following seven fallacies are common in attempts at manipulative persuasion.

1. *Intensifying short-term wants* so much that longer-term consequences are ignored. For example, the speaker describes the experience and prestige of owning a new car so vividly that the listener doesn't really think about payments with high interest for the next four years.
2. *Use of loaded language* that triggers automatic judgments and emotional responses but has relatively little objective meaning. Such language can be used by both sides to cloud any real issue in a dispute or event. For example, during the 1960s some people referred to the young people who opposed war as "communist pinko hippies" and "unpatriotic social degenerates," and some of those young people in turn referred to their detractors as "fascist warmongering plutocrats."
3. *Arguments based on personalities* rather than dealing with the issue at hand. In the following examples, there is no real connection between the arguments given and a rational basis for deciding the issue. "The husband of the woman sponsoring this equal rights legislation may have had business dealings with known Mafia figures, so we should reject the legislation." "This income tax legislation is good because it is supported by Senator Rankin, who was born on a farm, worked his way through college, served four years in the army, and visits his mother once a week."
4. *The "bandwagon appeal"*: the argument that since "everybody else" is buying this product or following this policy you should also. "Everybody cheats on their income tax, so why shouldn't you?" (You may have good moral and practical reasons for not cheating. And does "everybody" cheat?) "People choose Burp Cola three to one, so you should choose it also."
5. *Pressure to act now before you lose the chance.* "You'd better buy the suit now because if you shop around for a couple of days it will be gone." (How likely is it to be gone? And if it is, so what?)
6. *Asserting that a single cause alone is or will be responsible for a complex effect.* You could easily dispute the validity of the single cause asserted in each of the following examples. "Overpopulation is the cause of poverty in the world." "Eating diet candy bars will cause you to lose weight." "Raising admission standards will cause the quality of education at this school to rise."
7. *Assuming that there are only two alternative choices.* In each of the following examples there are actually several more complex alternatives between the two extremes given. "Either the Soviets are friendly and trustworthy or else they intend to wage war on us." "Either your friend is totally loyal or she is no friend at all." "Either we raise taxes or we cruelly abandon the disadvantaged people in our society." One of the several variants of this "two-valued orienta-

tion" is the "we-they" dichotomy: "We" (our ethnic group, nation, political party, or other grouping) are the totally good guys; "they" (the other ethnic group, nation, etc.) are the totally bad guys.

These seven are among the most common of many types of fallacies. Most fallacies rely on two basic tactics: *diverting* us from relevant reasoning about the real issues, and grossly *oversimplifying* the issues. The first five in the preceding list rely primarily on diversion; the last two rely on oversimplification. Fallacies are seductive types of pseudo-reasoning because many of them overlap with or resemble valid sorts of reasoning and because they appeal to our desire for simple, quick, emotionally satisfying answers.

The presence of fallacies in a message doesn't mean that we should automatically reject the message; but it does mean that material is being used, intentionally or not, that can lead us to invalid conclusions that are not in our real best interests. Their presence in a message should put us on guard.

Giving the Message a Fair Hearing   A healthy suspicion of persuasion should be counterbalanced by a second attitude: determination to hear (or read) the message accurately and fairly. You cannot really decide whether or not the speaker is validly proving that his proposal is in your interests unless you first hear his argument. In an argument with another speaker you are more likely to persuade neutral listeners if you first hear and understand your opponent's argument.

Thus in evaluating persuasion you need to be on guard but to delay judgment on the issue until you have heard the message. A system will help you evaluate the appeals in other people's persuasive messages.

A System for Evaluation

A listener is usually persuaded for one or more of three broad reasons: because of her faith in the speaker, because she is emotionally drawn to a certain decision, or because she is convinced that the decision is logical in view of the facts and her own beliefs and self-interest. Because all three reasons enter into our decision making, each needs to be evaluated.

Evaluate the Source   For speeches, the source is normally the speaker; in some cases, it might be extended to include the agency sponsoring the speaker or meeting. We need to know two main things about the source: real purpose and qualifications.

A speaker sponsored by the local utility company addresses various audiences on the topic of future demand and supply of electrical power in the city. We know from newspaper accounts that the company has invested heavily in a nuclear power plant under construction. We should hardly be surprised when the speaker's "informative" speech shows that future demand for electricity will rise sharply and the only adequate and efficient way to provide it is by nuclear power. A persuasive speaker may not always make clear the real purpose or his own motivations in giving the speech. You need to ask yourself two questions about the source's purpose: What is the intended effect of this speech on my attitudes and behavior? and, What motivates the speaker? The answers, of course, *may* be quite consistent with your purpose in listening to the speech, but they may also provide a much shrewder way of looking at the speech.

Even with a speaker whose purposes are open and reasonable enough, we still want to know if she is competent as a source. Does she have enough specific information about the issue at hand, enough experience with the general subject, and enough judgment to make sound decisions?

Evaluate the Emotional Appeal   Evaluating emotional appeal requires two steps. First, detect which emotional states or motives are being intensified. Second, determine whether such intensification is appropriate or relevant for the decision you are being asked to make.

Heightened emotions are not necessarily inappropriate. There are, for

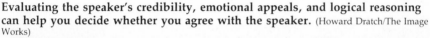

Evaluating the speaker's credibility, emotional appeals, and logical reasoning can help you decide whether you agree with the speaker. (Howard Dratch/The Image Works)

example, in the world around us and in our personal lives many injustices that should arouse our anger or pity. But even in these situations we need to test the link between a legitimate stirring up of emotion and the specific decision the speaker is asking us to make. We should feel pity for those suffering from hunger, but is the agency we are being asked to support making an effective or even an honest attempt to reduce hunger? We may well fear the horrors of nuclear war, but is unilateral arms reduction a viable way to reduce that danger? The answers to such questions usually depend on evaluating the logical reasoning in the speech.

Evaluate the Logical Reasoning   See if what the speaker says makes rational sense. You get some help here just by testing the speaker's content against your own knowledge and past experience, common sense, and self-interest. You can make shrewder judgments if you analyze the speaker's premises and the evidence she offers in support of her conclusions.

The Premises.   The premises, or assumptions, on which arguments are based are sometimes stated explicitly, but more often they are unstated. The evaluator needs to ask, What must I assume in order to draw this conclusion from the evidence given? A speaker, for example, offers convincing evidence that regular physical exercise significantly increases life span and concludes that therefore we should exercise. Most of us accept the unstated premise that a longer life span is desirable; and since we found the evidence convincing, we also accept the conclusion that we should exercise. (This doesn't necessarily mean that we *will* exercise, because to convince an audience is not necessarily enough to motivate them to action.)

Let's take another example. A compulsive child murderer is being tried for his crimes. He convinces the jury that he is not responsible for his vicious acts, that he is actually a victim of his own compulsions, and therefore he should be spared the death penalty. The unstated premise is that a person not responsible for his own acts should be spared full punishment. But the prosecutor, while accepting the evidence that the murderer cannot control his own actions, rejects this unstated premise. Instead he offers another premise: Anyone who cannot control his own murderous impulses is too dangerous to be allowed to live. The jury switches to accept the prosecutor's premise and votes the death penalty. Thus even when we accept the evidence, our decision to accept or reject an asserted conclusion should also depend on our reaction to the premise assumed in the argument.

The Evidence.   Evidence consists of the factual examples, testimony of experts, statistics, and other material given as proof that the speaker's assertions are logically valid. The evaluator needs, first, to realize that much detail offered in support of asserted conclusions does not function primarily as logical proof. A speaker asserts that for a career in high-technology industry, a college education is less useful than getting out on the job. To support this assertion he provides in compelling detail the case history of a high school dropout who amassed a fortune in a computer business. As evidence this case history is feeble: The speaker has based a broad generalization on only one example, and that is probably a very untypical one. The case history functioned primarily to provide a high level of interest and perhaps some emotional appeal in the speech.

When we have isolated the material functioning primarily as logical proof, we can then evaluate the quality, relevance, and quantity of this evidence in relation to the assertions it supports. To evaluate *quality* we ask questions such as these: How recent are the statistics? Was the source of the statistics or expert testimony unbiased? How expert is the "expert" the speaker quotes to support his point? Is the example a significant and typical case in relation to the generalized conclusion it is supposed to prove? Has the speaker summarized or quoted the evidence fairly? To evaluate *relevance* we ask, Is the expert really talking about this case or type of case? Do the statistics really apply to this case? To evaluate *quantity* we ask, Is the speaker drawing a key generalization from only one striking example, or is he, more convincingly, depending on a range of typical examples. Similarly several experts supporting a point are generally more convincing than one.

The main concern in this section has been to determine *the degree to which* we can rely on a persuader's influence when we are making a particular decision. The same framework of considerations would help us detect weaknesses when we must refute an opponent's case in order to convince a third party.

Listening as a Critic of Speechmaking

Skill in listening as a critic will enable you to respond more helpfully when a friend or associate comes to you and says, "I've got to give this speech in a couple of days. Would you listen to it and give me some pointers?" Equally important, skill in analyzing speeches as a critic will enable you to expand and refine your own speaking skills to fit later special needs. If, for example, you find yourself on the speakers' bureau of the company for which you work, you can pick up new techniques by analyzing what successful practitioners in that sort of speaking do and then applying what you learn to your own practice.

An Approach to Criticism

In class criticism your instructor will probably emphasize *technical* analysis based on such questions as these: What was the speaker's purpose, and how well was it achieved? What techniques, from organization of the speech to delivery, were used? What contributed to the effectiveness of the speech, and what needs to be improved? This approach is most useful for improving speech skills in class as well as giving you practice in observation and criticism that will enable you to improve later.

You should be aware, however, that technical analysis is not the only legitimate approach in speech criticism. Audience members often comment on a speaker's fascinating supporting material, clever language, or enthralling delivery, as if these qualities were themselves the aims of the speech. This *aesthetic* approach judges the speech as a pleasing experience in its own right without much regard to its informative or persuasive effects. (Given a choice, however, between a dazzling speaker whose message doesn't penetrate very deeply and a less spectacular speaker who does convince the audience, you will benefit more from studying the latter's techniques more closely.)

Speeches may also be criticized from an *ethical* perspective, in which the critic asks such questions as these: Was the speech worthy of the audience's time? Was the speaker's purpose in their best interests? Did the speaker really understand the topic well enough to make sound judgments and to treat it competently? Were arguments and other materials in the speech used to mislead the audience?

Although the emphasis in class criticism is on technical analysis, as fully developed human beings we cannot and should not ignore aesthetic and ethical sensibilities. Therefore neither of these other two approaches is entirely irrelevant or inappropriate, even in class criticism.

Suggestions for the Critic in Class

The following suggestions deal with how you can help your fellow students in class criticism.

1. *Aim to be helpful in your criticism.* Student speakers tend to make better progress if they feel that most of their classmates are really pulling for them, and this shows best when you point out specifically what worked well. Pulling for a person, however, also includes telling her specifically what didn't work and how to improve. This can be done in an honest but tactfully supportive way. If the delivery was energetic but the introduction didn't arouse audience interest, make *both* points. You do even better if you can explain *why* the delivery was effective and can *offer suggestions* for improving the introduction. Your ability to offer useful, specific, constructive criticism will increase during the course as you learn more speech theory.

2. *Avoid being dogmatic in criticism.* The dogmatic critic "knows" that his criticism is absolutely valid, and he isn't interested in the speaker's explanation of why she did something a certain way or what other listeners think. Actually, criticism is pretty subjective. You will occasionally see your class as critics split over such judgments as whether an introduction

or conclusion worked well or whether a topic was well adapted to the audience. Thus it is better to approach criticism as the art of making helpful suggestions, rather than as the science of pronouncing ultimate judgment.

3. *Be purposeful in criticism.* Assume that you are going to give the speaker some perceptive and useful comments. You can consciously observe some specific areas of technique, such as structure and transitions, or supporting material, or delivery, or introduction and conclusion. You can also combine your role as attentive audience member with your responsibility to make helpful technical comments by consciously monitoring your own reactions to the speech. Apply the four basic qualities that would make the speech effective for you as a listener: appropriateness, clarity, interest, and credibility. For example, does this speech seem appropriate to audience, occasion, and speaker? Why? Are you following it easily? Why not? Taking a few notes on each speaker can get you more actively involved in listening analytically, and it assures you of having something to say about each speaker, especially if the whole panel of speakers is critiqued together at the end of the class session. You may also want to accumulate these notes as a mass of specific observations, some of which will suggest techniques you can use to good effect in your own speeches in future rounds.

Summary

Listening skills enable you to obtain information efficiently from lectures and other oral presentations, to evaluate the validity of persuasion, and to improve your own speaking by learning from what other speakers do well. These and other aims in functional listening are better achieved if you listen to accomplish a particular purpose and if you remove your own mental obstacles to effective listening.

To get information by listening, you need to pay attention, understand what is being said, and retain the material. You can motivate yourself to pay attention better by reminding yourself of what you stand to gain from the lecture or discussion and by actively participating, at least mentally. You can understand better if you have a clear notion of what you are expected to get out of the presentation, if you try to spot key ideas and structure, and if you relate the presented material to your other knowledge and experience. You can retain material better by taking complete, organized notes and by reviewing your notes after the session.

To evaluate persuasion intended to influence your decisions, you need to be on the lookout for fallacies and other manipulative appeals; but you also need to hear the speaker out. Evaluate the speaker's real purpose and competence, the relevance of appeals to emotion, and the premises and evidence used to justify conclusions in logical appeals.

You develop your ability both to help other speakers and to learn techniques from these speakers by participating in class criticism. In this criticism, aim to be helpful and listen with your role as critic in mind.

Exercises

1. Be prepared to discuss or present in a two- to three-minute speech what you have learned by critically observing other speakers. Explain how you can apply your observations to improve your own speaking skill. Draw on your listening both in speech class and elsewhere.

2. In another course that depends largely on lecture presentations, casually interview several of your classmates to determine their sense of purpose and mental set when they attend the lectures. Do any have serious obstacles to attention and comprehension? Be prepared to present your results in a class discussion or in a two- to three-minute speech.

3. Observe an assigned persuasive presentation, preferably a persuasive speech on campus or in the community, but if necessary on television or videotape. Give a two- to three-minute presentation developing one of the following approaches:
   a. An evaluation of the validity of the speech, following guidelines for evaluating persuasion given in this chapter.
   b. An analysis of the persuasive techniques used, as might be done by someone wanting to learn how to improve his own skills in persuasion.

PART II

Techniques for Speech Preparation and Presentation

PART II

CHAPTER FOUR

Analyzing Situation and Deciding on a Specific Purpose

Consider the plight of the speaker for a high school commencement. She must come up with a topic for a speech that will be new to the audience, profound, interesting, inspiring—and somehow different from the thousands of other speeches given in virtually identical situations every year. Most speech students, faced with the task of discovering topics of their own, can sympathize with her problem. Yet these students have plenty of topics potentially available. The challenge is to locate these topics and then to narrow and adapt them into specific purposes appropriate for the particular assignments. It's a challenge that continues into later careers, although speakers then frequently have a narrower range of choices than in a speech class.

How can you meet this challenge without frustration? Begin by realizing that a perfect specific purpose rarely appears as an immediate, inspired answer to a speaking assignment. Instead, the speaker almost always begins with some initial idea from which the specific purpose of the speech is eventually shaped, and often the final topic and purpose are a long way from the initial idea. Let's see how the process might work.

A student is assigned to give a speech in class. The only specification is that it be eight minutes long. It can be either informative or persuasive. The student has taken some drama courses and performed in plays both on campus and in the community, so he decides to give his speech on what is happening locally in stage drama. He now has a topic area, but it's far too broad and vague for an eight-minute speech.

He considers several possible ways to narrow his topic. He could deal with play production or with appreciation of plays or with the history of campus or community theater. Finally, because his listeners are students on campus, he decides to deal only with plays presented on campus and to approach the topic from the playgoer's rather than the performer's point of view. Most of his classmates don't go to plays, so he refines the focus further to be "the rewards of attending plays on campus." Because his audience is likely to be doubtful about these rewards, he decides that he will persuade rather than inform.

To be sure that his specific purpose is clearly defined in his own mind he writes it out: "to persuade students in this class to go to plays on campus." For his audience he plans a tentative statement of focus "I'd like to urge you to see some of the stage dramas being presented on campus this year."

From this example, two important notions emerge. First, because a good speech fits the situation in which it occurs, your preparation is guided by your analysis of this situation. Second, rather than jumping randomly from idea to idea, you can follow a relatively efficient method for discovering a topic and then shaping your specific purpose.

Analyzing the Situation: Three Reference Points

A speech is a personal act of communication on a particular occasion to a specific group of listeners. Thus from initial search for possible topic areas onward through final preparation and presentation, three reference points guide development of the speech: the speaker, the occasion, and the audience.

Your Own Resources as Speaker

Insofar as you can within the particular situation, make use of your own inclinations and background. Try, for example, to pick topics in which you feel somehow involved because of the interest or knowledge you already have. Many student speakers, as they begin to get over their initial nervousness in the course, actually look on their speeches as chances to air their views or show their expertise on a topic.

Personal involvement with a topic gives you several important advantages. If you know at least a little about the topic, as one student put it, "you have somewhere to start and you know where to go." Thus you can save some time in research, and that time can then be spent polishing organization and delivery. As you go through the later steps in preparation, you continue to draw on your own resources. Your experience with a topic often enables you to use insights and specific examples that are just not available in printed sources. Personal knowledge and interest also increase the likelihood that your delivery will be more confident and enthusiastic. Also, the audience will respond with greater interest and respect if you can establish some personal connection, even a slight one, with the topic.

Analyzing and adapting to your own resources is realistic preparation for your later speaking. Most of the speeches you are likely to give will be drawn from your job or some other aspect of your personal concerns, even though in many cases you may have to search out additional information for the specific speech.

Occasion and General Purpose of Speech

It normally takes only the speaker's will to recognize and adapt to the two common requirements of occasion: Give the right general type of speech, and do it within the prescribed time frame. This meets, at least minimally, the listeners' assumptions about what will occur on the occasion.

People give speeches for such a variety of purposes and with such different and often subtle effects that any rigid division of all speeches into a few types, or general purposes, is likely to be more tidy than realistic. Nevertheless, it is important to establish some rough distinctions, because in the great majority of cases the occasion calls for a particular general purpose. For most of the speeches you are likely to give, the basic distinction in general purpose is between informing the audience and persuading the audience. This basic distinction, however, is not very meaningful for some other types of speeches that we will also consider.

Distinction Between Informative and Persuasive Purpose   Informative speeches provide objective information and insight. The instruction you receive in your courses or might receive in on-the-job training, for example, is presumably informative. Persuasive speeches attempt to change or reinforce audience attitudes on debatable issues or to get audience members to take some action.

In actual practice, marking the difference between "informative" and "persuasive" may be less simple. A speaker gives a speech explaining the early history of computers; his purpose is clearly to inform. He gives a speech urging his audience to buy a certain brand of microcomputer for their homes; his purpose is clearly to persuade. He gives a speech explaining how computer information networks can make available to anyone with access to one of the computers a great deal of private information about each one of us. The speaker feels he has given an objective informative speech, but many in the audience go away with deep misgivings about their privacy in the computer age. Was this third speech informative or persuasive? That is a neat question.

There is no neat answer. But this third speech does enable us to note a couple of important points about the distinction between informative and persuasive speeches. First, there are speeches that fall on the borderline: for some listeners they simply provide information; for others they significantly change attitudes. Second, even though a speech contains a great deal of factual information and does not announce a persuasive purpose, it may still be persuasive in intent and effect. One could argue that the third computer speech is persuasive, for two reasons: the absence in the speech of benefits of computer information networks, and the fact that the speech significantly altered some listeners' attitudes toward computers.

The following four considerations will help both speakers and listeners distinguish in practice between informative and persuasive speeches.

	Informative	**Persuasive**
Ultimate purpose and effect	To increase listeners' knowledge and understanding of the speech topic.	To influence listeners' attitudes toward the subject of the speech.
Selection of major ideas	Determined by the topic itself; the subject is covered in a reasonably balanced and complete way.	Determined by the speaker's intent to control the audience's perception and attitude toward the subject.
Supporting detail and language	Used merely to maintain a reasonable level of interest as well as clarity.	Used to stir emotional responses.
Audience perception	Audience sees the speech as objective and accurate.	Audience sees the speech as biased, as advancing only one of several possible views of the subject.

For the speaker who must maintain an informative rather than persuasive purpose, two further suggestions apply during preparation of the speech. First, try to know enough about your subject to avoid an unconscious bias created by limited experience or a few biased sources. Sometimes it is necessary to seek out a source or two, perhaps an interview, for views at odds with your own view of your topic. Second, in planning the structure of the speech, you may have to be especially vigilant to cover all major aspects of your topic, or at least enough to give the audience a balanced view. In the examples given earlier, the third speech would have been more safely informative if the speaker had discussed, for example, the restrictions on access to computer information banks or if he had pointed out some of the advantages of having so much information available.

Other Types of General Purpose $\quad$ Most other types of speeches contain elements of information or persuasion, yet neither of these aims accurately defines their purposes. As with information and persuasion, the type called for is usually determined by the situation rather than by the speaker's inclinations. We will look at four types.

$\quad$ *Ceremonial.* $\quad$ *Ceremonial speeches* occur in highly defined situations, and they are often judged mainly by how appropriately or imaginatively they fit the situation. They include speeches of welcome and commemoration, eulogies and award speeches, and chairpersons' introductions of speakers.

$\quad$ *Conflict Reduction.* $\quad$ Frequently in our society, factions oppose each other in ways that are unprofitable or that threaten the common good. Members of a union are divided on the issue of whether to strike, and emotions flare as the conflict intensifies. Even such an issue as where to hold meetings can create serious conflict within an organization. In the conflict reduction speech the speaker meets such occasions by attempting to reduce divisive tension and, if possible, to achieve compromise or agreement between the factions.

Program. The Rotary Club or the parent-teacher association asks you to be a guest speaker at their regular meeting two months hence. They may suggest a topic area, or one may be implied by your background or by the nature of the organization or particular meeting. Even when a certain topic area is indicated, you are usually given a great deal of leeway to develop your own views, ideas, information, and feelings on that topic. Sometimes the only specifications are a tactfully stated time limit and the implicit assumption that you will say something interesting about a worthwhile topic without being disturbingly controversial. In program speeches, the speaker may make listeners more informed about such topics as the challenges and rewards of being a public school teacher, the foibles of local city government, or different and amusing ways of looking at the way we use language. These speakers may also reaffirm and even inspire such beliefs as the value of initiative in business and public service, the need to pursue excellence in our daily tasks, or the rewards of travel or developing relationships with other people. Although program speeches may tend in either direction, neither "informative" nor "persuasive" captures the particular combination of serious purpose, varied and entertaining supporting detail, and informally expressed expertise expected in program speeches. And there are hundreds of thousands of them given every year, often by people who never expected to be public speakers.

Entertainment. Although many sorts of speeches should be entertaining—at least in the sense of being interesting enough to hold the audience's favorable attention—the term entertainment speech is used for speeches that are given primarily to amuse the audience through humor or highly novel material. The best-known subtype is the "after-dinner speech," of ancient and honorable lineage. An entertainment speech, unlike the patter of a stand-up comedian, usually has at least a vaguely defined specific topic. Many entertainment speeches even have a minor element of informative or persuasive purpose; but as this more serious purpose begins to dominate, the speech moves away from entertainment into another type. The entertainment speech is characterized by special skill with anecdotal material, vivid description, topical humor and satire, and spontaneous wit.

The remainder of this chapter and the five following chapters through Chapter 9 cover the basic means that apply to constructing and presenting any sort of speech. In these six chapters, however, these means are explained mainly in terms of informative speeches. Chapter 10 deals with the special requirements and techniques of persuasion. Chapter 11 has some suggestions specifically for speeches to reduce conflict and for some of the sorts of ceremonial speeches you may be required to give.

Additional Constraints of Occasion   Sometimes it is enough merely to give the appropriate type of speech in the stipulated length of time. At the opposite extreme, some occasions—such as an expert's report to a legislative board—narrowly define the speaker's specific purpose and treatment of material. Between these extremes are many occasions that influence the speaker's role with more subtle constraints. Here are three kinds of considerations you need to keep in mind:

1. Does the occasion call for an efficient, thorough treatment of a narrowly delimited specific purpose or for a relatively entertaining, less obviously structured speech? An oral report on a research project in an advanced history or psychology class, for example, would usually call for complete coverage of a precisely defined topic in a clear, efficient structure. On the other hand, a speaker reporting to the hiking club on her mountaineering experiences in the Cascade Range would be expected to provide a general sense of her activity and some interesting examples, rather than a complete, systematic report.
2. Are you expected to demonstrate some special expertise in your treatment of the topic? In later informative speeches in your speech class, for example, although you won't be expected to be a world authority, you will probably be expected to demonstrate a special knowledge of your topic—derived at least partly from research as well as perhaps from unusual background experiences you can bring to bear.
3. Will you be speaking in a more formal or a more relaxed and casual atmosphere? When presenting a special award, for example, are you expected to be jovial or serious?

Initial Analysis of Audience

As you begin preparation consider the characteristics of your audience that might guide your choice of topic and specific purpose. Adaption to audience characteristics should also guide your later development of the speech. Analysis should be done whether the audience is familiar or unfamiliar to you.

Characteristics of the Audience   By the very reasons for their being together in one place at one time, members of any particular audience are likely to have characteristics in common. Some of these characteristics are directly related to the occasion for the speech—a meeting of stamp collectors for example—while other characteristics, such as age or educational background, are more coincidental. If a speaker can recognize both sorts of characteristics, she has at least some clues as to how to select and treat a topic that might be interesting or useful to her audience. The following are three common bases for characterizing audiences.

1. *Age*: Perhaps we can still use Aristotle's notion that older audiences are more conservative and more interested in matters of security, whereas younger audiences are more idealistic and more interested in matters of challenge and achievement. At any rate, age does give clues to other audience concerns. A speech class of mainly seniors is likely to be interested in matters of the job market or graduate school, whereas a class of freshmen will be more interested in how to succeed in or enjoy college.

2. *Sex*: Roles and interests on the basis of gender are not nearly as clearly distinguished as they were even a generation ago. Nevertheless, a speaker addressing a mainly male audience would with some risk draw her topic from *Cosmopolitan* magazine, and another speaker might find a mainly female audience initially less than enthralled with his speech on modifying "muscle cars" of the 1960s. Few if any topics are inherently inappropriate for one or the other sex, but a speaker should be aware of the need to make special efforts to adapt some topics to both sexes in a mixed audience. The speaker on muscle cars could use as a major example, from his personal knowledge or research, at least one woman who gets great satisfaction from owning such a car. He thereby makes the subject seem less alien to many of his female listeners.

3. *Profession*: Listeners tend to identify themselves as members of a profession or vocational group, especially if the occasion for the speech is a meeting of their group. Groups of businesspersons are likely to be interested in computer technology, tax legislation, new management theories, or other developments that affect business organization and commerce. Present or future teachers are likely to be interested in methods and satisfactions of good teaching, but they may not react enthusiastically to a speaker deploring the "sad state" of public education. Union members are likely to be interested in the effects of robotics and other automation on jobs or on job security.

Other bases on which audiences can sometimes be characterized include educational background, leisure-time interests such as sports events versus fine arts, economic status, religious affiliation, and predominant social and political concerns. While such bases are often a useful way to begin analyzing an audience's interests and beliefs, they may not necessarily get at the important characteristics of every audience you face. Probably one important characteristic of your classmates, for example, is an interest in whatever affects the students or the reputation of your school. The point is: Seek characteristics that many of your listeners have in common as one way of discovering topics and treatments that will interest them.

Awareness of your listeners' background and interests, as well as their degree of knowledge about your topic, will guide you later in preparation when you plan your structure of main ideas, select and shape the supporting materials, and plan the introduction. The speaker's flexibility in adapting topic and treatment reflects a more general willingness to respect and be of service to the audience. A good speaker, for example,

Members of a classroom audience have many characteristics in common, but are also different from each other in many ways. (Elyse Rieder for Random House, courtesy of Pace University Speech and Drama Department)

treats a technical subject crisply for a group of experts and reduces his level of complexity and language for grade-school children. He takes both audiences seriously.

A word of caution: People are much more sensitive and self-conscious in audiences, especially small ones, than they may be in personal conversation. Do not embarrass your listeners or otherwise make them feel uncomfortable—for example, by your treatment of medical subjects, torture, or sex—unless there is some real point to be made. Even then, be as tactful and restrained as possible. What embarrasses an audience is seldom appropriate in a speech, whatever its purpose.

Familiar and Unfamiliar Audiences Students sometimes think that a speech class audience is somehow "artificial," as distinct from later "real life" audiences, and therefore is easier to talk to. Yet if for some reason you had to give a speech to another speech class late in the term, you would probably discover that the new speech class would be challengingly real—just as your present speech class actually is a "real" audience. The key difference is between an audience of familiar persons, to whom you can adapt almost intuitively, and an audience of relative strangers. You are likely later in your career to meet the particular challenges of both familiar and unfamiliar audiences.

Familiar Audiences.   With a familiar audience, you know more about what your listeners are interested in, and they know more about your background. This familiarity can produce an easy, almost automatic adaptation and a feeling of relaxed friendship. However, a common danger when preparing to face a familiar audience is that the speaker feels so comfortable he may get careless in selecting a specific purpose and working on the speech. In a speech class, this may result in a trite topic—for example, an offensive lineman on the football team choosing to explain the basic rules of football. Take advantage of interests in common and what you and a familiar audience know about one another. But when you do, use some creative and serious effort. The offensive lineman could more imaginatively have given his speech on how offensive players adapt to scouting reports on opponents or how players psych themselves up for games.

Unfamiliar Audiences.   Even a professional speaker is likely to be nervous preparing for an unfamiliar audience. Finding out about the audience in advance, however, can both reduce nervousness and increase the likely success of your speech.

Above all, you need to know what sort of speech the audience expects you to give: length, topic area, type of purpose, degree of formality. What interests bring members of the audience together, and how do they view the occasion? What other characteristics do they have in common? How do they view you: as performer, as technical expert, as welcomed guest, as program filler?

Obtain information about the audience tactfully from the person who arranges the speech with you. Get his or her telephone number in case you need further information about the audience when you are working on the speech. Perhaps you have an acquaintance who is a member of, or at least knows something about, the group. If it is a public group, such as a city council, you can observe the members in a meeting before you speak to them

As you begin the first step in preparation, then, you especially want to ask yourself these questions: What personal resources might you draw on for a topic? What sort of general purpose and other specifications are called for by the occasion? What audience characteristics might influence your choice of topic and specific purpose for the speech?

Method for Arriving at a Specific Purpose

In some situations, both in school and later, you will be given a topic area, but you will seldom be handed a perfect specific purpose. So there is some advantage in having experience with a method for moving efficiently, from even zero ideas for a topic area, to a specific purpose that will work well in the particular situation, and finally to a statement of focus. Before moving on to suggestions for doing this let's be sure we have a clear meaning for each major stage in the method.

1. *Topic area* is a general, often vaguely defined idea of what you could talk about. It is usually much too broad to cover in a single speech. Each topic area contains or implies numerous specific topics, only one of which you will use in the speech. Thinking in terms of topic areas lets you discover and explore your ideas without feeling that you have to produce the instantly "right" specific topic and purpose for a speech.
2. *Specific purpose* states the goal of the speech—that is, the effect you want to achieve with the audience. It delimits both the specific topic, or focus, and the type of general purpose, such as to make the audience better informed about the topic or to persuade them to a certain attitude about it. You write this out to guide your own preparation and perhaps for your instructor. Accomplishing this purpose is *why* you gather information and other material and then use it in the speech.
3. *Statement of focus* is your way of telling members of your audience the specific topic you intend to cover so they will know what to expect in the speech. It usually comes at the end of the introduction in the presented speech.

The following table illustrates these terms for an informative speech on drug smuggling, and a persuasive speech on campus plays.

General Purpose	Persuasive	Informative
Topic area	What is happening in local stage drama.	The federal government's attempts to control drug smuggling.
Specific purpose	To persuade students in speech class to go to some plays on campus.	To inform the audience about the federal government's special campaign against drug smuggling in Florida during the 1980s.
Statement of Focus	"I'd like to urge you to see some of the stage dramas being presented on campus this year. Consider the following reasons for attending campus plays."	"This morning I will describe the federal government's special campaign against drug smugglers in Florida during the eighties. I'll explain what was done and the effects it had."

Stage 1: Find a Suitable Topic Area

A student in a speech class knows that he is going to give several speeches during the term, so he sets aside a few pages in his notebook just to note down and perhaps explore possible topics for speeches. A few days later he hears a literature teacher mention Marshall McLuhan's notion that novelists and other creative artists are among the best people in society for interpreting the impact of technology. Somehow this seems relevant to the student's own interest in science fiction films and books, so he jots down some notes on the teacher's remarks and his own connection to science fiction, even though he hardly sees at this point how this provides a specific topic for a speech. Later, he decides to go just with movies, since in an earlier speech he told the class of his personal study of science fiction films. Eventually, he ends up with this topic area: how science fiction films warn us or prepare us for the technology of the future. It is still probably too broad and vague for a specific purpose, but it is something promising to work from when he must begin to shape up a particular speech.

Suggestions for Looking   Several general suggestions can be drawn from the example in the preceding paragraph:

1. Start early—"from day one," as one student put it—to look for topics, not just for your next speech, but for all the speeches you can foresee giving during the term. (Speakers who do a good deal of program speaking sometimes are shaping up topics long before they have particular assignments for which the topics will be used.)
2. Be open and alert to material you encounter in chance ways that triggers your own interests or knowledge, your curiosity, or your desire to talk about it to other people.
3. Jot down a note or two on a possible topic, perhaps explore the idea a bit on paper, in a notebook or other place you can readily find when you have to begin work on a speech. Try to accumulate notes on several possible topic areas so you have some selection.
4. Don't judge these general ideas for possible topics too hastily. You cannot be sure what specific possibilities are in a topic area until you start working with it. For example, noticing that you have trouble deciding what to wear one morning might yield an excellent speech on how clothes reflect mood and personality.

Places to Look   As a speech student now or as a speaker later, you may occasionally have some trouble finding topic areas when the situation permits freedom of choice. The following list may prove helpful. Realize that these suggestions are intended to trigger off ideas that already exist in your background or in which you might become genuinely interested, and that a triggered idea will probably require a good deal of refinement before it leads to a workable specific purpose for a speech. Move through the list fairly briskly; but when you come to a category that gets your attention, stop and let yourself think randomly about possibilities, even jotting some down on paper.

Topics Within Your Own Background

1. *Your past and present experiences*: Jobs, hobbies, living elsewhere, clubs, special training programs, contests. More specific sorts of topics include, for example, a job as athletic trainer, apprehending shoplifters in a discount store, the operation and atmosphere of a chess tournament or beauty pageant.
2. *What you do for self-improvement or social service*: Jogging, nutritional habits, volunteering for a charity organization, taking a particular nonrequired course.
3. *What you feel strongly about*: Complaints and gripes, values you hold, personal qualities and characteristics you esteem. More specific possibilities include complaints about dormitories, registration, and the attitudes of particular school officials toward students, techniques of teachers you admire, honesty and courage, either present or absent, in past or present political leaders.
4. *What you are curious to learn about*: What do you read about, or what would you like to read about if you had time? Have any interests been aroused in other courses? Are you curious to know how some organizations came into existence or operate or how some event in the past occurred?

Speech topics are often drawn from a speaker's own experiences. (Phaneuf/Gurdziel/The Picture Cube)

Topics from Public Affairs

1. *Social problems and political issues*: Campus, city, state, national, and international. Possible topic areas include taxation, crime and suicide, drug abuse, fraud and incompetence in government, environmental protection, allocation of public funds.
2. *Advances in science and technology, religion, or the arts*: Recent discoveries about primitive man, uses of lasers and computers, space exploration, genetic engineering.

Topics Suggested by Considering the Audience

1. *Of practical value to audience*: Student services on campus such as counseling or study skills, how to buy a used car, various sorts of home or car repairs, how to interview for a job.
2. *Promoting listeners' self-actualization*: Appreciation of some form of music, literature, film, art; special interest clubs on campus; new types of careers.
3. *Below the surface of something familiar to the audience*: History or beliefs of various cults or terrorist organizations, earlier careers of current public officials, psychological analysis of dreams, how movie theaters book films, history of some local area.
4. *Novel information*: Extrasensory perception, current theories about the Yeti or Bigfoot or the Loch Ness monster, famous local criminals.

A final comment on finding a topic area is mainly for you as a student in a speech class. Don't panic if you discover that another student is giving a speech in the same topic area before your turn comes up. The speeches are more likely to complement than duplicate each other, and this will increase interest in your speech. You can even adapt to the situation by alluding to some points the other speaker made. Such adaptation is especially impressive if both speeches are given on the same day.

Stage 2: Focus on a Specific Purpose

Very good student speakers who have learned the hard way give friends who are beginning a speech course this advice: Limit your specific purpose to a narrow part of your topic area. And limit it soon in preparation, even though you may have to modify it as you get further into research. These students have good reasons. The interest, clarity, and credibility of a speech depend heavily on depth of specific supporting detail, and the greater the depth of detail the less topic area you can cover in a given length of time. So you need to cut yourself out a task you can handle comfortably within your time limit. Also, you are unlikely to hold interest or impress an audience favorably if you ramble around randomly in a broad topic area like a nervous hunter in a jungle of ideas. As a final reason, the sooner you can narrow down to at least a tentative specific purpose, the less time and effort you are likely to waste thinking, reading, interviewing, taking notes, and doing other preparation that you will never use.

Our science fiction movie buff had arrived at a broad topic area: how science fiction films warn us or prepare us for the technology of the future. He is assigned to give a ten-minute speech that will be informative in general purpose. As he thinks about his past viewing, he notes several possible themes that have appeared in science fiction films: mutant monsters resulting from nuclear contamination, probes to other planets, wars fought in outer space, futuristic societies, and the significance of computers in some societies. He decides that the theme his audience will find most realistic and interesting is the depiction of computers in movies. He has made his first cut in reducing his topic area.

However, when he considers how many movies have depicted computers, from the 1960s through "Tron," "War Games," and subsequent films in the 1980s, he realizes that he still has far too much topic to cover. His original idea was to show how science fiction films prepare us for future technology, and among the film titles he has jotted down are three that dealt with computers in a six-year span just before general public awareness of the significance of computers. These films are "Alphaville" (Jean-Luc Godard, 1965), "2001: A Space Odyssey" (Stanley Kubrick, 1968), and "Colossus: The Forbin Project" (Joseph Sargent, 1970). He now has a specific topic: the depiction of computer technology in three films between 1965 and 1970.

Although he believes that these movies were brilliantly farsighted in pointing out how computers could really change or control people, he realizes that in this speech his assigned task is to inform rather than to persuade. Therefore he takes an objective slant of simply reporting how the films depicted the dangers of computers. He phrases the specific purpose like this: "to explain to the audience how three films between 1965 and 1970 portrayed alleged dangers of computer technology." Before moving on in his preparation he evaluates his specific purpose. He decides that it will be an interesting slant for the audience, that he has enough available information on the subject, and that it will fit his time frame well. He is a little concerned that "three films" might seem to be a vague focus, but he decides that in his introduction he can explain how these three are a good cross section of films ranging from popular to heavily serious, and he can rephrase his specific purpose as: "to explain how significant science fiction films between 1965 and 1970 portrayed alleged dangers of computer technology."

Note from this example that you go through four fairly distinct thought processes in moving from topic area to specific purpose:

1. *Think of several possibilities* in the topic area.
2. *Select one* that fits your needs in the speech.
3. *Shape and phrase it* as a specific purpose.
4. *Check it* for possible faults.

You may need to go through parts of this process twice or more before arriving at a manageable specific purpose. For example, after you have selected and phrased one possible specific purpose, you may discover that it is still too broad and thus needs to be broken down into even more limited possibilities.

Discover Possibilities in the Topic Area   There are several methods for slicing a topic area into narrower possible specific purposes. Whatever methods you use, write down the possibilities as you discover them. You will feel more confident about your specific purpose if you can choose from several possibilities actually written out in front of you.

One method is to think randomly about various aspects of the topic area, perhaps over a few days. A student who decided to speak about his job as a department store security guard might in two or three days discover several possible slants just on shoplifting: (1) How a security system detects shoplifters. (2) Don't try to shoplift. (3) The sorts of people who do shoplift. (4) You should report someone you see shoplifting. (5) The legal procedures followed in dealing with shoplifters. Because his assignment calls for an informative speech, he can scratch 2 and 4 as persuasive, leaving three choices.

Another method of searching the topic area for manageable topics includes jotting down a list of examples and other specific information on the general topic and then seeing if these items can be grouped into clusters. Each cluster will suggest a specific focus on some aspect of the topic area. The speaker on science fiction films grouped three movies, of many he thought of, into such a cluster to get his specific topic.

A third method is to discover possible specific topics by doing background reading or scanning some books or articles on your general topic. A student, having decided to give his speech on gunfighters of the old West, found a book treating the topic in a general way and with chapters on a dozen or so notorious individuals. The student realized that simply summarizing one of the chapters would hardly make a very creative speech. But by approaching the material more creatively and assuming he would probably do some additional research, he sorted out at least three good specific topics: to show how unstable and unhappy were the real lives of some of our Western heroes; to contrast the adolescent bravado of Billy the Kid with the vicious professionalism of "Killin' Jim" Miller as representing different types of gunfighters; or to tell the true story of the famous gunfight at the O K corral.

A fourth method is to find out from friends, especially if they are sample audience members, what sorts of slants they would suggest on your topic area. For a topic area on combining work with school, for example, one friend might suggest the speaker discuss the effects of having a job on grades and social life. Another might suggest instead a speech on what sorts of jobs are available and how to find the best ones. The speaker now has at least two specific topics that would be of interest.

Finally, a more systematic method is to arrive at a list of mainheads for a speech on the topic area and then view each mainhead as a possibility for the specific focus of your speech. Sometimes the topic area can be divided into mainheads on the basis of time. The idea of the impact of inflation in the United States, for example, could be divided into periods: after World War I, during World War II, and during the late 1970s. Sometimes the topic area can be divided on the basis of space: student uprisings, for example, in communist countries, in Western Europe, and in the United States; and the United States or any other of these areas could be further subdivided on the basis of space or time to arrive at even narrower specific purposes.

As you come up with these possibilities, don't worry if some overlap with each other, if some are still a bit fuzzy around the edges, and if some look less promising at second glance. At this point you are trying to line up possibilities, not a list of distinct and perfect choices.

Select One Possibility   Once you have some possibilities in front of you, it should not be hard to make a good choice if you keep in mind your reference points: yourself, the occasion, and your audience. You can apply these reference points at this stage by using the following five questions to evaluate your possibilities.

1. Which possibilities would meet the general purpose required for this speech?
2. Which possibility best fits your own inclinations and resources? Do you have more background or original ideas on one possibility than on the others? Pick a specific purpose that inspires rather than discourages you. Do you have better research sources on one possibility, such as friends or relatives you can interview, unusual opportunities for observation, or your own books or magazines? Is one possibility more appropriate for what the audience expects from you as speaker?
3. Which specific possibilities will your audience find most interesting? The speaker on shoplifting checked out his possible choices with a couple of prospective listeners. He had also noticed a recent front-page news story many of his listeners would have read, about a prominent citizen being indicted for shoplifting. As a result, he decided to speak on the sorts of people who shoplift. Audiences are more likely to be interested in specific topics that affect their own interests or that provide new information which can be related to what they already know.
4. How much information is your audience likely to absorb and understand within the time you have for your speech? To some extent this depends on how familiar they are with the general topic and how much detail they expect to learn in this particular situation. College students majoring in robotics might absorb a great deal of information from a thirty-minute detailed description of a particular robot used in the Japanese automobile industry, but a nonspecialist audience would be more likely to understand a speech merely explaining in general terms how most industrial robots rely on three main components. Avoid topics so broad that they must be

treated very superficially, especially if the audience is already familiar with the general topic. But also avoid topics that are too specialized to be easily understood or of interest to your particular audience.

5. Will your audience be asking questions? Many speakers learn to enjoy handling audience questions, and answering these can give you more opportunity to achieve your intended effect on the audience. You can attract questions by focusing on more controversial or novel aspects of the topic area as well as by arousing curiosity at one or two points in the speech.

Write Your Specific Purpose   Write down your specific purpose for your own use to check now and to guide the rest of your preparation. The easiest way usually is just to complete the sentence: "In this speech my purpose is to . . ."

The sentence should state a single central thought simply. The speaker who says, "My purpose is to explain what makes a successful track team and about the history of our track team" *may* mean that she intends "to show what past factors have contributed to the success of our track team." However, if a speaker cannot state clearly to herself how the two or three main parts of her speech fit together into a single unified focus, her chances of developing a speech with that single focus are not good.

Make your choice of words specific. When the speaker is going "to inform the audience of three *things* about flying saucers," is she going to inform us of three theories about their origin, three characteristics of most alleged flying saucers, three arguments against their existence, or some other trio of points?

If you have a manageable specific purpose clearly defined in your own mind, it will take you only a couple of minutes to write it down. The preceding speaker should be able to state her purpose: "to describe three theories explaining the origin of flying saucers." If you have trouble writing it out, you have a strong signal that you had better think through more carefully just what your aim is in the speech, at least at this point in its preparation.

Test and if Necessary Modify Your Specific Purpose   The following check-list summarizes major standards you have been working toward as you developed your specific purpose. Do apply the list. It usually takes only a few minutes, and it can save you trouble in later stages of preparation.

1. Do you have a clearly defined single purpose for the speech?
2. Do you find your topic and specific purpose interesting, something you want to talk about to this audience? As one student said bluntly, "If the speech bores you, the speaker, just think how the audience will react."
3. With your personal knowledge, research sources, and available preparation time, can you attain the level of expertise required in the situation?

4. Is your specific purpose likely to produce a speech that will be of interest or value to the audience?
5. Is it the type of speech—general purpose and level of seriousness—you are expected to give on this occasion?
6. Can you cover the topic fully with adequate depth of detail for your audience in the allotted time?

What should you do if your specific purpose fails to meet one or more of these standards? If you must shift to an entirely new topic area, do it now rather than later. Usually, especially if you have already invested time and effort in the topic area, you do better to shift your specific purpose within the topic area. Narrow the topic down further, for example, or shift to an approach that is less complex. Shift to an aspect of the topic that is likely to be more interesting to your audience or one in which you have a greater interest or better resources.

As you move into the next steps in preparation, use your specific purpose as a guide. Be flexible enough to modify it, but don't change every time you have a problem. Above all, in a late stage of preparation, avoid the temptation to switch to a whole new topic area. You almost always will have as many problems with the new topic area, and you will have less time to deal with them. If you are careful at this checkpoint in preparation, you should not have to change your topic radically later.

Stage 3: Plan Your Statement of Focus for the Audience

You write out your specific purpose for your own benefit. You plan a statement of focus for your audience's benefit. It should stand out clearly in the presented speech as stating the focus of the speech, and it should be easily understood by your audience. It may be worded quite informally, perhaps in two or more sentences, but the phrasing should be planned carefully.

If you can draft at least a tentative statement of focus for your audience now, you gain a further check on the appropriateness of your specific purpose: You should feel comfortable telling the audience simply and directly what you intend to do in the speech. If you find you cannot do this, you should reevaluate your specific purpose.

Summary

From initial selection of specific purpose through final preparation, the speaker needs to fit the speech to the situation in which it occurs. Three key reference points in the situation are the inclinations and resources of the speaker, the constraints on general purpose and length of speech imposed by the occasion, and the interests and expectations of the audience.

The most common general purposes for speeches are informative and persuasive. Some other types that do not fit neatly into either of these two categories are ceremonial, conflict reduction, program, and entertainment.

A speaker develops and defines a specific purpose most efficiently by going through three stages. In stage 1 she looks for general topic areas, insofar as she has a choice, especially ones in which she is interested and has background knowledge. In stage 2 she narrows down her most promising topic area to a specific purpose by discovering various possible specific topics in the topic area, by selecting from these one possibility that fits the audience and occasion, by shaping and phrasing that possibility as a specific purpose, and by applying a checklist to make sure it is appropriate for speaker, audience, and occasion. In stage 3 she phrases the specific purpose as a statement of focus that in the presented speech can be easily understood by the audience.

Exercises

1. Give a three- to five-minute speech with a clearly defined specific purpose that is fully manageable within this time frame. You may use research as well as personal resources. Know what type of speech you are giving. Make your specific purpose clear to your audience. Be prepared to explain, during class discussion of the day's speeches, how you arrived at your specific purpose and why you thought it would be an appropriate one for you, the occasion, and the audience.

2. Turn in to your instructor a topic area with three or four specific purposes for informative speeches derived from it. For at least a couple of the specific purposes, write a brief justification of the specific purpose, applying the checklist provided on pages 64–65 and giving any other reasons that make it a good specific purpose. The assumption here is that you are working toward a later major speech assignment; your instructor may provide you with useful feedback on this paper, so be realistic in your choice of topic area and specific purposes.

CHAPTER FIVE

Obtaining Material for the Speech

A student was impressed by a driver who stopped and helped him when his own car stalled in a severe rainstorm. From this evolves his tentative specific purpose for an informative speech: "To make the audience aware of how charitable acts are performed by ordinary people."

As soon as he has this specific purpose in mind, he begins jotting down random ideas as he thinks of them, and over the next couple of days he accumulates two or three pages of notes. He draws on other incidents in his own experience, such as a sales clerk who went beyond the call of duty to be helpful and a senior who volunteered to help him in computer lab. His knowledge of a friend's scholarship donated by a local citizen provides an example, and it also suggests that he might interview someone in the scholarship office to find out about other donors, why they give, and who gets the money. He considers possibly organizing his speech on the basis of "size" of acts: minor and spontaneous, significant contributions, and major commitments in life. Realizing that his notion of "charity" is itself fuzzy, he decides to read encyclopedia articles on "charity" and "philanthropy." Also he will later check the *Readers' Guide to Periodical Literature* under those headings to locate articles on charity as practiced by ordinary people. While gathering these random notes he remembers a recent newspaper article about a local shoe store owner who gives dozens of pairs of shoes to needy children. Not only does this article provide him with another example, but he could also interview the man. He decides to watch closely for other articles or letters to the editor that tell of local acts of generosity.

The fundamental point to be drawn from our example is this: In gathering ideas and materials, an efficient and creative speaker *thinks* about the topic *before* dashing off to interview experts or to do research in the library.

Note also that beginning with initial thinking, as illustrated in this example, and continuing through the rest of your research, you look mainly for the following three sorts of material:

1. *Major ideas,* from which you will select a pattern of ideas to form the mainheads and higher-level subheads in your speech plan.
2. *Supporting materials,* such as examples and experts' opinions, which will be used to make your major ideas clear, interesting, and credible.
3. *Sources,* from which you can get further ideas and supporting materials as well as a general understanding of your topic.

As you gather material for a speech, especially a major one, you are likely to get better results, with less effort wasted on relatively worthless sources and notes, if you go by stages. At first you are trying to get a sense of how the topic might be developed and what sources are available. This initial survey stage often overlaps the final shaping and defining of your specific purpose. In the second stage you get most, if not all, of the material you will need to develop the topic. By the end of this stage you are ready to move to the next steps in preparation: setting the basic structure of the speech in its likely final form and filling in much of the detail. A third stage may then be necessary, especially with speeches that depend heavily on research in print: You go back to your sources to look for additional supporting materials to fill in specific gaps in your outline.

Regardless of whether you spend a total of two or twenty hours gathering material, try to spread your time over as long a period of days or weeks as possible. This allows time for your research and your thinking to mesh, and for ideas to come up from the subconscious; it also permits you to follow up on leads and to encounter useful materials by chance.

Stage 1: Initial Survey

Since *you* are the one creating the speech, begin with what is already in your mind, as did the speaker at the beginning of this chapter. You may also want to survey especially for sources and for background information before moving into detailed research.

Survey Your Own Mind for Ideas and Other Material

An immediate random ransacking of your own mind is a relatively painless way of overcoming mental blocks and getting something down on paper. Getting something down early gives you confidence that you will have something to say. This confidence plus the base you now have to work from makes it easier to continue further planning. So take pen and paper in hand and ask yourself, just what do I already have on this topic? How do I feel about it? Why? What points could be made? How could I explain this idea? What examples do I already have? You may have to be more aggressive. Some students report getting this process of discovery started by forcing themselves to write randomly and continuously on the topic for ten or fifteen minutes.

Over a few days, more material may come spontaneously if you have your topic in the back of your mind. Once or twice review the notes you have already made to see if that generates new ideas and details. You can also stimulate ideas by thinking from your listeners' viewpoint: What aspects of the topic will they most want to hear about? How is the topic related to what they already know? What personal experiences do you have with the topic that might interest them?

Don't try to judge the material or fit it into a structure at this stage. Creative discovery is a different process from evaluating and selecting material, which comes later. Now you want to get out as much as possible, so you will have plenty to work with later.

Make at least a brief note on each item or idea that comes to mind, even if you have to write it on whatever scrap of paper is handy. More detail is better. Write out short blocks of the speech if that is the only way you can get started putting something down on paper. But avoid the temptation to try to write out the speech word for word or to become committed to your initial jottings.

Survey Especially for Sources

Usually you will need material beyond your own ideas and experiences. Therefore, ask yourself these sorts of questions: What books or articles do you own or know of on this topic? Whom do you know who might have information, books, or other resources on the topic? Are there experts or others whom you can interview? What opportunities, if any, do you have for direct observation on the topic? Might you be likely to find information in current newspapers, news magazines, or television programs? Note on paper any possible sources you come up with.

Although this initial survey for sources begins in your own mind, you may also want to check for possible sources in other ways. A friend who is more familiar than you are with the topic might be able to give you some helpful leads to additional sources. You might spend a half-hour or so browsing through the card catalog under your subject heading or in some recent issues of an index such as the *Readers' Guide to Periodical Literature* and jotting down any promising sources you encounter. This will at least let you know whether there are library materials available on your topic.

Seek an imaginative variety of possible sources. One student gave a highly effective speech urging his audience to buy a particular sort of car. As sources he used his own experience of problems with owning a car of a different sort, interviews with friends who owned the sort of car he was urging, the library for magazine articles with opinions of car designers and testers, dealers' pamphlets for material on gas mileage statistics, and his own field observation of sticker prices for both sorts of car. This range of sources made the job of doing detailed research more interesting for him and provided a great variety of supporting material. The range of sources itself did much to increase the interest and credibility of the speech.

Survey for Background Information

If you are not very familiar with your topic, you may need to get some background information before you can shape your concept of the speech clearly enough to direct further planning. If you can locate a faculty member or other expert on your topic and say what you have tentatively planned so far, he or she may be able in a few minutes to provide background information, suggest more specific topics, and even offer some ideas and sources to help you get started on a workable focus. You can also go to a book or a couple of articles that seem to cover the topic in a broad and easily comprehended way.

Note down ideas and useful sources you discover in such interviews and background reading, but don't get hung up doing detailed notetaking from these general sources before you are really sure of your specific purpose. When you survey for background information, you do it to improve your general understanding of your topic and to sharpen your specific purpose.

By the end of this initial stage in gathering materials, if it is for a simple speech that draws mainly on your present knowledge, you may be able to move on to planning the organization. If the speech requires greater depth in content, you will now need to do your main research. In either case, you can now do a couple of things to make your main research or further planning more efficient.

You can *make sure your specific purpose is still the best* you can draw from the topic area. You now have a fuller sense of what ideas and what sources of additional information are available on the topic. You may decide to narrow your specific purpose further or to refocus it in a way that will be more interesting to you or to your listeners or that will better fit the best sources of information available to you.

Insofar as you can, *begin to select main points* you are likely to develop in the speech, however tentative such decisions must be for now. Consider what supporting materials you need in order to develop these ideas to the satisfaction of your audience. Such thinking now will give you some notion of *what* you need to find in your main research, and from your survey of sources you have some ideas about *where* to look.

Stage 2: Main Research and Creativity

In this section we will look at two main ways to obtain materials: deliberate research in external sources and further use of your own knowledge, alertness, and inventiveness. Ideally, these two work together: research triggers your own ideas, and your own ideas direct the research. Your material from all sources grows as a physical accumulation. Keep it all together in one place—a clasp envelope, a file folder, a bundle of index cards, or at least a separate part of your notebook.

Do research to meet your real needs for the speech. You are now working more systematically than you did in the survey stage. Look for material that will make the specific topic and any likely main ideas clear, interesting, and credible to your particular listeners. As one student put it, "You do your research for the audience's benefit." It is a good idea to get two or three times as much material as you will use in the speech so you can select the best points to develop and the best supporting detail in final planning. But keep the total length and pace of the speech in mind: getting twenty items to support a point when you will have time for only two items is usually wasteful overkill in research.

Take fully useable notes. When you do note something, make the notes complete enough so you can use the material confidently. This applies to both the item itself and the source, and it applies to interviews, observation, those materials you run across by chance, and even ideas and examples that you happen to think of. Note enough detail on the example. Get the quote word for word if there is any chance at all that you will use it that way. For statistics, get down fully what they mean, who compiled them, and when. For expert opinions, both from print sources and from interviews, note any information on the positions held by and the achievements of the source, so you can state why he or she qualifies as an expert. Note the dates of your observations and interviews. For print sources, note date, author, title, and page numbers, as well as name of book or magazine; the test is, could another person readily locate the material in a library using your source notation? Getting it right the first time takes a little longer, but it avoids frustration and wasted time later or feeble vagueness in the presented speech.

If you use a great deal of research material, you will probably find it more convenient in the long run to take notes on 4 × 6 cards—one idea, one source, or one item of supporting material per card. Then you can later physically divide the cards, first grouping ideas and supporting materials under each mainhead, and then further sorting the cards for each main section according to its subsections.

Different specific purposes require different sorts of research. To be able to meet effectively the particular demands of any speaking situation, you develop skill in using print sources, observation, interviews, and chance sources as well as the resources already in your own mind.

Print Sources from Libraries and Elsewhere

You do not always find the most useful printed materials in the library. Don't neglect such sources as your own books and magazines, as well as those of friends, and current newspapers and periodicals. More than one speaker has found a key source while browsing at a newsstand or in a bookstore. If you

Libraries provide a wide array of research sources on speech topics. (Steven Baratz/The Picture Cube)

have a friend who has two or three years of *Omni, Discover,* or *Scientific American,* you have at least some sources on any one of several topics. The same notion would apply to a range of magazines on subjects from business administration to road racing or body building.

Despite the value of other sources, for many specific purposes a speaker can develop an adequate or impressive level of understanding and information only by doing a substantial amount of library research. Thus skill in quickly locating useful material in a library is a powerful tool for most public speakers. You want to know *what types of material* can be found and *how to find* what you need.

Your library may not have all the items listed below or may have them combined in different ways. Many libraries also have resources beyond those listed here or have special strengths. A city library, for example, may be the better place to go for material on local history, while a university library will probably be much stronger in special journals in each field of learning.

Types of Material in a Library There are various possible ways of categorizing the types of material in a library. The one used here is based mainly on physical type and location—the different areas you should look for as you begin to use a library.

1. *Books in the main collection*: The bulk of the library physically. Open shelves are much more conducive to source surveys than are closed shelves.
2. *Periodicals*: Ranging from popular magazines to very specialized scholarly journals. Current issues may be in one location, bound volumes for past years in another location, recent issues of newspapers in a third location.
3. *Reference works*: Vast amounts of condensed factual information in a variety of forms from encyclopedias and almanacs to such specialized sources as the *Dictionary of American Biography* and *Bartlett's Familiar Quotations*.
4. *Microform collections*: Noncurrent newspapers, earlier issues of magazines and journals, rare or older books and manuscripts. Especially useful for speakers are collections of articles on single topics in *Newsbank* and ERIC (Educational Resources Information Center) on microfiche cards. You will find the mechanics of using this material quite easy after a little initial direction from a library staff member.
5. *Government documents*: Includes detailed reports and committee hearings on a broad range of topics, as well as other sorts of material.
6. *Special collections*: Different for each library; may be regional history, original manuscripts, collections of material dealing with a single person or subject such as witchcraft or military weapons.
7. *Nonverbal printed materials*: Maps, paintings and reproductions, sheet music.
8. *Audiovisual material*: Tapes of speeches, plays, or music; films and videotapes. Oral history tapes also may be found in special collections.
9. *Interlibrary loan office*: Books and other materials from other libraries, by special request.

Means of Locating Material in a Library Skill in library research pays off by enabling you to mine the resources of your library on any topic efficiently and thoroughly. The following is a list of locating devices. As you learn to use them, be willing to ask for assistance from a librarian or more experienced researcher whenever you need it.

1. *Card catalog* (or electronic replacement): Indexes by title and author every book in the main collection and in some special collections. Nonfiction is also indexed under subject headings, which may lead you directly to several books on your topic. If you know of even one book on your topic, locate it under title or author card, and that card will tell you what subject headings in the card catalog the book is listed under. Looking under those subject headings will give you additional leads to other books. You can also go directly to the shelf (if permitted in your library) and look for other books in the vicinity of the one you looked up in the catalog.
2. *Readers' Guide to Periodical Literature*: Indexes by author, title, and subject all articles in about 150 serious general-interest magazines. Certainly the

most commonly used way of locating articles on a speaker's topic, but not always the most useful index.

3. *Special subject indexes*: Operate much like the *Readers' Guide* but cover a much more complete list of magazines and journals in a particular area of study. Examples are the *Social Science Index*, the *Education Index*, and the *Humanities Index*.

4. *Abstract annuals*: Operate much like the special indexes, except that they provide not only sources but also brief summaries, and most cover books as well as articles. Examples are *Psychological Abstracts* and *Microbiology Abstracts*. You can get some understanding of a topic just by reading several entries on it in abstract form, and you have a good idea of which articles or books are worth locating to read more fully.

5. *Linedex or some other alphabetized or topically organized list of the library's holding in periodicals*: Tells you quickly whether the library has a particular magazine or journal. Scanning relevant sections in a topically organized list may bring to your attention journals in your field of interest you never even knew existed.

6. *Other more specialized indexes*: Include the *New York Times Index*, which lists and abstracts by topic articles for each year in that newspaper, and the *Public Affairs Information Service Bulletin*, which is an index to government publications.

7. *Electronic source searching*: Your library may be equipped to run a computerized search for titles of books and articles on a given topic, and it may also have rapidly updated special indexes on microfilm or computer discs.

8. *The librarians themselves*: Those designated "reader's assistant" or some such title, and those in charge of departments such as reference, microforms, or government documents. Once you have the framework of your speech in mind and know what you are after, you may get help very efficiently from such resource librarians. For example, they may help you frame your search in words or phrases that fit the headings used in indexes and other guides.

Use Print Sources Efficiently and Accurately   In those cases in which you depend primarily on library research, begin with a *bibliographical list* of possible sources for detailed research. You may have spotted some useful books or articles in your initial survey stage, but now you are looking more systematically for a fuller range of library sources on your specific topic. You develop this list by using whichever indexes and other means listed above are appropriate for your topic and purpose. A skilled researcher can often locate ten or fifteen books or articles in an hour at the library. Make a bibliographical note on each source, including library call number or location, so you can readily locate it again. You may make a quick note of its likely value for your purposes, but do not at this stage take detailed notes on the content. The essential idea of the bibliographical list is that you move rapidly to discover a number of available sources so that when you begin your detailed research, you can go to the most promising sources first. You thus avoid wasting time reading and noting sources that have little value. In the end you might use only three or four magazine articles, but they might be worth more than the first six you encountered and would have used had you not done the list *before* doing your detailed reading and notetaking.

When you read and note material for your speech, go first to those books or articles that appear to meet these standards: Is the source right on target for your specific topic? Is it likely to provide the sorts of information and supporting detail you need for your purpose and audience? Is it at a level you can understand and use—as opposed, for example, to a highly technical journal? Is it a source you think is reliable—that is, competent and objective—and one that your audience is likely to respect? Is the source recent enough to be usable for your topic and purpose?

With a book, use the table of contents, index, and section headings to locate quickly what you might be able to use. With any print source, first scan or read rapidly, making at most only a few quick notes; then go back and take thorough notes on those items that are really likely to be useful to you.

You can save time copying source notations by keeping your complete source descriptions on a separate list or set of cards. Cross-reference each 4 × 6 notetaking card to its source by author or short title, and note the page number. For example, on a source card or list you have this complete description:

> Sherry Turkle, *The Second Self: Computers and the Human Spirit* (New York: Simon and Schuster, 1984); Turkle is a professor at Massachusetts Institute of Technology, and this work is "a field study based on many thousands of hours of interviews and observations all over the United States" (p. 7).

Then on each item of supporting material from that source, all you need note is, for example:

> Turkle, *Second Self*, p. 64.

Whether you use sheets or index cards for notes, always use quote marks to show your word-for-word quotations from a source as distinct from your summarizing or paraphrasing of content from the source. Separate your own ideas from quotations or summaries of research material by putting your own ideas and opinions in brackets [ ] or on a different set of cards or sheets of paper. Thus you can always tell which are items you have copied word for word, which are items you have summarized or paraphrased from a source, and which are items that are your own ideas or opinions.

Observation

If you are doing a speech on the use of persuasion or the quality of justice in a municipal court, or on nursing homes for the elderly or day-care centers for children, or on the misuse of city parks, or on the behavior of parents at little league ball games, go observe firsthand what you are talking about. One student went through the process of applying for food stamps in order to speak authoritatively on the screening process for applicants. Such observation can produce vivid and convincing supporting material, especially if you observe alertly and closely for details, such as how people act and what they say. Get complete notes, as soon as possible afterward if it is awkward to do so while observing. Go into the situation with some aims in mind, but be flexible enough to adapt to the unexpected.

Interviews

Professors, graduate students, store managers, detectives, people in city government, nurses, and a host of other people—including, probably, some of your friends or acquaintances—can provide material on a great range of topics. They may not tell you everything you need to know, but the insights, opinions, and examples they can provide from their personal experience and expertise are a strong sort of supporting material. Interview sources also may provide you with general understanding of the topic, the most up-to-date information, and leads to other print or interview sources. In fact, interviewing is occasionally far more efficient than library research, and some students and other speakers find it more interesting.

For credible opinions, factual information, and further sources, go to the best experts on your topic available to you. Do not, however, interpret "expert" too narrowly. Fellow students might be the most expert sources on the quality of food in a dorm cafeteria or on the various foul-ups that can befall a student in registration. A speaker may even design a short questionnaire and poll a sampling of students or other people in order to show what the prevailing opinion is on an issue.

When you interview someone, assume that his or her time is valuable. You may have to make an appointment in advance, and you may have only a very limited amount of time for the interview. Before the interview, think through your topic, as well as the particular qualifications of the source, so you know what questions to ask. Jotting down key questions in advance often helps the inexperienced interviewer. Adapt to the flow of conversation, and follow up on relevant and interesting unexpected points raised by the interviewee. But keep the pace reasonably crisp, and don't yourself indulge in aimless rambling or irrelevant conversation. Take some notes. You may even tape record if the interviewee agrees. Be alert for exact quotes that are phrased in striking ways or that may be used for expert testimony. Get these down accurately, and get permission specifically to quote directly.

Chance Sources

If a speaker on child abuse or on accidental shooting can cite a case from yesterday's six o'clock news, he has built-in interest value. One speaker

An expert on your speech topic may provide personal experiences and opinions, as well as more up to date information than other sources. (Bohdan Hrynewych/Southern Light)

on the home use of videotape encountered a video dealer by chance at a club meeting both were attending; the conversation produced much of the material the speaker needed. You encounter such "gifts" when something relevant to your topic comes up as you talk to friends, watch what goes on around you during the day, work at your job, watch television, or read the day's newspaper. If you have your speech plan roughed out a couple of weeks or more before you give it, you have that much more time to be on the lookout for chance material or even to slip your topic into a conversation with someone who could provide useful ideas or information.

The skill in using chance sources is to be alert for ideas and materials on your topic and to jot them down when they occur. One speaker on drunken driving may read in the morning paper of a fatal head-on collision at 2:00 A.M. caused by a person leaving a bar, and that evening may be annoyed by a weaving driver almost forcing him off the road, but the speaker's thinking about his speech is so isolated from the rest of his life that he doesn't even make the connections. Another speaker with the same topic would clip the article in the morning paper and would tail the evening driver as long as she safely could, mentally noting the driver's symptoms and hazards to other drivers. The second speaker has obtained two excellent examples simply by being alert.

Your Own Mental Resources

The thinking about your topic that began in your initial survey continues, in somewhat different ways, into main research. Often this thinking occurs as an ongoing interaction with your other research activity, but for some speeches you may find it useful to explore your mental resources in a more systematic way.

Ongoing Use of Mental Resources   Ideas may occur when you are mulling over the material you have gathered so far or when you visualize yourself giving the speech. Insights you have gained through research may suggest new points to be made or new ways to develop a main idea. Such insight may also suggest gaps to be filled in, either through further research or from your background knowledge and creativity.

For topics with which you are already familiar, be especially alert to draw on background knowledge to reinforce material from other sources. A speaker on sexual discrimination in management might use library research extensively but still draw her most vivid examples from her own experience as a junior executive in a large organization.

Use some creative imagination. Think about which aspects of your topic might be especially appealing to your audience or ways in which you can better adapt your research material to the listeners. Can examples or other supporting material from external sources be recast in ways that will be clearer or more interesting to your audience? Brief imaginative comments can make research material more personally relevant to the audience. In describing the effects of Japanese high-speed trains on commuting between major cities, for example, you could mention how these speeds would reduce commuting time between your campus and two or three nearby cities. Can you create a visual aid to emphasize a point or to clarify some statistics? Can an example in an article be replaced or reinforced by another real or made-up example that will be more vividly relevant for your audience? All such notions are worth jotting down in your notes as they occur to you.

Systematic Application of Mental Resources   At some point in gathering material for a speech you may decide to take a block of time, a half-hour or so, deliberately to draw on your knowledge and creativity. Perhaps early in main research you decide you will have a better sense of direction in research if you develop a largely personal treatment before going to other sources for additional support. Or perhaps you have already done a good deal of research, but the material isn't coming together in a very productive way. How can you tap your own mind efficiently and with some thoroughness?

Since the time of the classical orators, public speakers have used "topoi" to help them explore the resources in their own minds. A set of *topoi* is a guide or checklist of possibilities for what might be said about any one of a broad range of topics or purposes. Thus topoi can be used to trigger your memory or creativity to discover major points for the speech as well as items of supporting material such as examples and comparisons. Lawyers, politicians, and others often develop, whether consciously or intuitively, sets of topoi for the types of speeches they give frequently so they know where to begin looking when they must generate material for a particular speech.

The topoi provided here are an all-purpose set for a very broad range of mainly informative speeches. Realize that in any list some items will apply and some will not, so move through them to see which ones trigger something in your mind. The topoi you would use are in the left column; the right column merely provides examples to help clarify concepts in the left column. As ideas are triggered in your mind, jot them down.

I. Consider internal nature of the specific subject:

  A. What are its natural or possible divisions?

    1. Into types.

    Extracurricular activities on campus into athletic, cultural, social, organizational.

    2. Into parts.

    Components within the space shuttle.

    3. Into stages, as in time or in a process.

    Launching, flight, and return of space shuttle.

    4. Into degrees.

    Degrees of severity in mental illness: tension, neurosis, and psychosis.

  B. Description of subject:

    1. Physical aspects: sensory impressions; construction.

    Sights, sounds, etc. at a rodeo or an open-air market. Size and floor plan for new campus building.

    2. Mental and other non-physical aspects of subject.

    Full description of child abuse would cover both physical and psychological types of abuse.

  C. Good and bad characteristics of subject: moral, physical, economic, psychological, etc.

    Good and bad economic, environmental, and psychological aspects of a policy of using nuclear sources for energy.

D. Real or created examples of subject, drawn from your experience, imagination, broad reading, conversation, or observation.

Examples of specific clerks who impress customers favorably, contrasted with examples of other clerks who annoy customers. (Examples can, in turn, suggest idea headings.)

II. Consider subject in relation to external factors.

A. As in a chain of cause-effect relationships:

1. Causes of subject?

What causes teen-age shoplifting?

2. Effects subject has had, now has, or will have—on whom or what?

What effects does juvenile crime have on the criminals, on parents, on other teen-agers?

B. As falling in a certain class of things, and yet being different from other things in that class.

How is chess a sport? an intellectual exercise? different from other sports or intellectual challenges?

C. As being in sharp contrast or opposition to other things.

Computers as contrasted with, and in conflict with, resourceful human heroes in science fiction films.

D. As fitting in a larger scene in which it occurs:

1. Physically, spatially, geographically.

Indian cliff dwellings located geographically, structurally fitted to terrain, and placed in relation to each other.

2. Historically or sociologically.

Computers as one aspect of humanity's increasing dependence on technology.

E. As being better or worse than other things.

What exercises is jogging better than? Why is stealing books worse than some other sorts of petty crime?

III. Consider subject from varied perspectives:

A. From points of view of different people involved with the subject.

Used car sales from both salesperson's and customer's points of view.

B. How audience member might be involved with topic: use it, be affected by it, respond to it.

How listener might use described procedures to appeal a traffic ticket. How listener might be affected by loss of privacy in computer age.

C. Coldly factual versus human interest perspective.

Statistics on deaths, injuries, and property damage caused by drunken driving, versus description of specific accident and effects on one family. (Both perspectives may be combined in a speech.)

To see how this system can operate, let's return to the speaker whose purpose is "to make the audience aware of how charitable acts are performed by ordinary people." After gathering some initial survey notes and beginning his main research, he decides to try systematically to tap his own knowledge and creativity. He spends about thirty minutes going through the preceding outline of topoi. The topoi trigger the following ideas in his mind. (Enumeration in parentheses refers to the item in the topoi outline that caused him to think of the particular idea.)

Possible types of contributions to others include money, time, energy, and sympathetic interest and concern. (I.A.1.)

What causes or motivates people to do charitable acts? (II.A.1.) What motives come up in articles and interviews, and in the speaker's own experience?

Can a charitable act be explained as a form of personal achievement by the doer? (II.B.) How is it different from, better than, or not as good as other forms of personal achievement? (II.E.)

Charitable acts can be considered from the point of view of the recipient as well as that of the doer. (III.A.) Possible effects on the recipient are to enable survival, pursuit of goals, or feeling less lonely or more confident. (II.A.2.) What other effects on recipients come up in research? Examples of effects on recipients?

What opportunities are there for students, if they wish, to become involved in ordinary, everyday acts or in campus organizations engaged in charitable acts? (III.B.)

Some of these ideas, of course, will be transformed, combined with research material, or eliminated later in preparation. But by stimulating his own creative thinking, the speaker has developed new ways of looking at the research material he is gathering and has increased the stock of ideas and supporting materials from which he can select as he plans the speech.

For most speeches you will give, your research and inventiveness so far will probably provide all the raw material you need for a speech. On some topics, however, even if you were conscientious when you did your main research, you might have wanted to avoid compulsively taking notes for every point and subhead that could possibly be used in the speech. So what do you do if you discover later that you don't have the material in your accumulated notes to develop a particular point that you now plan to use?

Stage 3: Filling in Gaps

As you did your research in print sources, you probably ran across material that seemed of possible value but not worth the labor of copying or detailed noting at that point in your research. However, if you checked those sources out of the library, borrowed them from friends, or even photocopied some portions, you now have them at your fingertips even if you don't have notes on them. The advantage *now* is that you can go through them rapidly because you know exactly what you are looking for.

If you have not checked out or photocopied the material, you may still locate what you need, from your initial survey for sources or your bibliographical list of library materials. Library or other print sources that didn't seem worth consulting when you were doing your main research, even possible interviews, may now seem to be precisely what you need.

Sometimes, if you think about what really has to be done at a particular point in the speech you won't have to return to sources at all. If a speaker is trying to make interesting and vivid the notion that electronic technology may affect job opportunities even for professional workers, she might go to expert testimony and other research material. However, she might more effectively create a hypothetical example to fit the profession in which her listeners are employed or training:

> How would you feel if you had spent five years in college preparing to be a teacher plus several more years on the job, you had a family depending on your income, and you faced this threat. More and more, your students' needs would be diagnosed by computers, and the students would be taught individually by modules using videotape presentations and computer testing. And every year more and more funds would be shifted from traditional teachers' pay in order to provide equipment and the technicians to run it. Wouldn't you begin to argue that in your profession something harmful to humans was happening?

Summary

From the beginning, in gathering material, look for major ideas and understanding of your topic, for specific supporting materials to make your main ideas clear, interesting, and credible to your listeners, and for sources of further material. In gathering material, especially for a speech that requires considerable research, think of your research in stages.

In the first stage, survey your own mind for ideas and information. Develop a list of possible sources for further research. If you lack general familiarity with your topic, do some broad background reading. At the end of this stage evaluate what you have gathered so far and rethink your specific purpose and plan for the speech.

In the second stage, you do research to meet your specific aims in the speech. If you use library sources, do a bibliographical list first so you can concentrate your detailed reading and notetaking on the best available sources. Don't neglect interviews and observation if appropriate for your purposes. Be alert for chance sources of information. Continue to use your own background and inventiveness to interact with research material, and perhaps use topoi to explore your mental resources more systematically.

The third stage of research, if necessary, is done after organization of the speech is well under way; you return to sources to fill in specific gaps in your outline. You can prepare for third-stage research when you do your main research by, for example, checking out or making a bibliographical note on possibly useful library materials.

Regardless of what sources or method you use, some general suggestions for efficient research can be gleaned from this chapter. Keep your *aims* clearly in mind at each point in your research. Try, insofar as appropriate for your specific purpose, to use a *variety* of sources. *Think* about your topic and about the research materials you turn up. From initial brainstorming to library research, get complete *notes* on whatever you might use; don't trust to memory.

Exercises

1. Present a two- to four-minute speech in which the supporting material is drawn mainly from personal experience and creative thought, *or* from interviews and observation, *or* from print sources.

2. Hand in to your instructor your sources for a major speech you are working on and the research notes you have accumulated so far. (This is a continuation of exercise 2 in Chapter 4.)

CHAPTER SIX

Planning Basic Structure

If you have ever been held way past the end of a class period while an instructor raced to finish his lecture or been tested on material that he didn't cover because he ran out of time, you can appreciate one reason for organizing a speech. In almost any speaking situation you, as speaker, will have a specific purpose and a more or less fixed time within which to accomplish it. Tight planning enables you to select the key ideas and supporting detail which will best accomplish that purpose within the time limit.

Careful advance planning can also give a speaker greater confidence and force in delivery. As one student put it, "The most important thing I learned about public speaking was organization. Organization took half my fear away. That fear was about getting up in front of the class and not knowing what to say or how to say it." Moreover, if you see your speech as a logical pattern of ideas, rather than just some random things to say about a topic, you are more likely to emphasize the most important ideas by your voice and gestures. Increased confidence and your sense of the ideas make your delivery more energetic and varied.

Effective organization can do a great deal for your listeners. Usually an audience, unless especially motivated, will grasp and remember only a few points from a speech, so you need to organize the speech in a way that will enable listeners to see clearly what the main points are. When members of an audience can follow a speaker's line of thinking and feel they are on the same wavelength, rather than being lost and confused, they are more likely to be interested in the speech. They also usually have more confidence in a speaker who is able to organize his material into an efficient, clear structure. Thus if you organize your speech reasonably well, the audience will give you fuller and more favorable attention, and this in turn will make your job as speaker more pleasant.

A speaker should make the rigor and obviousness of the organization appropriate to the particular audience and purpose. A general audience for a sixty-minute public lecture may expect to perceive and remember only three or four main ideas and a few miscellaneous details, whereas a class listening to a lecture in a history course may expect to get several pages of clearly organized notes for future study.

To make organization work for you in any presented speech, you first select the best ideas and supporting materials and put them in the right order. Important as this planning is, it is not all. You also have to plan how to help the audience follow that organization easily and clearly by the way you phrase key headings and use transitions. The tool for both sorts of planning is usually an outline.

Why Use an Outline?

The famous American author Mark Twain was much in demand as an after-dinner speaker. His audiences were impressed that he could come up with so much humorous material on the spur of the moment when giving a speech. Twain gave this impression because of his technique of starting a speech with a couple of jokes or humorous remarks relating to something that had happened that very evening. Then, without the audience noticing, Twain would slip into the bulk of the speech, which had been prepared in advance with meticulous care, continuing with relaxed delivery and an occasional ad-libbed remark. Twain—and many modern professional speakers—set the standard to aim for in the presented speech: delivery which is so natural and conversational that the speaker seems to be creating the ideas at the moment of utterance, whereas in reality the speech has been tightly planned in advance.

The best way for most speakers to get this combination of naturalness and tight planning is by working out the plan of the speech in outline form on paper. Few people can plan even a short speech in their heads. If a speaker cannot sketch the plan out on paper in some detail, it is unlikely that he really has a plan, and both the speaker's confidence and the effectiveness of the speech will suffer. Although a good outline is a great source of confidence, do not be tricked by this into writing the speech out word for word like an essay, especially when you are working on organization. Writing out everything in paragraphs actually conceals rather than reveals the *structure* you are planning.

An outline abstracts the framework of ideas and materials in a speech; it reveals the skeleton, like an X-ray. Thus the speech planner can keep his attention on structure. He can select and shift around the ideas and items of supporting material without getting bogged down with all the detail and language that will later fill out this skeletal framework.

Process in Planning Organization

An outline showing organization for a particular speech evolves over time from initial plans and rough sketches that are checked, revised, and filled out until

Organizing research and ideas for a speech is a creative process. (Hazel Hankin)

the speech takes final shape. Good results are more likely if this evolution can be spread over at least a few days. The speaker who assumes that his first attempts at outlining will have to be changed and expanded is likely to save time in the long run. He doesn't suffer from that paralysis of the pen which afflicts the planner who thinks he must have it right as soon as he puts words on paper. So feel free to experiment and revise when you begin planning.

As you plan structure, remember also that *you* are in charge. You are the one who makes the creative decisions that shape the strategy of the material to fit your purpose and your audience's expectations. Three people might organize a given mass of material in three different ways, and all three plans might be almost equally effective. Certainly, there are such things as wrong decisions, and the suggestions in this chapter will help you avoid them. But don't be afraid to make your own decisions.

In organizing a speech, aim first for a *basic structure* of the few main sections into which you will divide the speech and the important ideas you intend to develop. This basic structure will be shown in your mainheads and major subheads—usually the highest two or three levels of your outline for the body of the speech, as in the following example.

> **Specific purpose: to inform the audience how three important science fiction films between 1965 and 1970 portrayed alleged dangers of computer technology.**

I. The three films all depicted physical dangers of computers to humans.
   A. Machines that place little value on human well-being are given control of the environment.
   B. The machines will kill humans in order to preserve themselves.
II. More subtly, the films depicted political dangers of computers to humans.
   A. Humans lose freedom of choice because the computers make all important policy decisions.
   B. Humans lose even the ability to make decisions because only computers can store and comprehend the relevant information.
   C. Humans lose the right to an alternative form of rule because they dare not pull the plug on the computer.
III. Perhaps most realistically, the films depicted spiritual dangers of computers to humans.
   A. The human spirit was weakened because people became willing to trust computers to solve their problems.
   B. The human spirit was weakened by the apathy people feel toward each other when they no longer need to cooperate for their mutual welfare.

How you develop the basic structure for a speech is the topic for the rest of this chapter. Chapters 7 and 8 explain how you fill in the basic structure with supporting detail and other material for a fully planned speech.

Think of your development of basic structure as occurring in three stages: planning a pattern of mainheads, one for each main section of the speech; planning the structure of principal subheads within each main section; and checking to improve this basic structure.

Stage 1: Plan a Pattern of Mainheads

Look over the ideas and materials you have gathered so far. If you are lucky, or inspired, the entire structure of mainheads and many of the subheads may fall into place, at least roughly, with a few minutes of thought. If such an inspired organization does come, get it down on paper as fast and as completely as you can. You may already have had such inspirations while gathering ideas and materials, and in fact your later research may have been guided by your tentative plan for mainheads. Whether from earlier or presently inspired insight, you would now have a plan to check over, if necessary to revise, and then to fill in with subheads and detail. Incidentally, such "inspiration" becomes more likely as you become more familiar with conventional patterns such as those described on pages 91–98.

But what happens if, as is more commonly the case, no great flash of inspiration has occurred? You are staring at a pile of material. You know that somewhere in it is a pattern that will work for your audience, but you don't know where it is. What do you do? Search through and think about your material to discover *possible mainheads*. After you have explored the possibilities *decide* on your mainheads. Then resolve any remaining problems about the *sequence* in which to put the mainheads. The result should be a workable pattern of mainheads. Let's look more closely at each part of this stage.

Search for Possible Mainheads

Go through your notes and make a special mark by each item that seems to be an important general idea, as distinct from an example or other item of supporting material or an item for the introduction or conclusion. You are looking for the ideas that might end up forming the top two or three levels of your outline. (Eliminate entirely ideas and materials that are clearly not relevant to your specific topic.) Get these possibly useful *major ideas* by themselves on a separate sheet or two of paper. Can you locate any possible mainheads among them? Can you put together two or three ideas that seem related, so as to form one main section and then write a mainhead for that section?

If you cannot locate major ideas in your notes, try to combine specific points you do have into some set of categories that will make sense. A speaker wants to tell his audience about various attractions to see on a trip to San Francisco, and he has come up with a list of a couple of dozen items: the wax museum, the zoo, the art museum, the natural history museum and aquarium, the U.S. mint museum, particular places to eat and do special shopping, and convenient trips to places near San Francisco, such as the University of California campus in Berkeley. A list of two dozen items, each of which is dealt with briefly and rapidly, is not going to be very easy to follow, so he considers grouping them in different ways: by geographical area, *or* by type of activity (shopping, entertainment, and cultural), *or* by the time of day a person would be most likely to enjoy the activity. Any *one* of these ways of grouping the points would provide a basic structure that would give listeners the sense that the speaker had control over his material and was not just bouncing from one miscellaneous point to another.

After you have tried finding key headings and groupings in your raw material, try working from the other end. Ask what major points you need to make, or what areas of information you need to cover, in order to fulfill your specific purpose. How can you divide your specific topic into a few subtopics?

Perhaps you discover that you have to add some major ideas in order to fulfill your specific purpose or provide your audience with everything they would want to know. A speaker might, for example, have as a purpose to describe a local hard-rock dance hall. She realizes that physical descriptions of the place and its patrons don't cover all she wants to say, but only after thinking about what is likely to interest her audience does she realize that the other part of her speech is the psychological aspect of the dance hall experience, so she adds that as another possible mainhead. In a speech explaining how to raise tropical fish for fun and profit, the speaker might rather quickly decide to explain the habitat for the fish, feeding them, protecting them from hazards such as each other, and breeding new generations—four main divisions of the topic. However, a little thought about what the audience would need to know would show him that he also had to explain where to buy good stock and how to sell the fish.

Don't worry about final decisions as you begin to think through the possibilities. You are just trying to discover possible mainheads and patterns, using roughly three approaches: (1) locate mainheads in your notes; (2) combine more detailed ideas in your notes into mainheads; (3) discover what mainheads you might need to add for complete coverage of your topic. You may, in fact, sketch out two or three possible patterns of mainheads for the speech. If so, fine; you have increased your chances of coming up with the best pattern.

Decide on a Set of Mainheads

There does come a time in planning when you must say, These are the mainheads of my speech. This is often the crucial stage in planning the speech, but you have prepared for it in the preceding stage and you are in charge of the structure of the speech. This stage covers only the *highest* level of headings, the roman-numeral level in regular outline form.

Aim for three or four headings; sometimes only two will do, and you should almost never have more than five. Our tropical fish breeder, for example, finds himself with a half-dozen blocks of information he needs to cover, but he realizes that the audience will not comfortably follow that many separate blocks of information. So he wisely divides his topic into three main sections: getting started by buying fish and setting up tanks; raising and expanding the stock; and marketing the fish.

Try to divide the speech into main sections according to one governing principle. If the listener can say, "Ah, yes, I see she is covering this as stages in a process," or "She is explaining each important type of these things one type at a time," it is much easier to follow the speech than if the listener doesn't know what sort of mainhead is coming next. Also, try to make the mainheads of roughly equal importance.

Go back to the possible mainheads you have discovered. Can a group of these be selected or reworked so that each covers a separate aspect of the topic and together they cover it fully? Do they together form a consistent pattern? Do they cover what you really want to say about the topic?

You can also take advantage of conventional patterns for basic structure. Later in this chapter, on pages 91–98 several such patterns are provided. Look over these patterns and see if one seems to fit your topic and purpose. Often, once you discover a workable pattern it becomes fairly easy to locate within your material the mainheads you need to fill out the pattern. If one of these patterns is helpful, use it; but don't feel that your basic structure must fit one of these models.

Arrange the Mainheads in a Sequence

The order in which you cover the main sections in the body of the speech is sometimes determined by the nature of the material itself. In describing a historical event you would normally begin with the initial point in time in the event and proceed to the final point in time. The speech on the attractions in San Francisco, if it were organized on the basis of area, would probably begin with the downtown area; the next main section would deal with the outlying areas of the city; and the last main section would cover adjoining areas, such as Berkeley. Thus the speech would move in concentric rings from a central point outward. The speech might have proceeded from north to south, or according to some other scheme. The important notion here is that the speech should appear to move through a series of main sections according to some consistent and logical plan.

Sometimes you may look at your mainheads and decide that there is not any particular order natural to the material itself. There is, however, usually some order that will seem best adapted to helping the audience follow the material with interest and clarity. Consider the following possible strategies for sequence.

Deal with the more general aspects of the topic before the more specific aspects. For example, explain the general purposes and orbit of the space probe of Saturn before main sections on the more specific findings. Define the scope of the problem of high school dropouts before going into causes of the problem. The initial general information provides the audience with a background or perspective within which they can fit and better understand the more specific information.

A second possible strategy for sequence is to *begin with the more familiar and move to the less familiar* aspects of the topic. This makes the audience comfortable with the topic before the speaker moves into more difficult parts.

A third possible strategy is to *begin with the aspect of the topic that will be most interesting or significant to the audience.* The audience early in the speech finds the content interesting or useful, and their interest continues through the rest of the speech; in addition, their initial favorable feedback inspires the speaker to a more conversational and confident delivery in the rest of the speech.

Note that the standard patterns now to be described provide ideas for sequence as well as division into main heads.

Possible Patterns for Informative Speeches

The patterns that follow are some of the more common organizational strategies for speeches. If you understand the logic behind each pattern, you will be better able to choose and adapt one that will meet your needs for a particular speech. You want a pattern that will seem natural for the material, that will help your listeners follow the speech easily and with interest, and that will emphasize the points you think are most important on the topic.

Note that at this point you are looking for the best *structure*. The exact phrasing of the key headings and the use of transitions to clarify that structure to your audience can come later in planning. You should, however, write each heading fully enough so you define clearly what you intend to cover in that main section. Only two or three words per heading is usually too vague even for your own best use as you check and refine the structure.

Although we are here primarily concerned with the pattern of main-heads, these sample patterns may also suggest ways of organizing subheads within a main section. A speaker will often use one pattern for the mainheads and a different pattern within each main section. For example, a speech on raising tropical fish for profit might follow an overall process pattern: first, you get some fish; second, you raise some more; and third, you sell some. But within the second main section, the pattern of subheads would be topical: habitat, feeding, breeding, and protecting.

Natural Order Patterns

Natural order patterns depend on a logical sequence, or order, that is inherent in the material itself and that the speaker should follow consistently. The speaker must, of course, decide on a beginning point and an ending point. The greatest challenge in natural order patterns often is to divide the sequence of material into a *few distinct* main sections. Such a division gives the listeners a few key points under which they can group and thus better understand and remember the more detailed material.

Time Pattern Time patterns are used when one important aspect of the subject is its progression or change over time. Thus one way for the audience to get a grasp on the topic is to see it as divided into stages in time. The pattern may be used for topics as different as the proliferation of nuclear weapons in the world, Picasso's career as a painter, or how a college campus grew in size from its founding to the present. Three or four distinct main sections make the ideal pattern for the audience to grasp. The speaker in the following use of the pattern decided, however, that her material could be divided most logically into five main sections.

Specific purpose: to describe the historical evolution of smallest-particle theory in physics.

I. Democritus's theory of atoms as smallest particles, about 400 B.C.
II. First unified theory of types of atoms and molecules, about 1800.
III. Discoveries of construction of atoms from three more elemental types of particles, from late 1890s to early 1930s.
IV. Discoveries of great variety of subatomic particles, beginning in late 1930s.
V. Theory of quarks as most fundamental building blocks, from about 1965.

Space Pattern   If your purpose is to enable an audience to understand the physical nature of the subject, often your best approach is to give them an overview of the subject in your introduction or the first main section and then deal with each main area or physical part separately in the following main sections. The space pattern can be used in describing a large geographical area, a more limited area such as a college campus or a factory, a building, a room such as an auditorium, or a very limited area such as a computer keyboard. It also can be used to describe a plant or an animal or a machine. For instance, you might describe improvements in a new sports car model moving from the body shell, to the interior, to the mechanical controlling devices such as brakes and steering, and finally to the power train. You should be able to divide the subject into three or four mainheads, as in this example:

Specific purpose: to describe this city in relation to its location on a river.

I. The original river front is presently a tourist area.
II. The central business district is next to the river front area.
III. Next come the older residential areas.
IV. Finally, farthest from the river are the newer suburbs.

Process Pattern   Process patterns can be used to show your listeners how they can do something step by step. It may be a mental process, such as using positive thinking in facing a challenge, or a physical process, such as doing a set of aerobic exercises. The patterns also may be used to show the means by which something is normally done by others, such as open-heart surgery, or the stages or steps by which some result, such as tectonic formation of the continents, occurred or was achieved in the past. Topics may be as trivial as how to mix a drink or as relevant to the audience as in this example:

Specific purpose: to explain how to succeed with essay exams.

  I. Day-by-day preparation throughout the term.
 II. Final preparation before the exam.
III. Attitudes and techniques when taking the exam.

One common sort of process speech tells the audience how to construct or repair some object: making Christmas decorations, tuning a car, or repairing an electric outlet, for example. Often this sort of process speech follows roughly the following structure:

  I. Planning the project, or determining the repair to be made.
 II. Gathering the necessary tools and materials. (I and II may be combined in one section: I. Preparation.)
III. The actual construction or repair. (This is usually the longest main section. Its separation into a *few* distinct subdivisions is important for clarity.)
IV. Using or evaluating the result. (If this is not an important part of the process, it may be handled only briefly as part of the conclusion.)

Cause-Effect Patterns   There are a number of ways to use cause-effect patterns. You may explain causes of a present situation, such as water pollution. You may explain the projected effects of a present situation, such as space exploration. You may cover both the causes and the effects of a past situation or event, such as the causes and effects of the urban riots of the 1960s.

Most stated cause-effect relationships, at least outside the physical sciences, are somewhat speculative. Some, in fact, are so debatable that the speaker's primary task is to convince the audience that the asserted causes or effects are really the true causes or effects—to convince the audience that leniency with first offenders is really a major cause of juvenile delinquency, for example. Such speeches become persuasive in purpose. Nevertheless, this pattern is legitimate for informative speeches if the speaker depends on reliable sources and analysis of the topic, and if he is aware that the causes or effects he asserts are usually only a probable and incomplete description of reality.

This pattern is frequently used to explain both cause and effect when there is particular interest in how an event came to happen and what the result is. For example:

Specific purpose: to explain the rather sudden increase in women engineering students at this university.

  I. The increase was caused by special recruitment and scholarship programs for women, aimed at high schools in this area.

II. The effect was a significant increase in both the quantity and quality of local women high school graduates majoring in engineering here.

The recruitment program is described in some detail in section I, and in section II the effect is explained with both statistics and examples. The same basic structure can be used for a topic in which there are several causes and several effects. In a speech on the causes and effects of communication breakdown within families, for example, the first main section could explain several causes and the second section could explain several effects.

When you use this structure to describe more complex cause-effect relationships you should distinguish, for yourself as well as for the audience, between serial items and parallel items. In a serial relationship one cause produces an effect that becomes the cause of another effect, and so on through a chain of cause-effect links. For example:

Specific purpose: to explain a possible harmful effect of rapid introduction of medical technology into underdeveloped countries.

  I. Introduction of medical technology into underdeveloped countries causes rapid reduction in death rates from some diseases.
  II. Reduced death rates cause rapidly expanding populations.
  III. Population growth outstripping food production causes famine.

In a parallel relationship, all causes contribute directly to the effect, or all effects flow directly from the cause. In this example all causes contributed directly to one effect:

Specific purpose: to explain what caused the "Wild West" to be wild.

  I. The adventurous independence of many people who accepted or fled to the challenge of new country.
  II. Absence of clear legal jurisdictions in much of the country.
  III. The instability of social structure in boom towns.

Topical Patterns

Often you will have to separate a mass of material into a few categories, or main sections, that will serve your purpose and make sense to your audience. Sometimes the separation of material into main sections is quite obvious or traditional, such as the treatment of the federal government in terms of three branches: legislative, executive, and judicial. Other times, there appears to be no natural separation of the examples or other information into categories—for example, in a speech on alleged photographs of unidentified flying objects (UFOs). Nevertheless, the audience is likely to become confused and bored if you merely provide a string of examples or other data, so you have to impose some categories on the material. The UFO photos, for example, could be grouped according to type of UFO in the picture *or* according to categories of pictures ranging from obvious fakes to those for which there seems to be some verification.

There is great variety in topical patterns; but when you are working out your specific purpose and main sections, perhaps the most useful distinction is between patterns based on *partition* and those based on *classification*.

Partition Pattern   Use of a partition pattern assumes a precisely delimited subject which is then sliced up into main sections that together cover the subject *completely*. In a speech explaining the intercollegiate athletic program's income last year, for example, there is a specific amount of income, and the speaker's task is to arrive at some meaningful categories within which to explain the entire income. He might perhaps use student body fees, ticket receipts, donations, and such special income as television rights. If there was some income not covered by these categories, he would have to rework the categories. Similarly, a speaker explaining the elements of composition in good portrait photography would need to cover *all* significant elements.

Classification Pattern   Use of a classification pattern commits the speaker only to cover some major aspects of the subject. A speech classifying the sorts of customers a waitress encounters may draw on a vast number of examples and observations, but the speaker cannot hope to account for every possible type of customer. Therefore, the speaker selects *some* types of customers to discuss, and these types form the basis for the mainheads of the speech—for example, shy customers, friendly customers, demanding but fair customers, and hostile customers. Similarly, a speaker might explain *some* important types of jobs that robots can do or *some* of the more practical ways citizens can become involved in crime prevention.

Deciding Whether to Partition or to Classify   A speaker's choice of specific purpose within a topic area usually determines whether she is committed to partitioning the subject into divisions that cover it completely or whether she has the flexibility of classifying a number of items into a few categories she selects to cover for this particular audience and situation. She might, for example, commit herself to cover *all* the types of resources in her college library—human, print-paper, microform, and electronic—as in this example of a *partition pattern*:

Specific purpose: to describe the resources provided by the library of this college.

   I. Human assistance in each department of the library.
  II. Print-paper materials, such as books, serials, maps, and prints.
 III. Microrecorded materials, such as microfilm and microfiche collections.
 IV. Electronic resources, such as audiovisual materials and computerized systems.

On the other hand, the speaker might decide to point out only *some* of the more useful library resources for her particular listeners, as in this example of a *classification pattern*:

Specific purpose: to describe some library resources a student might find especially useful.

   I. Books, indexed in the card catalog.
  II. Periodicals, indexed by the *Readers' Guide* and other indexes.
 III. The reference section, for condensed, convenient information.
 IV. The microfilm section, for past issues of newspapers and older magazines.

Whether you use partition or classification, cover your material in three or four clearly defined main sections. Also give some thought to the sequence in which you put those main sections. Note that in the outlines for the library speech, both patterns begin with resources that are easily used and familiar to the audience. Thus the speaker gets on comfortable ground with the audience before moving on to more specialized or unfamiliar aspects of the topic.

Psychological Patterns

Psychological patterns are based more on adaptation to the thought processes of the audience than on any logical sequence in the material itself. In some of these patterns the order is based on providing listeners first with what they need to know in order to understand what comes next.

Inquiry Pattern   The inquiry pattern is a rather specialized one that leads the audience through a natural progression of understanding. The purpose of an inquiry speech is to enable the listeners to make their own informed decisions on an issue. Before they can evaluate specific decisions or solutions to a problem, they must have standards that an ideal solution would meet, and before they can understand these standards they must know something about the problem. Thus a full inquiry pattern usually falls into three main sections: explanation of problem or point for decision, setting forth standards against which to measure solutions, and explanation and evaluation of each solution.

Specific purpose: to clarify the choices this city faces if it is to assure itself a supply of usable water in the future.

I. Problem: the city is now using water faster than the supply is being replenished.
   A. Effects of present and projected rates of water use.
   B. Factors contributing to present use of water.
II. Standards: an ideal solution would meet the following standards:
   A. Would assure a permanently adequate water supply.
   B. Would be publicly acceptable and enforceable.
   C. Would be technically feasible in the near future.
   D. Would be low in cost.
III. Solutions: explanation and evaluation of each possible solution against the standards. (The city is not likely to pay for all three solutions, so the citizens must make a choice.)
   A. Legally enforced conservation of water.
   B. Construction of plants to recycle used water.
   C. Adding more sources by use of long-distance pipelines.

An inquiry speaker should realize that no one solution will meet all the standards perfectly. If one did, he would have found the perfect solution and there would be no reason for inquiry. Inquiry speeches are to help audiences in those frequent situations in life in which we must make a choice from among several less-than-perfect options. A group of recent graduates in accounting, for example, might listen to a speech clarifying how they could apply their personal standards in choosing among three career options: working for a large corporation, working in a specialized accounting firm, or striking out on their own. After this, or any other inquiry speech, listener Smith might pick a different solution than listener Jones because he valued certain standards differently than did Jones. Each picks the solution that seems best to meet the particular standards he thinks are most important.

In other psychological patterns, the order is based on first arousing an anticipation in the audience and then satisfying that anticipation. When a speaker spends the first part of a speech telling us about the origin and procedures of a recent serious search for the Loch Ness monster, we assume that in the latter part of the speech he will tell us the results of the search. When we are told about the development of a bloody conflict between factory workers and management in local history, we expect in the latter part of the speech to be told how the conflict was resolved. The speaker can exploit the dramatic possibilities in the topic by first explaining the search, mystery, or conflict. Then, when audience interest has been aroused, she can present the resolution in the last main section. It works a bit like a plot in a suspense story.

Problem-Solution Pattern   The problem-solution pattern is probably the most common psychological pattern. It provides members of the audience early in the speech with what they need to know in order to understand later parts, and it also arouses anticipations that are met later in the speech. In fact, the problem-solution pattern is so potent as a psychological strategy that it is frequently used in persuasion (and we will consider it more fully in Chapter 10). However, it can be used in informative speaking, as a simple two-part pattern: I. Discussion of problem; II. How problem was solved. For example, a speaker might: I. Explain the nature and extent of book theft in the college library; II. Describe what the library staff is doing to curb the thefts. Or a lecturer on business management might: I. Describe past symptoms and causes of declining morale among newspaper carriers; II. Describe three things the circulation manager did to improve morale.

The problem-solving pattern can also be used more flexibly, as this sample illustrates:

> **Specific purpose: to explain the construction of the Golden Gate Bridge.**
>
>   I. Problem: developing a span of sufficient length and strength.
>   II. Theoretical solution in design of the bridge.
> III. Actual construction of the bridge.

Stage 2: Plan Structure Within Main Sections

In the preceding stage, you were working with the overall unit: purpose statement plus mainheads. In this stage, you fill in under each mainhead the next level or two of subheads. Each subhead in your speech should fall under a mainhead and be related to that mainhead—as a subdivision of it, as supporting argument or proof for it, to clarify it by more detailed explanation, or in some other way. In a very simple speech you may go directly from mainhead to specific supporting materials, but in most speeches you will have at least one level of subheads between your mainheads and your specific detail.

To locate these subheads, begin by dividing your raw material according to main sections. Go through all your idea notes and research materials, and label each item, in pencil in the margin, with a roman numeral showing which mainhead it goes under. If you took notes on 4 × 6 cards, you can now deal the cards out into stacks or rows according to mainheads.

If an item doesn't seem to go under any mainhead by this stage in planning, it probably should be eliminated. Most decisions about which mainhead to put material under should be rather quickly obvious. For others, you should be able to make a choice without agonizing over it or risking seriously faulty structure. If you encounter very many hard choices about where to put material, perhaps you should go back and rework your pattern of mainheads to conform more closely to what you really want to cover in the speech.

Once the material has been sorted out among the mainheads, you can work on each main section. A speaker on camping, for example, has divided his subpoints and supporting materials among the following three mainheads:

Specific purpose: to describe how to have a safe and enjoyable three- or four-day cross-country camping trip.

  I. Prepare carefully in advance.
 II. On the trail be sensible and cheerful.
III. Camping each night poses special duties.

He is ready to work on the next level or two of this outline.

Approaches to Structuring a Main Section

How do you divide the material in a section into subsections and determine the subhead for each subsection? You can use one or more of the following four approaches. If the structure within one main section is especially hard to work out, you will often save time in the long run by getting together, perhaps in abbreviated form, all your items for that main section on one sheet of paper before applying these approaches.

Start with the Mainhead One approach is to start with the mainhead itself. What major points are needed to cover it fully? or does it divide into? In the speech on camping, the speaker had only to glance through his notes and draw on his personal knowledge to decide on the subheads within the third main section.

III. Camping each night poses special duties.
     A. Setting up camp involves three jobs.
        1. Put up shelter.
        2. Gather firewood.
        3. Store supplies.
     B. Cooking and cleaning up are other special duties.
     C. Breaking camp requires a few final duties.

Look for the Most General Points   A second approach is to look for the most general points among your items for the main section. See if these suggest a pattern of subheads, then see if other subheads are needed to fill in the pattern. When the speaker on camping looks through the material for his first main section, he sees a long list of items such as flashlights, good boots, maps, lightweight and nourishing food, example of the time he went out with a poorly designed backpack, importance of proper equipment, first-aid supplies, example of friend who got a bad cut two days out, supplies for all likely needs, and so forth. Two items stand out as more general and, in fact, as including most of the other items: proper equipment and necessary supplies. Maps, however, don't seem to fall clearly into either category, and they actually suggest a different part of complete preparation: know about the terrain in which you are going. He has his structure for the first main section.

> I. Prepare carefully in advance.
>   A. Use proper equipment.
>   B. Obtain information about the area you are entering.
>   C. Obtain supplies to meet every likely need.

Group the Items   A third approach is to group most of the items into two, three, or four categories and then devise a subhead for each category. Any item that doesn't fit into one of these categories should be eliminated; if such an item is necessary for the speech, you have to rework the categories. Even if in his raw material for section I the speaker had not noted "supplies" and "equipment," he would realize that he had to group the various specific items on his list into some sort of categories. Experimenting with different ways of grouping would probably lead him to the distinction between permanent, reusable items (equipment) and items that are likely to be used up on a trip (supplies). Some items, such as first-aid supplies, can be almost arbitrarily put into either category. But maps don't seem to fit into either category, and the item is clearly too important to discard, so he would create a third category. Again, by a somewhat different method, he would have arrived at the structure shown above for the first main section.

Scan the Topoi and Pattern Lists   A fourth possible approach is to scan the list of topoi on pages 79–81 and the list of possible patterns on pages 91–98 to see if either of these lists will suggest a pattern for organizing within the main section. For the second main section ("On the trail . . .") the speaker had a list of suggestions ranging from being considerate of other hikers and being positive when the going gets rough to avoiding steep, gravelly climbs and not trying to go too far in one day. But he can't discern any general points or ways to categorize the items. Scanning the list of topoi, however, he notices one division of items into "physical" and "mental." This suggests the key to organizing the second main section.

> II. On the trail be sensible and cheerful.
>   A. Be a physically sensible hiker.
>   1. Avoid taking foolish risks.
>   2. Pace your endurance.
>   B. Be a mentally positive hiker.
>   1. Be considerate of both your companions and other hikers.
>   2. When problems arise, try especially to keep in a good humor.

For a major speech, you should end up with at least a two-level outline of ideas in rough draft.

Stage 3: Check to Improve Basic Structure

Now you should have a rough outline of your basic structure: specific purpose, mainheads, and a level or two of subheads under each mainhead. Don't fill in the supporting materials yet. You can see and revise the organizational strategy more easily if you have it outlined on one piece of paper than if it is spread over several pages with the supporting materials added in.

Your basic structure may be perfect. But if it isn't, now is the time to improve it. You can develop a stronger speech, and you can avoid wasted time and other frustrations later in preparation. As you check it over, be ready and willing to change it in at least four ways: by *cutting* out idea headings and even whole sections, by *adding* in new mainheads or subheads, by *rearranging* the sequence of mainheads and subheads, and by *rephrasing* headings.

Guidelines for Checking Structure

As you look over your outline, try to imagine how the audience will respond to the speech. Are you developing the topic in a way that they will find interesting and that will help you accomplish your purpose? Will the organization seem natural and logical so that your listeners can follow it easily? The five guidelines that follow are not intended as rigid rules for their own sake, but rather are to help you adapt the structure to serve your own purposes and the needs of the listeners in the best possible way. They are aims toward which you work during the process of developing the basic structure for a speech. Try deliberately applying them one by one to your rough draft outline. The order in which they are given here is as good an order as any to use.

Guideline 1: Does the structure emphasize the main points you want your audience to understand?   To judge this *you* first have to know clearly what your main points are.

Look at the mainheads (I, II, etc. in the body) and the first level of subheads (A, B, etc.). Within these two levels should be the main ideas you would want your audience to carry away from the speech. If the main ideas are missing or are down on the lowest levels of the outline, then you need to get those ideas into the top levels and rearrange the rest of the organization to fit.

Sometimes you have to take a more fundamental approach: Does the structure reflect the focus you really want to develop on the topic? A speaker may, for example, have tried to organize her speech on the basis of "two advantages and two disadvantages of solar energy" when what she really wants to discuss are "three techniques for tapping solar energy." She will be more comfortable when she restructures the speech on the basis of the latter focus.

Guideline 2: Will the body of the speech fulfill your statement of focus?   In your statement of focus in the presented speech you, in effect, promise your audience that you will cover a specific topic and purpose fully.

Do the mainheads together meet that promise? A speaker states that her purpose is "to analyze Ingmar Bergman's film *The Seventh Seal*." She has planned remarks on the plot and characters in the film and on the specific film techniques used. Only now, checking the structure, does she realize that she also needs to deal with the thematic meanings of the film in order to cover all major aspects of her announced purpose. (Well, better late than never!) Her choice—and yours in a similar situation—is either to narrow down the announced specific purpose or to add in the needed section. And this leads us to consider the maximum time limit for the speech.

Will you have time to go into enough specific detail under each main heading to make your ideas clear and interesting to your audience? You can get a very rough estimate by dividing the number of major sections into the time allowed for the speech. Remember, you also need time for the introduction and conclusion. You can almost always add specific supporting materials to your present points, so "too short" is usually not a problem. But if your time limit is going to force you to develop your ideas too briefly and thinly for your particular audience, you probably should cut out some sections and, if necessary, revise your specific purpose to fit what you have left.

Guideline 3: Is the speech divided into a consistent pattern of main sections? A speaker might describe the operation of a cannery by using a space pattern in which he explains what happens in each area within the cannery, *or* he might use a process pattern describing step by step what happens to the produce from the time it arrives in the cannery until it leaves in cases of cans. But he should not mix the two sorts of mainheads if he wants the audience to follow the speech easily. Your purpose and material may not always permit a simple consistency of pattern, but approach this aim as closely as you can. It has great advantages.

Using a single basis for the pattern of mainheads helps you achieve some other aims of good structure. You should check specifically for these aims: First, *avoid overlapping*, in which the same particular point seems to turn up in two or three different main sections. Second, make your main sections of roughly *equal importance*. Third, present the main sections in a *rational sequence*—a sequence in which what comes before seems to pave the way for and lead naturally into what follows.

You can also check for these aims *within* each main section. Not all the main sections in a speech will be organized in the same way, although such parallelism in structure among main sections is an advantage if there is no good reason not to use it. Regard each main section separately as a

The rough outline of a speech should be evaluated to make sure that it meets the audience's needs and the speaker's purposes. (Rae Russell)

sort of "minispeech," and see if the subheads (A, B, etc.) add up to a consistent, rational pattern developing the mainhead under which they fall.

Guideline 4: Is the basic structure as simple as it logically can be?   As a student put it, "The simpler you can make it to yourself, the easier it will be for your audience to understand." This means as few mainheads as logically possible, seldom more than four, and as few subheads as possible under each mainhead. If necessary, eliminate some ideas and group others together to get a basic simplicity that an audience can follow clearly and comfortably. Simplicity also means having as few levels of organization as possible between your mainheads and your lowest levels on the outline where the supporting materials occur.

Guideline 5: Is the speech unified?   This guideline requires that every idea in the body of the speech supports your purpose in the speech. You can rather quickly test for logical relevance by seeing if each mainhead does state a part of your topic, and if each subhead is a part of or supports in some way the mainhead under which it falls.

If you discover that a section of material seems irrelevant to your statement of focus, the best solution usually is to eliminate the section. You can use the time thus saved to develop more fully the ideas and sections that are relevant. Sometimes, however, the solution is to rephrase the statement of focus or a mainhead so that the material does become clearly relevant.

It must be admitted that in longer speeches a speaker sometimes will digress into an example or even a brief line of thought that does not seem relevant to his specific purpose. Occasionally this is effective because the material, although not logically relevant, does advance the speaker's purpose indirectly, perhaps by increasing the audience's general interest in the speech or by creating a closer feeling between audience and speaker. Such digressions should be used with great care, however. The purposeful digression is not the same thing as sloppy organization, and perhaps the beginning speaker does best to develop skill in tight organization before he begins to experiment with digressions. Digressions run the risks of distracting the audience from the main points and of making the speaker appear careless or unsure of his material.

The Guidelines in Action

A student has drawn on her experience working three summers as a lifeguard at a swimming pool, to get ideas and materials for a speech describing that job. She also interviewed and obtained some printed material from the city official who oversees the city swimming pools, and she interviewed two friends who worked as lifeguards at different pools.

She sifts through her notes, combines examples and other detail, and uses her own knowledge to discover major points for the speech. She arrives at this outline of basic structure.

> **Specific purpose: to describe the job of summer lifeguard at a municipal swimming pool.**
>
>   I. Requirements must be met for a job at a city pool.
>   A. Certificate of advanced swimming skills.
>   B. Special certificate from training program in rescue skills.
>   C. Certificate for successfully completing special first-aid class.
>   II. There are some disadvantages in being a city pool lifeguard.
>   A. Preventing drowning is a very heavy responsibility.
>   B. Sometimes you have to deal with some obnoxious kids and parents.
>   C. Sitting at a pool all day can get rather boring.
> III. There are some good points in having a summer job.
>   A. You can make money.
>   B. Almost any job is more interesting than sitting at home with nothing to do.
>   C. A summer job can give you various kinds of experience that can help in a later career.

The outline looks pretty good to her. It is a structure, and it covers most of what she wants to say about the job. But she has the initiative (and the courage) to see if the structure can be improved.

First she considers whether this basic structure shows the major ideas she wants to get across to the audience (guideline 1). Under mainhead I she has the official requirements for a lifeguard job, but she also wants her listeners to realize that there are important less tangible requirements, such as having a sense of responsibility and being able to deal with people tactfully. Therefore, under mainhead I she adds a fourth subhead:

>   I. D. Less tangible requirements for the job.

Still applying guideline 1, she discovers that there are some special advantages of lifeguarding that don't fall under any of the subheads she now has in section III. For example, you can get some healthy exercise being around a swimming pool. So she adds:

> III. D. There are some special good points about lifeguarding as a summer job.

Glancing back over section I as it now stands, the speaker senses something wrong: She has three relatively specific subheads on the training and certificates officially required, but she has only one subhead to cover several unofficial requirements. This seems to be an inconsistent and poorly balanced pattern of subheads (guideline 3) within section I. She could add the unofficial requirements as subheads D, E, and F, but guideline 4 suggests that she go for a simpler set of subheads, so she decides on this pattern:

I. Requirements must be met for a job at a city pool.
   A. There are official requirements for training and certification.
   B. There are unofficial requirements for personal qualities.

The specific requirements will be given as supporting material to clarify A and B.

Applying guideline 2, she discovers that her specific purpose promises to describe a job and yet the body of the speech doesn't even describe the duties of that job! Therefore, she decides to add a main section on duties. But what will be the subheads? Going through her notes and thinking further, she produces three main duties. She adds this main section to her speech:

II. A lifeguard has three main duties.
   A. To prevent people from annoying or endangering themselves or others.
   B. To be ready to rescue a person or handle a medical emergency.
   C. To keep the pool equipment operating and the pool area neat.

When the speaker thinks ahead to how she will explain the performance of each of these duties, she realizes that she is likely to use some of her material on requirements for the job. For example, a lifeguard is able to handle a major medical emergency because he or she is required to be certified in advanced first aid. So section I on requirements will overlap with section II on duties, and she doesn't really need guideline 3 to tell her that this could be a flaw in structure. But in another way the requirements one has to meet in preparing for the job are separate from duties on the job. What should she do?

At this point the speaker begins to get a little discouraged. It seems that in some cases solving one problem in structure only leads to another problem. But she rallies her courage, takes another look at the five guidelines, and attacks the outline again.

To the problem of section I and the new section II partly overlapping, she applies guideline 4: When in doubt, simplify. She combines the two main sections by using parts of "requirements" under "duties." Eliminating other parts of her detail on requirements also will help her stay within the time limit. (Another speaker might have kept the two sections because he saw a natural distinction between "requirements" to qualify for the job and "duties" on the job. His structure might not have been as efficient as hers, but it would not necessarily have been wrong.)

As she routinely applies guideline 5 to make sure everything in her speech supports her specific purpose, she suddenly notices that as presently phrased her last mainhead, on good points of *summer* jobs, isn't even relevant to her specific purpose. She needs to refocus this main section to be on the good points of a *lifeguarding* job. The subpoints under the original mainhead plus other points in her notes, such as being able to make extra money giving swimming lessons, produce a dozen or so good points about the lifeguarding job. She combines these, following guideline 4, into four subheads. She also changes "good points" to "advantages" in order to parallel "disadvantages" in mainhead II (guideline 3).

In a last check-through she sees that in II.C. she gives as one disadvantage of the job that it is "boring," and in III.C. she gives as one advantage that it is "interesting." This is a flagrant inconsistency. Or is it? She thinks back to the reality of her subject: Some lifeguards do find the job very boring at times, and other lifeguards or even the same ones at other times find it more interesting than most summer jobs. Her solution here is not to rework the structure to make it consistent like some problem in abstract logic, but rather to rephrase the headings to state more accurately what she means and then to explain each subhead in her supporting material.

Finally the speaker decides she has an outline that will work and it is time to move on to the next step in preparation. So she won't have to work with a mess of crossouts and scribble-overs, she takes ten minutes to write a clean draft of the basic outline. She is mainly aiming for two levels of headings, but if she has decided on some third-level headings she will put them in also. Here is her final outline:

Specific purpose: to describe the job of summer lifeguard at a municipal swimming pool.

I. A lifeguard has three important duties.
   A. The main, routine duty is to prevent behavior that could annoy or endanger people at the pool.
      1. Common types of disruptive or dangerous behavior.
      2. How the lifeguard prevents such behavior.
   B. A second, more dramatic duty is handling rescues and medical emergencies.
      1. Examples.
      2. Special training and certification required of lifeguards.
   C. A third, less glamorous duty is maintenance of the physical equipment and pool area.

II. There are some disadvantages to a summer job as a municipal lifeguard.
   A. Preventing drownings or other serious accidents is a heavy responsibility.
   B. Sometimes you have to deal with obnoxious people, both kids and parents.
   C. Some lifeguards find that sitting at a pool all day is sometimes boring.
III. There are some advantages that lifeguarding has as a summer job.
   A. With regular hours plus other opportunities you can make fairly good money.
   B. It's healthy.
   C. Some people find the variety of people and situations interesting.
   D. You get some kinds of experience that might be useful in a later career.
      1. Dealing with people.
      2. Teaching and coaching.

When you have finished a rough draft of your basic structure, do as this speaker did: Take at least a few minutes to check the structure for possible improvements. You may not make it "perfect," but you may make it a lot better. Be flexible enough to change even some of your initial revisions, as this speaker did, in order to solve further problems in structure. But also realize that sometimes you must choose among apparently equally valid ways to organize a section, so make a choice and then depend on your phrasing of key headings and transitions to make that structure clear and coherent to your audience.

Summary

Well-planned organization of a speech serves both speaker and audience. Outlining is a tool that enables you to work out and check this organization on paper as it evolves over a period of time. You begin by planning the basic structure—purpose statement and mainheads—and then usually a level or two of subheads.

You can plan a pattern of mainheads more efficiently by following a process roughly stage by stage. First, think through your topic and the material you have so far to discover possible mainheads. Second, decide on the mainheads you intend to use in the speech. Third, arrange the mainheads in a sequence.

Often the pattern you need can be found among these common patterns: natural patterns, such as time, space, process, and cause-effect;

topical patterns, whether partition or classification; and psychological patterns, such as inquiry and problem-solution.

Plan structure within main sections by first placing each relevant item in your notes under the appropriate mainhead. Then within each main section decide on the highest level or two of idea headings needed to develop that mainhead.

As you plan, you work toward certain guidelines for effective structure, and when you have a rough draft of the basic structure you can test it against these guidelines to discover possible ways to improve it.

1. Do the major headings state the main ideas you want to convey to the audience?
2. Will you cover all necessary parts of your topic, and in enough detail within your time limit?
3. Is the speech divided into a consistent, logical pattern of main sections?
4. Can you make the structure any simpler and thus easier to follow?
5. Is the speech unified so that all major headings clearly contribute to your purpose?

Exercises

1. Give a four- to six-minute speech clearly exemplifying one of the patterns on pages 91–98. On your outline state the pattern used. Be prepared to explain why this pattern was appropriate for your material, purpose, and audience.

2. Turn in a tentative basic structure for a major speech you are developing as the class moves through Chapters 4 through 9. (This is a continuation of exercise 2 in Chapter 5.

CHAPTER SEVEN

Filling in Basic Structure

A student has decided to give a speech on suspense film maker Alfred Hitchcock. Drawing on her experience seeing his films, some of them several times, and reading relevant parts of five or six books she checked out of the library, she arrived at the main ideas for her speech. She decided to arrange her ideas under three mainheads in the "classification" pattern. Although at this stage she is not aiming for a polished outline, she does write out some main ideas as complete sentences in order to have a more precise sense of what each heading is to cover.

Statement of focus: I'm going to describe three sorts of techniques Hitchcock used in suspense films to manipulate audiences.

I. Plot action is one sort of technique.
    A. Hitchcock was interested in emotions, not logic of plot.
    B. Surprise—is not predictable.
    C. Suspense—is predictable.
    D. Combines suspense and surprise.
II. Hitchcock played on his audience's deep psychological fears and impulses.
    A. Bizarre and horrible events erupt in bright, cheerful surroundings.
    B. He makes audience identify with criminals.
III. Hitchcock used cinematic techniques within shots and in editing the film together.
    A. Pictorial composition and movement on screen.
    B. Editing:
        1. Expand time.
        2. Rapid editing.

As we look over the headings in this outline, we realize that many of them, by themselves, do not communicate much. How can Hitchcock combine surprise and suspense if they are opposites in regard to predictability? What are "shots" and "editing"? Why should her listeners believe that Hitchcock makes his viewers identify with criminals? She realizes that if the speech is to be effective some of these ideas will need proof, even though her speech is informative, and most will need to be at least clarified. She also is aware of the needs to make the speech interesting and to convince the audience that she knows what she is talking about. To meet these needs, she will use examples, quotations from experts, visual aids, and all those other sorts of developmental detail called "supporting materials."

As would most effective speakers, during her research and thinking she accumulated more items of supporting material than she can use in her ten- to fifteen-minute speech. She labels these items according to the mainheads and major subheads for which each could be used. If she is lacking supporting materials for any idea, she goes back to the books she has checked out of the library or to her memories of the films.

Now she performs the crucial part of step 4 in preparation: She selects which items of supporting material to use, and she begins to decide how much detail to use and how to shape each item. She records her planning on an expanded rough draft of the outline, the first main section of which is shown below. Her wording for the items of supporting material may not communicate much to a reader, but they tell her *what* items she plans to use *where* in the speech. Note, however, that at this stage she does make some improvements in the phrasing of some idea headings. (We will see how this content might be further revised and actually worded in the sample presented speech at the end of this chapter.)

I. Plot action is one area of Hitchcock's technique.
    A. He views plot only as a way of working on emotions.
        1. Hitchcock quote, ". . . logic is dull."
        2. Example of *Psycho*, quoted from Hitchcock.
    B. Keeps audience fearful of nasty surprises.
        1. Kills off heroine in *Psycho*—detailed example: star; all rules off.
        2. Kills off heroine in *Frenzy*—brief example.
    C. Uses suspense, when audience does know what is likely to happen.
        1. Hitchcock quote: must give audience information.
        2. In *Psycho*, detective found Norman's mother.
        3. Sister searches for Norman's mother—detailed example: tension builds.
    D. Combines suspense and surprise.
        1. In *Frenzy*, example of waiting for scream, being distracted by girls.
        2. Example of Norman not finding and then finding newspaper with money.

What is true of this speech on Hitchcock will be true of most of the speeches you will give: The potential worth of the speech may be in the ideas, but the effectiveness with which those ideas are actually communicated, as well as the popular appeal of the speech, will depend largely on skillful use of supporting materials. You develop this skill as you learn what supporting materials can do at each point in a speech and as you learn how to draw on a variety of types of supporting materials.

What Supporting Materials Do

When you give a speech, you feel better if the audience understands your ideas and is interested in what you have to say. Beyond minimal standards for clarity and interest, different speaking situations place emphasis on different responses. A program speaker at a civic club luncheon usually is most concerned with being interesting; a speaker instructing in lifesaving first aid is more concerned with making the important ideas clear and memorable; a persuasive speaker may be more concerned with emotional impact and establishing a credible image. Even within a single speech, the skillful speaker is aware of which points need to be clarified, which are more in need of proof, which require a special effort to make them interesting. He selects and shapes each item of supporting material to accomplish one or more of six functions.

To Clarify   A speaker asserts, "The silicon chip brought about the revolution that is replacing calculators with computers in homes and small businesses, and that is permitting massive, flexible computer-aided instruction in schools." To the speaker, a senior in applied computer science, this is a perfectly clear statement. To the listener who knows virtually nothing about computers, the sentence is far from clear. A speaker begins to clarify the assertion by defining "silicon chip" and explaining how these chips operate in computers, by contrasting computers with calculators, and by explaining what computer-aided instruction is, perhaps using a hypothetical example of how such instruction might be used in a course familiar to the audience.

As a speaker you don't want to keep clarifying that which is already clear to the audience, but most inexperienced speakers err in the opposite direction by not using enough clarifying supporting materials. And there are relative degrees of clarity. Why let an important idea be "sort of clear" when you could use an example or a comparison or a visual aid or a fuller explanation to make it crystal clear?

To Arouse Interest   As popular periodicals from the *National Enquirer* to *Time* magazine show us, new, surprising, and specific information, even about familiar topics, arouses interest. Be alert for such novel, detailed information when you research your topic. Visual aids and detailed examples are other reliable ways to increase interest. Material that is personally related to the speaker or to the listeners is likely to increase interest. In a speech on the benefits of nursery schools, the speaker drew repeatedly on her experience as an enthusiastic nursery school teacher, and the speech kept a high level of attention. Listeners also tend to be more interested in events close to them in space or time. In dealing with victims of accidental shootings, an example that occurred a few days earlier in the vicinity of your school is likely to arouse more interest than a similar example years ago in another state.

A rather specialized way of keeping audience interest is the use of humor. More than most skills in public speaking, the ability to use humor is probably a natural talent that people have in widely varying degrees. For speakers who have no great talent, the set joke is rarely effective, unless it is used aptly to illustrate a specific point. Jokes or quick witticisms that fail to get expected laughter, however, may still relax the audience, so don't be afraid to give it a try. (It may also be comforting to know that one doesn't have to be a humorist to be a highly effective speaker.) The only intolerable error a speaker can make when using humor is to show bad taste—which embarrasses listeners and brands the speaker as lacking in judgment. Much effective humor occurs spontaneously in the speaking situation, and much of it comes from speakers who don't take themselves too seriously—though they may take their task very seriously.

To Make the Ideas Memorable   The listener remembers a striking item of supporting material and thereby remembers the key idea associated with it. Therefore, the idea should be built right into the item of supporting material. A speaker on dangers to safety in the home illustrated each of his four main dangers with a humorous sketch—a man lying in a bathtub with a television set propped on his knees was one example. A young woman advising her audience to pursue their ambitions despite difficulties used a vivid comparison, which she stated in the body of the speech and again in the conclusion: "When you reach the end of your rope, tie a knot and hang on."

Types of supporting material commonly used to make ideas memorable, as these cases suggest, are visual aids, detailed examples, vivid comparison of idea to tangible act or object (the idea of steadfast determination compared to the physical act of hanging on to the knotted end of a rope), and a quote from literature or a familiar saying.

To Increase Emotional Impact   We are most affected emotionally by what we experience directly, such as being involved in or witnessing a bad car accident, winning a hard-fought game or race, or being treated with contempt by some official. The speaker can cause us mentally to experience or witness events that arouse our fear, anger, pity, happiness, confidence, or other emotion. The primary tool is vivid description, which sets the event before our eyes:

> I was studying when I heard the crash on the road near our home. It was raining lightly, and I guess the woman driving the big station wagon hadn't realized how

slick that made the streets. Her car had struck one end of a concrete bridge abutment. The first thing I noticed when I ran up to the car was a piece of battery thirty or forty feet ahead of the car. The woman who had been driving was pinned between the front seat and the steering wheel. She was moaning, softly crying for help. All I could do was try to reassure her, to tell her that help was coming. The woman on the other side had smashed her head into the windshield. She was unconscious and bleeding a lot. One of the kids in the back had been thrown halfway into the front seat, sort of jammed between the two women. One of them must have been his mother. He just stared in one direction, but I knew he was alive. When the ambulance arrived, they had to go in through the rear door of the station wagon. When they got to the boy, one of the medics said, "There's no use worrying about this one." They pulled him out from between the two women, roughly it seemed to me. I never knew if his mother had heard them say that. And I never found out if the boy lived or died.

Other sorts of supporting material may contribute to emotional impact. A speaker may draw a comparison, or analogy, between his topic and something that carries a strong emotional charge in the audience's minds—for example,

Verbal supporting material can contribute to the emotional impact of a speech. (Kathy Bendo for Random House, courtesy of Pace University Speech & Drama Department)

comparing callous disregard for starving children in the world now to the starvation of helpless children in the Nazi concentration camps. Or the speaker may quote from a source that arouses strong feelings, usually positive, in the particular audience. To an audience of civil rights advocates, for example, the speaker might quote from a famous civil rights leader such as Dr. Martin Luther King, Jr.

Some supporting materials for emotional impact come from research in printed sources, but often you can discover and shape examples using vivid description and comparisons from your own experience, observation, and creative imagination.

To Gain Trust and Respect for the Speaker   Do you have teachers who state obscure facts, or refer to experts they have talked to or books they have read, or mention personal experiences, partly at least to let you know that they know what they are talking about? Using supporting material to gain your listeners' trust and respect is a perfectly legitimate aim.

There are several ways to use supporting material to increase audience confidence in you as a person, without being boastful or too obvious in your intent. Draw on a variety of sources for supporting material, and let the audience know about the different sources you have used. Comparisons or other references to people and events in history or literature, and quotes from poetry or other sources, tell an audience that here is a speaker with some broad background knowledge and some imagination. A speaker who can explain researched ideas with examples he designs for his particular audience demonstrates that he really does understand the ideas and that he wants his audience to understand them. A speaker's image is often enhanced simply by the use of abundant factual data, by personal examples and other references to personal experience (if done tactfully), and by carefully prepared visual aids.

To Provide Proof   Even in an informative speech and even when the audience has general faith in your credibility as a speaker, they may find some of your major ideas hard to accept. You should spot those ideas in advance and back them up by quoting experts, by statistics, or by factual examples. An audience might question the statement that a relatively conservative and early film maker such as Hitchcock could really be regarded as "the master" of suspense films. For proof, the speaker could cite two experts and point out that one is a movie critic and theorist, and the other the author of a book on thriller movies. A statement that persistent flirtation by male employees can be a type of sexual harassment for working women was supported by four factual examples of working women who were seriously disturbed by such unwanted attentions. Sometimes just explaining an idea fully enough to make it clear will make it acceptable to the audience.

We can think of memorability and emotional impact as two more intense sorts of interest used in special situations. And credibility is increased both by the speaker's image as a person whose knowledge and judgment can be trusted and by the proof offered for asserted ideas that might otherwise be questioned. Thus we end up with the basic aims of clarity, interest, and credibility, with appropriateness to speaker and audience a pervasive aim.

Types of Supporting Materials

Classifications of supporting materials into different types are not always tidy. One *item* of supporting material may actually combine two or three *types*, as with a visual aid showing statistics provided by an expert. Nor does the list that follows cover every variety of supporting material. But this list will give you some notion of several major types and how to use them.

Why should you know even a modest list of major types of supporting materials? One reason is to make it easier for you to discover and develop material for a speech. A speaker who knows what an apt quote is will be more likely to note such an item in his research. A speaker who understands how to use hypothetical examples or visual aids is more likely to think of developing them in a speech. A second reason is that if you understand how different types work, you are more likely to select the best type to accomplish the intended functions at each point in a speech. Finally, technical understanding of supporting materials helps you learn from other speakers. When they use supporting materials with unusual effectiveness, you have a handle for getting at exactly what they did and then applying it to your own practice.

Verbal Supporting Materials

We will consider nine separate types of verbal supporting materials grouped into three categories. The first category contains four major types of examples and comparisons. These are drawn both from research and from the speaker's knowledge and creativity. Next are direct means of clarifying ideas, by explanation and definition, usually drawn from or shaped by the speaker's mind. In the final category are three types of specific data and quotations, usually drawn from research.

Examples and Comparisons

Factual Examples. The audience usually finds the individual case more interesting, easier to understand, and more convincing than the general idea. So the speaker uses the individual case—the example—to illustrate the idea. A speaker states that television viewing can break down conversational contact and mutual support within families. The audience passively agrees. Then the speaker spends nearly a minute on a narrative example: In high school he had an ongoing conflict with a teacher, and it was distracting him from his other studies. Finally the tension erupted in a shouting match with the teacher, and the student was deeply disturbed. That evening he raised the matter at dinner, and his parents were temporarily interested, until it was time for the evening game shows, followed by a *Laverne and Shirley* rerun. The example concluded with the student in his room feeling desperately alone. Now, at least some listeners are beginning to understand the speaker's point.

The preceding illustration shows how examples may follow a *narrative* format, often with a bit of suspense and climax. Other examples rely more on the sensory detail of *vivid description*. (How would you classify the car wreck example on pages 113–114?)

Often a single example will not prove a general point to an audience's satisfaction, and sometimes a single example will not even clarify an idea adequately. The example can be reinforced with other types of supporting material, or you can use two or more examples on a point. When you use two or more examples in a series, the audience will often get the general drift from the first example, and subsequent examples can be developed more briefly.

Specific Instances. Specific instances are an extremely efficient form of supporting material and are often used in a series. In this type a speaker uses only a word or phrase to trigger off listeners' recognition of examples that are already in their minds. A speaker might state that many of the most popular television shows of all time reflected an underlying positive and compassionate view of human beings while showing people's individual foibles, and then back this up simply by listing *Family Ties, Star Trek, M*A*S*H,* and *The Cosby Show.* The listeners get some enjoyment and satisfaction using their own knowledge to fill in and understand the speech. This also is true of specific instances in the form of allusions to recent news items or to literary or historical figures or events.

The speaker should be sure that the audience does in fact have the necessary knowledge to understand the specific instances. A speaker asserts: "Even in modern times, serious people still search for mystical creatures, such as sea serpents, the Abominable Snowman, the Loch Ness monster, Sasquatch, and the Mokele Mbembe." The first item—sea serpents—and perhaps the next two would communicate, at least vaguely, to most audiences; but the last two instances would fail to communicate at all unless the listeners had the needed special knowledge. Such failures to communicate frustrate listeners, so if in doubt about your audience's special knowledge, cover yourself by expanding the specific instance to a brief detailed example: ". . . and the Mokele Mbembe, which is a large brontosaurus-like dinosaur supposedly living in a 50,000 square mile swamp in the Congo basin."

Hypothetical Examples.   A speaker wants to support a point with the specific detail of an individual case but does not have a factual example that fits his purpose. With a little imagination he can make up an example—admitting to the audience, of course, that it is not a real example:

> Imagine a person who wants a painting of the scene outside his window. He describes the scene over the telephone to a painter, and the painter follows his description as closely as he can. Now, no matter how complete the description and how competent the painter, that painting will not be like a photograph of the scene. Minor objects will be missing. Shapes of trees or buildings will be changed. Colors will be changed. Words, no matter how many are used, just can't describe precisely all the detail we see—much less what we hear, feel, or think.

A speaker may envision the listener in the hypothetical example, as in this example of a person coming home to find his residence burglarized:

> You arrive home after work. As you go up to your front door you see it is open. But you know that no one is home. As you go inside, you already have a sick feeling of suspicion in the pit of your stomach . . .

Do not, however, envision your listeners in situations or roles they would find offensive, as one speaker did in a speech on littering: "You are driving down the highway, throwing your hamburger wrappers and beer cans out the window, too dumb to care what you're doing to the environment."

The great advantage of hypothetical examples is flexibility. You can create one to fit exactly your need to make a particular idea clear and interesting. (You may also in your research discover useful ones other people have created.) Hypothetical examples, however, are rarely convincing proof; and even in an informative speech, the speaker who doesn't combine factual information with hypothetical examples may lose some credibility.

Comparison and Contrast.   Often, the speaker with an idea that is new to her listeners or difficult to understand will compare that idea with information that is more tangible or familiar to the audience. A speaker might use these comparisons (adapted from *NASA Educational Briefs*, No. EB 81-4) in explaining the tremendous density of the "black holes" that some astronomers believe exist in space:

> A mini-black hole may be so small you couldn't even see it under an ordinary microscope. Yet it may contain more mass, may weigh more, than

Mount Everest. If it suddenly decompressed, it would be as if millions of hydrogen bombs were detonated all at once.

Your use of comparison and contrast depends largely on your creative imagination in connecting your idea to other material outside your specific topic area. This is especially true in the use of two special forms of comparison: literal analogies and figurative analogies.

In a *literal analogy*, you can compare the thing you are talking about with another thing that is similar in all essential respects. Usually, literal analogies are used to prove. You assert that some point you are making about your subject is true because it is known to be true in the analogous case. For example:

Even though our football coach is having a losing season, things will only get worse if we fire him in mid-season. Last year at State College they fired a losing coach in mid-season, and in the rest of the season they suffered six disastrously one-sided losses.

In a *figurative analogy*, the thing you are talking about and the analogous thing are similar only in respect to the one point or the few points on which you are comparing them; the things are not really of the same sort. Thus figurative analogies, unlike literal ones, are not valid as proof (although sometimes they can seem surprisingly convincing to audiences). They are more properly used for clarity and interest, often by putting an abstract idea in concrete, physical terms that an audience can visualize. For example, the abstract notion that listening is an active rather than passive process becomes clearer when likened to catching a thrown ball:

The person catching the ball doesn't simply hold up his glove and assume the ball will hit it, and it's the thrower's fault if it doesn't. Rather, he tries to anticipate how the ball is coming and adjust his physical position to catch it. Similarly, we try to anticipate where the words are coming from—that is, the speaker's purpose—and we try to shift our mental position in order to catch the speaker's meaning accurately.

As another example, a speaker attempting to make memorable the idea that the family unit is important compared families in the nation to cells in the human body: if too many cells fail the body collapses, and if too many families fall apart the nation will collapse.

Explanation and Definition

Explanation. A speaker says, "A term paper writer who is overwhelmed by his own research notes probably didn't do enough early preparation," or "If your car won't start in the morning check the battery thoroughly." Listeners may passively agree, but it is unlikely that they really understand the connection between early preparation and too many research notes or how one checks a battery thoroughly. Explanation is an efficient way to clarify ideas that are new or complex to the audience.

Often the best approach to explanation is to break the thing to be explained into its parts. A process such as checking a battery or treating a case in juvenile court can be broken into separate steps. A speaker explained "positive mind control" as occurring in three steps:

> First, define your goal clearly. Second, mentally rehearse achieving the goal. Third, in the actual situation open yourself up to achieving the goal by clearing all the negative debris from your mind.

Other explanations may divide the idea into a series of cause-effect relationships:

> For the writer, lack of initial brainstorming on the topic results in a vague focus and no clear-cut main ideas to guide research. Because he lacks a clear guide to research, he feels he must take notes on everything that is relevant to his topic area. As a result, he ends up overwhelmed by his own notes.

If dividing the process, concept, or other idea into its parts won't clarify it adequately, go into further detail on each part using other sorts of supporting material, such as visual aids, factual or hypothetical examples, and comparisons.

Definition. Three main sorts of terms can reduce your clarity in communication unless you either avoid them or define them. Two of these sorts are technical terms. They are likely to occur when you as a specialist in your topic area are addressing an audience of nonspecialists. Scientists are not the only specialists; stamp collectors, literature teachers, auto mechanics, and numbers runners (to use a series of "specific instances") are all specialists, and no doubt you yourself are a specialist on some of the topics you might choose to speak on to your class. One sort of technical term is the *unusual word*, part of an obviously specialized vocabulary. It is easy for an audience and for a sensitive speaker to spot. As a speaker, you do better to avoid the term if you can use instead a roughly synonymous word or phrase that will communicate directly with the nonspecialist audience. If you must use the technical term itself, be sure to define it in a way that will really communicate rather than simply adding more technical jargon. The same suggestions apply to the other sort of technical term, except that it is not so easy to spot because it is a *common word used in a special sense*. In a technical discussion about computers, for example, such words as "basic," "memory," and "bit" can seem to be used in ordinary ways when the speaker intends a specific technical meaning.

The third sort of term is often the most deceptive in sabotaging communication. These are *nontechnical words that have a great breadth of meaning*. Both speaker and listener may interpret the word in a reasonable way yet be miles apart in their meanings, as illustrated by a story from the Russian Revolution: A capitalist whose factory had just been occupied by Bolshevik revolutionaries rushed up to the local Bolshevik commander, shouting, "I demand *justice* now!" So the Bolshevik commander administered *justice*; he shot the factory owner dead. The results will not be so drastic for you; still, when you use such terms as "personal rights," "fairness," "love," "bureaucrat," "administrative hostility," and a host of others, be sure your audience catches your specific meaning, even if you have to define the sense in which you are using the word.

There are many ways to define a term, and we will consider only five. One way may suffice, or you may need to combine two or three to make your meaning clear to your audience. The most common form of definition is to place the term in a class of things and then show what characteristics distinguish it from other things in that class: *"Genre films" (class) are those popular motion pictures (class) that use formula plots and conventional heroes and villains so the audience always knows roughly what to expect (characteristics that distinguish genre films from other popular motion pictures). Familiar movie genres include westerns, tough cop movies, musical comedies, and disaster movies.* The preceding sentence illustrates a second form of definition: use of a series of specific instances or a real or hypothetical example of the thing being defined. A third form is by how the thing operates or what it does: *By "virtue" I mean that quality which causes a person to do things that are consistent with his own honor and with the welfare of other people around him.* Fourth is by listing the parts that make up the thing being defined: *By "personal independence" I mean being on your own financially, setting your own career goals, and making your own decisions about personal behavior.* A fifth form of definition, by negation, is particularly useful if your audience is likely to misunderstand your term in a distinctly wrong way. You tell them what the term does not mean: *By "personal independence" I do not mean ignoring the advice of others, isolating yourself from other people, or having no moral standards.*

Specific Data and Quotations

Statistics.   Numbers may be used as simple figures in description: the height of a building, the nearest distance from Earth to Mars, the number of kilowatt hours of electricity used in your home last month. When we talk about the average number of kilowatt hours used in homes in your city last month, we are summarizing information about a large number of examples, of which your home is one—that is, we are using statistics. Because statistics do summarize great numbers of individual cases, they are a powerful source of proof. And contrary to some people's opinion, they can be made very interesting, have emotional impact, or make ideas memorable—if they are made clear and significant to the listeners.

You will use both simple figures and statistics effectively if you follow two basic rules: Be sure *you* know what the numbers mean. Then make sure the *audience* knows what they mean.

Let's start with the first rule. When a speaker tells us that the illegal pornography business grosses two hundred to three hundred *billion* dollars a year, he is telling us that this business accounts for about ten percent of the total goods and services produced in this country. This number won't be credible to the audience—and it shouldn't make sense to the speaker. He probably means two to three hundred *million*. But that's not what he said, and to alert listeners that one slip may cost the speaker some credibility.

When a speaker tells us that the average income in the United States is about $26,000 a year, does he mean per family of four, per household, or per person? Let's assume he means per family. By "average" does he mean the total national personal income divided by the number of families (the arithmetic mean), or does he mean the income point at which exactly half the families earn more and exactly half earn less (the median), or does he mean the income bracket in which more families fall than in any other single bracket (the mode)? Does he mean just earned income, or does he include income from all other sources such as interest on investments? If the speaker himself knows the answer to such questions, he has a much better chance of making this a meaningful statistic for his audience.

The speaker should also know where the statistics come from. Are they timely rather than obsolete, and do they come from a source the audience will accept as reliable? Take the extra couple of minutes needed to note and understand the time period, original source, and full meaning of the statistic when you research it.

The speaker who knows what the statistic stands for, why it is reliable, and how it is relevant to his idea can convey all that, as needed, to the audience. This is, however, not always enough to make statistics clear, much less interesting, to an audience. Four additional techniques can be used to increase the effectiveness of statistics. First, *round off numbers*, unless precision is required. "About twenty-six thousand dollars" communicates. "Twenty-five thousand, eight hundred and ninety-four dollars and thirty-seven cents" is a string of figures that won't register at all with many listeners. Second, *restate the key statistics* in different terms:

> In 1970 the Brazilian government spent five hundred million dollars building the Trans-Amazon road to open up the Amazon rain forest for settlement. They expected a million families to settle by 1980. Instead they have eight thousand families. *This is less than one percent of what they expected.* A project expected to cost about five hundred dollars per family has instead cost the

government *more than one hundred times that much*, about sixty-five thousand dollars per family. (Adapted from "Crosscurrents" column, *Science 82*, January–February, 1982, p. 87.)

Such restatement can sometimes be used to relate the statistics more directly to the audience:

> There were seven thousand burglaries and other property thefts in this city last year. That is one for every twenty households. Statistically, one person in this room will be hit this year. In the next ten years half of us can expect to have our home, car, or business robbed.

A third technique is to *compare the figure or statistic* with something concrete or more familiar to the audience:

> The giant star Betelgeuse has a diameter of three to four hundred million miles, about four times the distance from Earth to the sun. If our sun were in the center of this star, our Earth's orbit would be only about halfway out from the center to the star's surface.

Finally, a speaker can *use visual aids*—usually prepared graphs on chartboard—to make statistics clearer and more memorable (and showing statistics visually also often seems to make them more convincing). The average-mean family income for the lowest fourth, the low-middle, the high-middle, and the highest fourth of the U.S. population could each be represented by a vertical bar in which one inch would equal $2,000 income. The relative heights of the four bars would show graphically the relative income levels among the four groups.

Expert Testimony.   On topics about which we have little or no knowledge, we are at the mercy of other people for information and opinions. A speaker adapts to this by citing "experts" as sources or support for information and opinions given in the speech. Experts are not necessarily nationally known figures. Local store managers, for example, would probably be experts on how department stores cope with employee crime.

As a speaker, you may locate expert testimony in printed sources or in interviews. Either type of source may itself be the expert or may provide you with the testimony of other experts: "Last Tuesday's *New York Times* states . . ." or "In last Tuesday's *New York Times* I read that our ambassador to Mexico stated . . ." You may quote the expert word for word, or you may summarize or restate the expert's remarks—as long as you do so accurately—in your own words.

Expert testimony is used most commonly to increase credibility in a speech, and this may be necessary in informative as well as persuasive speeches. Thus as speaker, your most important consideration is that such supporting material be accepted as reliable by the audience, especially if these listeners are likely to question your main ideas. In a speech on the possibilities of intelligent life in outer space, a speaker spent several sentences explaining the qualifications of one of her major experts, astronomer Carl Sagan, so that his opinion would have more convincing weight. A message arguing that unwanted animals should be put to death not only cited the local animal shelter manager's supporting opinion but also suggested her competence and good character:

> Ms. Velasco, who has been with the animal shelter for eighteen years and was this city's 1977 Humanitarian of the Year, said that although animals are kept as long as possible, after a few months they often become depressed and stop eating. Thus, according to Ms. Velasco, it is kinder to destroy them.

Will the audience believe that you are reporting the expert testimony honestly and accurately? If you have doubts here, in your speech document your source fully—down to specific date and page number, or date and location of an interview—and quote word for word rather than putting the expert's statement in your own words.

It is usually easier to convince your audience that your expert testimony comes from a source who is objective and highly competent on the topic if, in fact, your expert does have these qualities. So for expert testimony, try to use highly reliable and respected sources, at least on serious or controversial issues.

Apt Quotes.   The main value of using apt quotes as supporting material is in the source's particular choice of language in phrasing the idea; thus the material is always quoted word for word. The lines may be taken from poetry, drama, novels, songs, proverbs and folk sayings, or famous speeches; or they may be just a particularly striking way your source phrased an idea. For a decade or more, one frequently used apt quote was from President John F. Kennedy's inaugural address: "Ask not what your country can do for you; ask what you can do for your country."

Apt quotes are used to increase interest, often to make a main idea or the focus of the whole speech memorable, as when they appear near the end of the conclusion. Their use also tends to enhance the speaker's image in the listeners' minds, and they can be used as pseudo-proof. A speaker, for example, urges support of public education to avoid the consequences of a poorly trained, underemployed and crime-ridden society. She closes with a Biblical quote, "As ye sow, so shall ye reap." Another speaker begins a speech by quoting science philosopher and fiction writer Stanislaw Lem, "The primary obligation of intelligence is to distrust itself." Then she explains the implications of this remark, paving the way for a speech on extrasensory perception and other paranormal phenomena.

Visual Supporting Materials

Audience interest is almost assured when a speaker uses a well-prepared chart or gives a demonstration or shows objects—such as small animals, car parts, or scuba diving equipment. Listeners also appreciate being able to get information easily, quickly, and clearly, as occurred when a speaker used both a plastic model and a large cutaway chart to explain the operation of the space shuttle. Listeners can remember key points more easily if those points are associated with striking visual aids. Visual aids—for example, large photos of traffic accidents or drawings by emotionally disturbed children—can be used for emotional impact or proof. Just the fact that the speaker has taken the trouble to prepare a good visual aid can cause the audience to respect and like the speaker more.

A speaker, especially a beginning speaker, with a well-prepared visual aid is likely to be more at ease because he has something to handle and move around with and because he has at least one major thing he is sure will work well in the speech. In addition, the positive audience feedback produced by an effective visual aid increases the speaker's enthusiasm and confidence.

Despite all these advantages to both audience and speaker, visual aids are often underused and misused by speakers. In many of the speaking situations you are likely to face, especially with small audiences, even a simple prepared chart would be an asset, and some of those situations will virtually demand the use of visual aids. Thus it is useful to have some notion of various types of visual aids and some practical guidelines for using them effectively. Hopefully, enough students in your class will take the initiative to use visual aids so that you can learn from observation as well as practice.

Four Recommended Types of Visual Aids   Consider using one of the following four types of planned visual aids which are frequently employed in a variety of situations.

Prepared Charts.   Two big advantages of prepared charts are that they can be done neatly and precisely on chartboard or white butcher paper and the speaker can rehearse with them in advance to gain confidence. Charts can be used to diagram machines, processes (such as the four stages in commercial canning), playing fields (such as in a speech showing offensive strategies in soccer), and objects (such as the interior of the great pyramid of Cheops). They can be used to show statistical relationships visually in bar, line, and pie graphs, and to show foreign terms or symbols. They can also be used as sketch maps that focus attention on the particular geographical relationships you want to emphasize better than would an ordinary map. Charts can even be used to list a series of key concepts and a bit of information about each one, as in a speech describing four main factors in academic success.

Figure 7.1 **This chart shows the number of shoplifters apprehended and the total value of goods in their possession in a sampling of four types of stores over a three-month period. The speaker uses the chart to reinforce visually some data indicating that the frequency of shoplifting and the value of goods stolen varies widely among different types of stores.** (Random House photo by Stacey Pleasant)

Occasionally, a speaker will want to reveal a chart in stages or build it up as she goes through a major part of her speech. One way to do this is by masking, with opaque paper attached by masking tape, the parts of the chart to be revealed later. One student comparing regular costs with special tour prices for two trips masked all the data on the second trip and also the special tour price for the first trip. She explained the regular cost of the first trip, then unmasked the special tour price for that trip while she explained it. Then as she moved through the second example, she first removed the masking over the regular price and then the masking over the tour price. She ended up with a visual aid showing two convincing examples of the price advantages of the special tours, and she had precisely controlled her audience's attention as she revealed the visual aid part by part. A speaker can also build up a visual aid, by showing the chart with the basic diagram and then adding in additional lines or other items with a felt tip pen or other heavy marker. The items to be added can be planned in advance in faint pencil lines the audience won't see. A speaker can also tape onto a chart small cardboard objects prepared in advance.

Photos, Maps, Posters, and Artwork. A poster of Dracula in a speech explaining the origins of the myths about the count served as a minor item of interest. However, in a speech explaining a trend in modern art, reproductions of artworks in that trend, backed up by careful explanation and perhaps by art works from other trends or periods for contrast, would be the core of the speech. A student explaining what made portrait photographs artistic relied on two or three enlarged photos to illustrate each of her four main ideas. If a photo or map is too small to do the job, your purpose can occasionally be served by making a larger sketch based on the original. You can also use your own sketches for other purposes, such as emphasizing each main idea with a cartoon or other sketch.

Demonstrations. Demonstrations can be used as supporting material for only one main part of the speech, as when a speaker demonstrated traditional stances and strokes as part of a speech on samurai swords. However, some speeches—on how to do a series of slimnastic exercises for example—rely so completely on this type of visual aid that they are called demonstration speeches.

Figure 7.2 **This chart diagrams the process of drilling for oil.** (Random House photo by Stacey Pleasant)

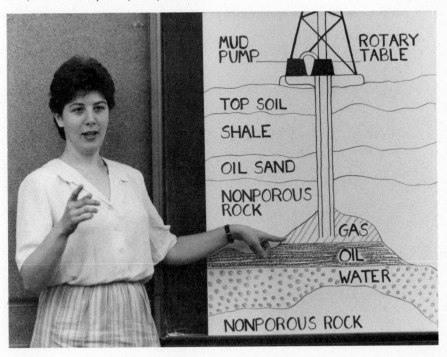

The speaker may use herself as demonstrator or she may work with another person, as when demonstrating a detailed process of stage make-up, taping up a runner's ankle, back massage for relaxation, or various sorts of first aid. In these dual demonstrations, working with a volunteer from the audience can add interest, but working with a prearranged confederate gives the speaker better control over the situation, especially if the demonstration is rehearsed in advance.

Another sort of demonstration speech explains a process such as making stained glass objects, tooling leather, or cooking some particular food. In this sort of speech, the speaker doesn't actually go through the process; rather he has objects, perhaps combined with charts, to represent each stage of the process as he explains it.

Demonstrations are perhaps the most fun to use and the surest form of supporting material for holding an audience's attention, but bear two cautions in mind when using them. First, they profit from tight advance preparation and rehearsal more than most people realize, and even then

Figure 7.3 **This bar graph shows the share of total family income in the nation in 1985 earned by each fifth of the population, from the highest paid to the lowest paid. The speaker is contrasting high-income families with low-income families.** (Source: U.S. Bureau of the Census, Current Population Reports, Series P-60, No. 154. Random House photo by Stacey Pleasant)

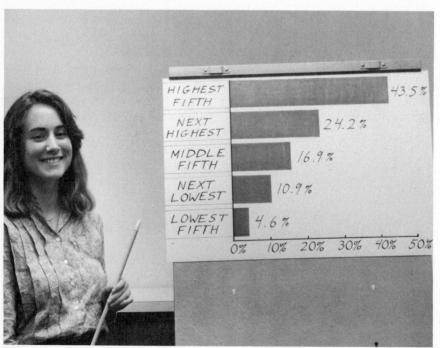

Figure 7.4 **This line graph is used to illustrate the speaker's discussion of the period of time when the number of females enrolled in college surpassed the number of males.** (Source: Statistical Abstracts of the United States: 1986. Random House photo by Stacey Pleasant)

the speaker has to be prepared to take the unexpected in stride with unflappable calm and a sense of humor. Second, don't let the demonstration overwhelm the situation so much that the *ideas* of the speech are lost or the audience is made uncomfortable. In the samurai sword speech, for example, the front row of the audience became more concerned with self-preservation than with the nuances of the sword strokes.

Three-Dimensional Objects. In addition to their use in demonstrations, physical samples and models may serve as independent items of supporting material. When used well, they add interest and a sort of tangible credibility to the speech. A small sampling of possible objects includes animals, musical instruments, models of the human head or other anatomy, artifacts such as Indian pottery and rugs, camping equipment, and models of buildings or other large constructions. Models may be ready-made or created by the speaker; and some students have made appropriate use of models from commercial kits. One ambitious student speaking on percussion musical instruments filled the front of the classroom with every type of percussion instrument available from the school orchestra. Another

Figure 7.5. **This pie graph shows how the entire student programs office budget was divided among six major components. It visually reinforces the speaker's comments on the ratio of overhead cost to programming purchased and the relative balance among types of programming. The speaker explains each component in greater detail.** (Random House photo by Stacey Pleasant)

speaker explaining the cost of outfitting a youth league football team didn't really need to show each item of a uniform as he explained its cost (which he also had listed on a prepared chart); yet showing the items added to interest and reminded the audience of the speaker's personal connection, as a coach, with the topic. Mild advantages are gained when a speaker holds up copies of important books on his topic—especially if they are his personal books—when he is quoting from them or recommending that his audience read them.

Other Types of Visual Aids In addition to the preceding four, there is an almost endless array of other types of visual aids, from felt boards to staged bits of dramatic action. We should note at least three additional types.

The Chalkboard. For quick, simple diagrams, for lists or outlines that are put up one point at a time, and sometimes for fairly complex diagrams that are constructed part by part at intervals during the speech, the

Figure 7.6 **A single chart is prepared with parts masked in advance. In this case the chart is a list of key words used to emphasize each of the speaker's four main points on how to reduce stress. The chart is shown in the first stage when the speaker begins the first main section, on controlling diet. Masking is removed to reveal the second stage when the speaker begins the second main section, and so on until all four points are shown when the speaker begins the fourth main section, on why and how to "have fun" to reduce stress.** (Random House photo by Stacey Pleasant)

chalkboard may be more flexible than prepared charts. Keep the visuals simple, and especially avoid putting up very much at any one time. You can thus maintain reasonably consistent eye contact with the audience and a fluent flow of words, rather than becoming enthralled with your own work at the board. Plan ahead. Even with simple numbers, sketches, or terms, know *what* you are going to use *when* in the speech. For more complicated visuals, try to rehearse a time or two with a chalkboard if a really smooth presentation is desired; at least, sketch out the visuals on paper. Before you begin your speech erase everything already on the board, so it won't distract the audience. Make the visuals neat and large enough to be seen easily. Avoid nervous doodling or aimless additions to the aid. In sum, if you are going to use the chalkboard, use it with authority and skill.

When in doubt as to whether to use the chalkboard or a prepared chart, you usually do better with a prepared chart. It gives you better control over the visual aid both in presentation and in preparation, and it usually creates a better impression on an audience. Especially, if you have to take time out to draw a complicated visual aid on the chalkboard you should have prepared it on chartboard to begin with. In addition, in some later speaking situations you won't have a chalkboard; it will be prepared charts or nothing, so there is something to be said for getting some practice with them now.

Electronic Audiovisual Aids.   Electronic audiovisual aids include tape recorders, overhead and slide projectors, and movie projectors. They require a bit of technical expertise, and they tend to dominate a short speech, sometimes turning it into some other sort of presentation. In a public speech, however, slides may do the job of photographs more effectively, and tape-recorded bits of music or responses to an interview question may well support major points in a speech. (Your instructor may welcome more ambitious efforts using audiovisual equipment.) A speaker using such equipment should select the audio or visual material carefully, with the total time frame of the speech in mind, and should cue each item in advance precisely. The following sorts of questions may help avoid last-minute disaster: Is the sound quality of both tape and recorder adequate? For visual projection, can the room be made dark enough? Is there a workable stand for the equipment suitably located? a screen? Are there electric outlets—that work—sufficiently near? If you are using unfamiliar equipment, do you or your assistant know how to work it—for sure—and is it in working order? It is often a good idea to use a technical assistant, especially if the equipment must be operated some distance from the speaker's stand. If you do so, rehearse together. Speak loudly enough to be heard easily above any equipment noise. With so many precautions, it may seem that using electronic media is hardly worth the trouble. On the contrary, it can be well worth the effort; taking these precautions helps make the use of these media professional and effective.

Handout Materials. Probably the best general rule for handout materials is: Don't use them. The sort in which one item is passed through the audience is especially frustrating because at the moment you are talking about it part of the audience hasn't even seen it yet and those who have are no longer much interested in it. When you give each audience member a copy or sample, you are then competing with the aid for the listeners' attention. When you must give each listener a handout, distribute the aid at that point in the speech where you will be discussing it, and explain it fully then. Of course, you can always wait until the end of your speech to hand out the fascinating brochures, but this is not a friendly thing to do to the next speaker.

Guidelines for Use of Visual Aids The guidelines for selecting and shaping supporting materials, near the end of this chapter, apply to visual aids as well as other types. Visual aids, however, have their special requirements for both preparation and presentation if they are to be used effectively. The following eight "rules" are a quick checklist that will help you meet those special requirements. The first four apply mainly to preparation of the aid.

1. Design the visual aid so that all members of the audience can see what it is supposed to show. Incredible as it may seem, probably the most frequent flaw in use of visual aids is lack of adequate visibility. So don't take it for granted. Is the item itself large enough? Postcards and snapshots almost always fail. Are lines, letters, numbers, and other details large enough and dark enough to be seen from the back of the room? Using various colors to show different aspects on chartboard is fine, but be sure all colors contrast with the chartboard color; pale red lines on yellow posterboard won't do for the people in the back of the room.
2. Use only aids that contribute to your purpose. The aid need not be vital; it may only reinforce or add a little interest to a point. But it should be relevant to your ideas, and the presentation time taken and impact of the aid should be at least roughly proportional to the importance of the point it supports. Because visual aids are so interesting to an audience, if they don't work for your purpose they will work against it.
3. Design the aid carefully and neatly. Whether it is a set of slides, a demonstration, a series of quick sketches on the chalkboard, or a prepared chart, make sure the aid is complete, efficient, and tidy. Your class or other audience will respect a modest professional quality, rather than a rambling demonstration or a sloppily prepared chart.
4. Plan in advance how you will use of the aid. The more complicated the aid is, the more advance planning is needed. At least, know what aids you are going to use when in the speech. If possible, rehearse with the aid. Ideally, rehearse where the speech will be given. At a minimum, look the physical situation over carefully in advance with your use of the aid in mind. Where will you put the aid before and after using it? Where will you display the aid or do the demonstration so that all can see it? More than one speaker has been frustrated by having a great aid and no

place to set it or no way to attach it to a wall. Incidentally, don't be the first person in your class to discover that a rolled-up chartboard will not suddenly flatten out to lean firmly on an easel or chalkrail.

The second four rules apply to the actual presentation, though the speaker works toward these when practicing the speech.

5. Show the aid at the appropriate point in the speech. The greatest interest value of the aid is when you first expose it. That's when you want to be talking about it. Therefore, keep it concealed until you come to the part of the speech it supports. It is also often useful to put it back out of sight after you have used it, though occasionally a speaker will leave the aid up as a type of ongoing reinforcement for a key idea or series of points.

6. Position both yourself and the aid so that all the audience can see the aid easily. The lectern is not transparent, and neither are you. Charts can be placed on an easel or chalkrail to one side of the lectern so you can move freely between lectern and chart. Don't hold an aid so low or at such an angle that part of the audience can't see it. Higher is better for people in the back of the room. It may be worthwhile to bring a cardboard box so as to show a small model or a demonstration higher than the top of an available desk or table.

7. Explain the visual aid. Very few aids are clear without supplementary verbal explanation. Even if a chart, for example, is self-explanatory, it will take some time for the audience to figure it out, and the speaker would do better to reinforce it verbally rather than stand awkwardly silent for several seconds, or, worse, rush on to the next part of the speech while the audience is still trying to understand the chart. Explain all parts of the chart or sketch; if the information is worth putting in a diagram, it's worth making sure the audience understands it. Although a complete explanation is not always feasible with physical objects, at least explain any aspects of an object that will otherwise distract the audience by confusing them or making them curious. When explaining any visual aid, point distinctly to the part you are dealing with at the moment; a pointer (it could be a pen or a ruler) is helpful for this.

8. Keep your eyes and your mind on the audience. With some rehearsal you probably won't need more than quick glances at your visual aid, so talk to the audience about the aid. Don't give the impression of examining the object or chart while mumbling aloud. Be sure to look at *all* sections of your audience.

Suggestions for Selecting and Shaping Supporting Materials

The following three general suggestions will help you more effectively select and shape your supporting materials. These apply to your use of material from interviews, observation, chance, and your own creativity, as well as from print sources.

Select and Shape Materials on the Basis of What the Audience Needs   Try to anticipate where in a speech the listeners might be confused or bored or doubtful, and then select your supporting materials to meet these needs. Try to put the greatest *quantity* of supporting detail under those headings where there is the greatest need. Select the *types* of supporting material that are most likely to meet the particular sorts of audience need on each point. If, for example, the need is to prove to the listeners the validity of the point, you are likely to use expert testimony, factual examples, and statistics. Once you sense what the supporting materials need to do at a particular point in the speech you can use the section "What Supporting Materials Do," earlier in this chapter, for suggestions on how to accomplish that function.

On a larger scale, the speaker adapts the overall nature of supporting materials to the general motives and inclinations of the audience in that situation. If the listeners seek a close understanding of the topic, perhaps because they plan to apply the information themselves, the speaker is likely to rely on carefully planned explanation often backed up with hypothetical examples and visual aids. If the audience's inclination is to be interested and perhaps inspired, the speaker is likely to rely heavily on detailed examples, as did Russell Conwell in his famous speech "Acres of Diamonds," which inspired his listeners to take advantage of opportunities around them. So successful was Conwell's adaptation to his listeners' inclinations that he gave the speech hundreds of times to paying audiences in the late nineteenth century, earning a total of several million dollars.

Use Variety, Depth, and Specificity in Supporting Material   These qualities are useful especially to emphasize your most important ideas and to increase the overall interest and force of your speech. Variety in types and sources of supporting material itself increases interest. To the speaker, one item of supporting material may clarify or prove an important point; but it may take two or three items to convince the listeners or even to give the point time to "sink in." Variety and depth come together in the technique of using a combination of types of supporting material on a particular point: statistics plus a detailed real example—as to show both scope and emotional aspect on the point that elderly people on fixed incomes suffer during inflation; real examples for credibility plus hypothetical examples with which your audience can identify—as to clarify causes for college dropouts; following a detailed example with several brief examples or specific instances—as to illustrate how courageous journalism has contributed to the public welfare; combining real examples with expert testimony—as to prove the value of special textbook-reading skills. And other combinations are possible.

"Positive mind control" can be defined in one sentence. It can be briefly explained in three or four sentences. But will a listener really understand the technique or be much interested until you describe in specific detail an individual case, such as your use of the technique when having a job interview, or a friend's positive mind control when taking a history exam? In addition to detailed real and hypothetical examples, comparisons and visual aids also tend to increase specificity.

Select Supporting Materials to Which You Personally Can Relate   The audience is not reading about your topic in a magazine article; rather, they are listening to *you* talk about it. Therefore, insofar as it's possible, establish your personal connection with the topic and the supporting material. If you have personal experience with the topic, draw on that experience for some of your supporting material, and let the audience know that you are doing so. If you did some especially creative research, such as interviews or observation, let them know about it.

Use supporting material that you are comfortable with and understand. Almost any speaker is more comfortable with visual aids she has prepared, telling the story about the time Aunt Tillie scared away the burglar, or impressing the audience with an apt quote she really believes. She is less comfortable parroting examples or statistics she doesn't really understand and finds boring. Of course, another speaker might find the statistics fascinating and want strongly to help the audience understand them. Using supporting material you enjoy conveying to the listeners makes you more interested, confident, and energetic in delivery.

Sample Speech: Structure and Use of Supporting Materials

The speaker whose outline on Hitchcock was discussed at the beginning of this chapter has selected, shaped, and placed her supporting material. In the final planning step she would improve structure and key phrasing and add an introduction, a conclusion, and transitions; and in rehearsal for delivery she would continue to refine the supporting material and the phrasing of key headings. (These final parts of the process of speech preparation are discussed in Chapters 8 and 9.) However, for now we are going to skip over final planning and rehearsal in order to look at a written record of the speech as it might finally occur. The speaker herself would *not* be likely to write the speech out in this form; instead, she would probably work from a detailed outline and rehearsal. This written version is only a two-dimensional record of the living, three-dimensional act of the speaker talking to the audience. This record will, however, serve our present purpose of seeing how various supporting materials are worked into a pattern of major ideas.

(Title)	**THE MASTER AT MANIPULATING AUDIENCES**
(Introduction)	(1) We are all familiar with, and most of us have seen "women in danger" movies like *Halloween*, occult
Specific instances, for interest.	suspense shockers like *The Exorcist* and *Carrie*, and more restrained mystery suspense movies like *Blowout*. We pay our money to be led through an exciting experience, and that experience is created through the film-maker's techniques.
	(2) The master of suspense movies, from whom most of the makers of these other films learned many of their tricks, is Alfred Hitchcock. Movie critic and theorist Andrew
Direct quotes as *expert testimony*, for credibility.	Sarris called Hitchcock "the supreme technician of the American cinema." In his book *Thriller Movies*, Lawrence Hammond refers to one of Hitchcock's movies, *Psycho*, as the "most successful suspense film ever made." In Hitchcock's films we can discover the techniques that produce the excitement we pay our money for.
(Statement of focus)	(3) This morning I'm going to describe the sorts of techniques Alfred Hitchcock uses to lead his viewers through an exciting experience. I will draw my examples from two classic Hitchcock suspense films: *Psycho*, made in 1960, and *Frenzy*, made in 1972. Although I cannot cover all of his
(Preoutlining transition)	specific techniques, I do intend to cover three main areas: how he uses plot action; how he works on people's deep psychological feelings; and how he uses the resources peculiar to the film medium.

(First mainhead)

Expert testimony,
  for credibility.
Example, for clarity and
  credibility; example
  includes direct quote
  and comparison.

Example—entire
  paragraph—for
  credibility.
Explanation, for clarity.

Example, for clarity
  and interest.

(4) Plot action is probably the most obvious main area of technique. Hitchcock views plot strictly as a way of manipulating the emotions of his audience. To viewers and critics who quibble about the logic of his plots, Hitchcock's reply is "I always say logic is dull." In an interview in *Movie* in 1963, he goes on to explain that characters and events in *Psycho* were "all designed in a certain way to create this audience emotion. Probably the real *Psycho* story wouldn't have been emotional at all; it would've been terribly clinical."

(5) Hitchcock does have a police psychiatrist in *Psycho* explain how the murderer, Norman Bates, has a split personality. One part is the mild-mannered son devoted to a mother who died several years earlier. The other part of Norman *is* the mother, who has a tendency to murder young women. Norman even keeps Mommy, the product of his taxidermic skill, still about the house. But this explanation of the logical aspect of the plot occurs at the end, after the audience has experienced the film, and even Hitchcock admits that it's pretty superficial.

(6) How does Hitchcock use plot action to keep his viewers keyed up? For one thing, he keeps the audience fearful of nasty surprises. Suspense movies usually follow rather predictable formula plots, but Hitchcock often makes his movies much less predictable. Perhaps the most famous example occurs in *Psycho*. Hitchcock has a character, Marion Crane, escaping her frustrating life with forty

thousand dollars stolen from her employer. We identify with Marion, who is played by glamorous star Janet Leigh. We know she will somehow return the money, and all will end happily. Right? Wrong! A third of the way through the movie, Mommy-Norman stabs Marion to death in a shower, and that's the end of the star of the movie. Suddenly, all rules are off, and the audience doesn't know what to expect.

Expert testimony, for credibility.

"From that point on," as Hitchcock put it, "the audience's mind is full of apprehension"—which is putting it mildly.

Example, added proof, for credibility.

(7) Hitchcock used the same device, though less dramatically, in *Frenzy*. The most likely candidate for heroine, Babs, makes it only about halfway through the movie before trusting the villain, with fatal results.

(8) Oddly enough, another Hitchcock device in plot action works precisely because the audience *does* know, roughly, what is going to happen. As Hitchcock said in his 1973 television interview with Richard Schickel, "The essential fact is, to get real suspense, you must let the audience have information." Again, *Psycho* provides a classic example. As Marion's sister searches the old mansion for Norman's mother, we know she will find the mother, probably in the fruit cellar where Norman has put her. We also know that the coming encounter will be unpleasant, because a private detective's similar search earlier in the movie ended with him being murdered by Norman as his

Expert testimony, for credibility.

Example, for clarity and interest.

mother. As the sister searches the upper rooms, where the detective met mother, tension mounts. As she starts down into the fruit cellar the tension becomes almost unbearable. And that's still true with audiences more than twenty years after he made the movie.

Example, for clarity and interest.

(9) Hitchcock seems to delight in his ability to manipulate audiences by a combination of suspense and surprise even in minor bits of plot action. In *Frenzy* the villain has just murdered a woman in the victim's second-floor office. The woman's secretary returns from lunch, and as she goes into the building, the camera remains outside on the street focused on the building. Suspense mounts as we imagine the secretary climbing the stairs and entering the office. We tensely wait for the scream we know will come. Then a couple of attractive girls come around the street corner, and we are distracted. At that moment the expected scream comes—catching us completely by surprise!

(Major connective transition)

(10) Surprise and suspense in plot manipuate the emotions of the audience. This occurs on the surface of the movie. To see more fully how suspense films operate, we must see how Hitchcock probes the psychology of his audience and how he uses the resources of his medium.

(Second mainhead)

(11) The second main area of technique is Hitchcock's probing of his audience's deep psychological fears and impulses. Of our many mental quirks that Hitchcock works on, I'm going to discuss only two: the vague anxieties we

(Transition, preoutlining second main section)

may feel in even the most ordinary of situations, and a repressed temptation to identify with criminals.

Example, for clarity.

(12) In Hitchcock films, the most bizarre and horrible events are likely to erupt in surroundings that seem ordinary, familiar, even cheerful. In *Frenzy*, for example, a woman going about her business in a sunny office on a well-traveled street suddenly becomes the victim of a brutal assault and murder.

Comparison and contrast— rest of paragraph—for clarity.

(13) This inconsistency between event and setting has an unsettling effect on audiences. When we see a monstrous villain doing his evil deeds in a creaky old castle with lightning flashing outside the windows, we can dismiss the whole thing as fantasy. But, as Andrew Sarris points out, "When murder is committed in a gleamingly sanitary motel bathroom during a cleansing shower, the incursion of evil into our well-laundered existence becomes intolerable. We will never be quite as complacent again."

Expert testimony, for interest and credibility.

(14) Just how effective Hitchcock's combination of bizarre event in ordinary setting can be was shown by a story told me by a friend while I was working on this speech. Several years ago a wife and husband stationed in Germany saw *Psycho*. A couple of days later the husband decided to play a joke on his wife. He dressed up with a stocking over his head and approached her with upraised knife while she was in the shower. The wife did recover from her shock. But she was so

Example, for interest.

mad she left her husband and flew home to the States. It was a month before they were reconciled and she flew back to Germany. The husband's joke cost him something over a thousand dollars just for his wife's air fare.

(15) We have seen a continuation of Hitchcock's technique by other directors in movies in which terrifying events happen at the high school prom or to baby-sitters in quiet, tree-lined, middle-class neighborhoods.

Brief examples, for interest and proof.

(16) Hitchcock also probes our deep psychological tendencies when he manipulates us into identifying with criminals.

Example, for clarity and proof.

(17) In *Frenzy*, it is night and the murderer is in a truckload of potatoes trying to pry an incriminating tie pin out of his latest victim's hand. The victim is stiff with rigor mortis, and the murderer is in constant danger of being discovered. We get so involved in this challenging task that we share the murderer's anxious moments and frustrations. We know that this man has committed several gruesome murders and his latest victim, the present corpse, was about the only appealing character in the film. Yet, we are, as Hitchcock accurately puts it, "rooting for him all the time to get that tie pin back."

Brief example, added proof, for credibility.

(18) In *Psycho*, the character that has the audience's strongest sympathies is the girl who has stolen forty thousand dollars. Movie analyst Raymond Durgnant may overstate the case when he says that to enjoy *Psycho* "is to stand convicted of a lurking nostalgia for

Apt quote, for interest.

evil." But an awful lot of people must stand so convicted, because they identify with Hitchcock's criminals.

(Third mainhead)

(19) I'm now going to deal with the third area of technique, and that is how Hitchcock uses the film medium itself. At its simplest me-chanical level, a movie consists of a series of "shots" that are edited together one after another. Each of these shots is a single bit of uninterrupted film. The camera is started, runs for awhile, often only a few seconds, and stops. That's a shot. Then the camera shifts position, perhaps only a few feet or inches, and starts an-other shot. There are usually more shots in a scene than the typical viewer realizes. You might recall a minute or so of conversa-tion in a film as one continuous shot, whereas actually you saw first a shot of one speaker, then a shot of the other speaker, then both of them, and so forth in a half dozen separate shots. Hitch-cock uses both the pictorial quali-ties within shots and the way he edits shots together to excite and involve the audience.

Explanation—rest of paragraph—for clarity.

Definition, for clarity.

Hypothetical example, for clarity.

(Transition)

Examples—two in paragraph—for clarity.

(20) Let's look first at some things he does within shots. When Marion is fleeing in her car with the sto-len forty thousand dollars, she encounters a thunderstorm at night. (Show chart-sketch 1.) In shots taken from inside the car, as this sketch shows, the rain beat-ing on the dark windshield pro-duces an intense vertical pattern while the lights of oncoming cars add bright, irregular zigzagging patterns over the vertical patterns.

Visual aids, for clarity and interest.

Even as an abstract pattern of light and dark and movement, this is really disturbing. A little later in *Psycho* a less abstract example occurs. When Marion wakes up in her car her first sight is the face of a highway patrolman, wearing apparently opaque dark glasses, looming over her, almost filling the movie screen. (Show chart-sketch 2.) Because of the way the patrolman is shown from Marion's point of view, we identify with her fear. We wouldn't feel this shock if the scene was shown neutrally from a few feet away, as in this sketch. (Show chart-sketch 3.) However, we would get the same basic information in either version. Camera position creates the emotional impact.

Comparison and contrast, for clarity.

(21) Hitchcock sometimes edits shots together in such a way as to expand time in order to increase suspense. In *Frenzy*, for example, when the hero is climbing a flight of stairs for his final showdown with the villain we don't just see him walk briskly up the stairs. Instead, Hitchcock shows us his feet on the stairs, then his face, then his hand on the railing, then back to his feet, and so forth, as tension builds for probably two or three times as long as it would actually take him to climb the stairs.

Example, for clarity.

(22) Hitchcock is also a master of another common editing technique: the use of a rapid series of very quick shots to create an almost physical sort of excitement. Perhaps the most famous example is the murder of Marion in the shower in *Psycho*. It's one of the

Example, for clarity.

Statistics, for clarity.

most memorably gruesome scenes in movie history. Yet we never actually see knife touch flesh. Instead we see separate shots of knife in the air, upraised arm, horror-stricken face, knife again, blood on tiles, et cetera—altogether seventy-eight separate bits of film in a scene that lasts forty-five seconds. This averages out to a separate piece of visual information, usually violent, about every six-tenths of a second. It overwhelms our senses.

(Conclusion)

(Summary)

(23) I've not, of course, covered all the specific techniques used by Hitchcock and later makers of suspense movies. But this sampling will give you an idea of the ways in which these movies manipulate us psychologically to give us the thrills we pay for. Next time you are tense or scared or excited in a movie, ask yourself if it's because you don't know what is going to happen . . . or because you do know. Is it because ghastly events are happening in surroundings that are uncomfortably ordinary and familiar? Are you being tricked into identifying with someone you really shouldn't want to be like? Or is it the sorts of movement and the angles at which you are seeing things on the screen that are making you uneasy? Or is it the way those separate shots of film are put together that causes your neighbor to scream and throw his popcorn in the air? For whatever reason, when you get your money's worth from a suspense film, you owe something to the man who was the master for nearly half a century, Alfred Hitchcock.

Statement of Sources

1. Raymond Durgnat, "Inside Norman Bates," in *Focus on Hitchcock*, edited by Albert J. LaValley (Englewood Cliffs, N.J.: Prentice-Hall, 1972), pp. 127–137.
2. Lawrence Hammond, *Thriller Movies* (London: Octopus Books, 1974), pp. 107–113.
3. Roy Paul Madsen, *The Impact of Film* (New York: Macmillan, 1973), pp. 283–287.
4. Andrew Sarris, *Interviews with Film Directors* (New York: Avon Books, 1967), pp. 241–252.
5. Richard Schickel, *The Men Who Made the Movies* (New York: Atheneum, 1975), pp. 271–303.
6. Interview with Prof. C. Ramirez Berg, on campus, Feb. 8, 1987.
7. Conversation with Ms. Rose Alvarez, about Feb. 10, 1987.
8. Films viewed: *Psycho* at least four times, most recently on Jan. 29, 1987 in the University Film Series; *Frenzy* three times, most recently on TV Channel 7, Jan. 22, 1987; many other Hitchcock films, most recently *Family Plot* and *The Thirty-Nine Steps*.

SUMMARY

From the stock of raw material he has gathered, the speaker selects and forms the specific items to support the main ideas in his speech. Usually, each item of supporting material is selected to serve one or more of the following six uses: to clarify the idea under which it falls; to increase interest in the speech, to help the audience remember main ideas, to increase emotional impact, to cause the audience to respect and trust the speaker, to prove an idea asserted in the speech.

Some major types of verbal supporting material are:

1. Factual examples, which may be brief or very detailed, and which often use narration and vivid description.
2. Specific instances, which in a few words cause the audience to remember examples they already know.
3. Hypothetical examples, which the speaker creates to fit the situation.
4. Comparison and contrast of the speaker's idea with something similar and more familiar to the audience; special forms are literal analogy and figurative analogy.
5. Explanation, often by breaking an idea into its parts and then clarifying each part by other sorts of supporting material.
6. Definition of technical terms and of terms with broad, vague meanings.
7. Statistics, which often require special care to be made clear to an audience, as by rounding off, restatement, concrete comparison, and visual aids.
8. Expert testimony, which is used to increase the credibility of a speech; the audience should have faith in the expert.
9. Apt quote, in which the phrasing by another person is used to give an idea greater interest or impact.

Visual supporting materials include prepared charts, maps and art work, demonstrations, and objects and models; they require special care in preparation and presentation but can have great advantages.

The speaker gets most benefit out of supporting material by following these three suggestions: First, use supporting materials that are appropriate to the listeners' expectations for the speech and that will meet their needs at each point in the speech. Second, use as much variety in types and sources, specificity in detail, and depth in quantity of supporting material as your time and resources will permit. Third, insofar as you can, use supporting material to which you have some personal connection, or that you at least understand and will enjoy using.

EXERCISES

1. Present a three- to five-minute speech using at least five different types of supporting material. In the margin of your outline, label each item of supporting material: indicate which type it predominantly is and which function(s) it performs.

2. Turn in an outline for one main section of a major speech on which you are working. Indicate fully the items of supporting material you intend to use under each subheading in this main section. For at least some of your planned supporting material, briefly explain why you are using these particular items. (This is a continuation of exercise 2 in Chapter 6.

CHAPTER EIGHT

Final Planning

At this point in preparation, you have roughly planned the body of the speech: statement of focus, a pattern of mainheads and subheads, and supporting materials in place. If you are confident of your plan for the body of the speech, the rest of preparation usually is downhill.

To make the job easier, final planning is divided into six parts. In your later experience these parts may merge and overlap; but in your first major speeches, force yourself to spend at least a few minutes on each part.

1. Check over the length and structure in the body of the speech as you have planned it so far.
2. Plan an introduction for the speech.
3. Plan a conclusion for the speech.
4. Plan some major transitions in the body of the speech.
5. Try to improve the phrasing of mainheads and key subheads.
6. Prepare a final draft of the outline, using a form that is most appropriate for your purposes in the particular speech.

Check the Body of the Speech

At this stage you are looking over the body of the speech with two aims in mind: improving the body itself, and discovering what you will have to do in the introduction, transitions, and conclusion to make the speech work well.

For the first aim, make any obvious improvements in structure, such as simplifying the basic pattern of headings or rearranging the order of main sections. Go through the body of the speech aloud—even if you have to jump awkwardly back and forth among your notes—in order to estimate length at least roughly. If you need to cut very much, you will probably do better to cut one or more main sections, and this may require you to reform the statement of focus. If you have to make the speech longer, the best way usually is to add more items of supporting material to important sections. To obtain more or better supporting material, return to your notes and review Chapter 7 for suggestions about types of supporting material. If necessary, return to the third stage of research described at the end of Chapter 5.

Your second aim is to discover, from the body of the speech, some of the things that should be done in the remaining steps of final planning. What, for example, needs to be done in the introduction? The statement of focus, "I'm going to explain how to set up the apparatus for Kirlian photography," may meet all the tests for a good statement of focus and still not work because some listeners have no idea what Kirlian photography is or that its purpose is to photograph the energy auras allegedly radiating from people and other matter. So the introduction has to provide that background information. If your topic and purpose require that your treatment of the body will be relatively dry and impersonal, you should make a special effort to arouse interest and relate the topic to the audience in the introduction.

Where is the audience likely to become confused following the organization of the speech or to lose sight of your main points? Those are the places where you will have to give special care to planning transitions. If the pattern of ideas in the body of the speech is complicated, but it is important that the listeners understand the material clearly, you probably should plan a detailed summary in the conclusion.

Plan the Introduction

It may be an exaggeration to say, as one student did, that "the first sixty seconds of a speech make it or break it," but the confidence and the positive feedback from the audience that an effective introduction produces certainly start the speaker off with an advantage. Therefore, plan an introduction that will work effectively in the particular situation, and have it well enough in mind to get off to a smooth start in delivery.

What an Introduction Can Do

In virtually any situation the speaker is wise to plan at least two or three sentences leading up to the statement of focus. This avoids an abrupt or slip-shod beginning that is likely to make a speaker seem careless, unskilled, or lacking in composure. Speakers use introductions for the following four purposes:

Arouse the audience's interest in the topic.
Create a favorable personal relationship with the audience.
Provide background information.
State the focus of the speech.

A well-planned introduction makes a good impression and gets a speech off to a good start.
(Karelle Scharff)

You do not necessarily do all four of these in any given speech, although the fourth, the statement of focus, is almost always done in some form. The important thing is that you accomplish whatever is necessary or useful to pave the way for the rest of the speech in that situation.

Arouse the Audience's Interest in the Topic   Ask these sorts of questions: What is novel or original about your topic? How can your topic be of practical benefit to the audience? How is your topic related to something they are already interested in, or at least know something about? What is the most interesting or surprising fact, quote, statistic, example, or possible visual aid that you've encountered in your research, and could it be used in the introduction? Such questions can lead to some of the following ways of hooking audience interest in your introduction.

Appeal to the desire for novel information by suggesting the unusual nature or surprising aspects of your topic, as in this opening:

> Even when most scientists in a field of study agree, can we assume that they are correct? Most paleontologists did agree that in 1912 at Piltdown, England, a very significant discovery was made. For more than forty years parts of a skull found then were regarded as among the most important discoveries ever made for the study of the evolution of man. Then in 1953 the skull parts were shown to be phony—a total hoax. In fact, the Piltdown Man was one of the most famous hoaxes in science. I'd like to explain how the Piltdown hoax occurred.

Show the listeners how the topic affects them or can be of value to them. This can be done very directly: "In my speech today I'll show you how you can save money on car repairs." Or it can be done more subtly by using an example with which the listeners can identify:

> You're waiting outside a manager's office to be interviewed for a job. You really want the job. Another person waiting to be interviewed for the same job is obviously flustered and is not really thinking about what he can do in the interview. But you're calm because you know what kinds of questions you will be asked, what the interviewer will be looking for, and how to create the best honest impression. How do you gain that confidence? You learn to handle the job interview to your advantage by following the four simple rules I'm going to explain.

You also arouse interest if you can *link your topic to something the audience is already interested in*, such as some ongoing or striking event in the news or some local or campus issue.

> I'm sure most of us are aware of the big debate over whether the movie *Pink Flamingos* should be shown in the free university film series. How could we not be aware of it? It's been front-page news for two weeks in our campus newspaper, and even the city papers are picking it up. The dean of students says he won't permit student fees to be wasted on a movie that he calls crude, filthy, and with no redeeming artistic value. The film selection committee and a lot of other students are claiming censorship and violation of civil liberties. This made me wonder who picks these films, what their standards are supposed to be, and who legally has the final say in selection. So I checked it out. Now I'm ready to tell you how the free university series films get picked.

Ask a question or series of questions that will cause listeners to respond mentally or will arouse their curiosity: "Why did you get up this morning? Why are you sitting in this class right now?" to lead into a speech on what motivates people in their everyday decisions.

Surprising or shocking statistics or vivid examples also can be used to arouse interest. Statistics are especially effective if they can be related to the audience's self-interest: "Research has shown that seventy percent of people in the kind of careers we are training for are satisfied with their professional life. Thirty percent are not. What will increase your chances of being in the satisfied seventy percent? That's what I'm going to discuss this morning." An especially vivid and typical example is a way of arousing attention, and it is readily available on many topics: a recent example of an abused child to open a speech on child abuse; a brief narrative example of the speaker's first trip in a balloon to introduce a speech on hot air ballooning as a hobby; a frustrating experience with slow service and bad food in the school snack bar to begin a speech urging improvement in that food service.

Finally, when a speaker has a close relationship with an audience, simply *explaining how the speaker herself came to be interested* in the topic may be sufficient to make the listeners interested.

Create a Favorable Personal Relationship with the Audience You have a favorable personal relationship with your audience if they like you and if they respect you as a credible person. In some situations, such as when you as expert are providing important information to an audience, the listeners' faith in your credibility, especially your competence, is more important than their friendly feelings. In other situations, such as most program and ceremonial speeches, their liking for you is more important.

To get listeners to like you, show that you like them and want to do a good job for them. If you really enjoy or appreciate the opportunity to speak to them, say so. If you can honestly and tactfully praise them, do so. Refer to relevant common ground and similarities between you and your audience—and there is always some basis for common ground. For example, in speech class, you are all college students, all (including your instructor) members of this particular speech class, and all associated with your college. Note how this speaker addressing a parent-teacher association both identifies himself with the audience and uses subtle praise to secure good will from them:

> Like most of you I have children in grade school, and I too want my children not just to learn skills but also to be happy and emotionally healthy. Your presence at this meeting tonight demonstrates that you do care deeply about your children. With this sort of care you have already taken the first step toward assuring your children's emotional health. But, alas, we don't always know how to show our children we care. Sometimes we're unsure whether to praise our son or daughter for doing well or to reprimand them for not doing better. I hope my remarks tonight will give you a few more ideas on how to show a child that you really care about him or her.

To gain the audience's respect for your competence, refer to any particular experience relevant to the topic you have had or to any special research you have done. The following speaker refers to both her experience and her research:

> Last spring I worked half-time for a candidate for the U.S. Congress. Several times I got to sit in on meetings between the candidate and his campaign staff. Supposedly these meetings were on the issues, but to me they seemed more concerned with how to build the right image for the candidate than with where he really stood on the issues. Wondering if this was standard practice in campaigns, I decided to do some reading, in Theodore White's books, for example, and in a book on Richard Nixon's campaign titled *The Selling of the President*, and in Kevin Phillips's book, *Mediacracy*. On the basis of this research and my experience, I'd like to explain how image building works in political campaigns.

A woman in speech class speaking on how to discipline small children significantly increased her credibility simply by mentioning that she had raised three children.

A confident, fluent, pleasant delivery in the introduction also does much to tell your audience unobtrusively that here is a speaker who is competent to do his or her job and who thinks enough of the audience to take some effort in preparing to address them.

Provide Background Information   As with the speech on Kirlian photography mentioned earlier, occasionally an audience will need some explanation of a larger context in which your specific topic occurs. You may need to explain a scientific theory or a social issue. Or you may need to locate your topic geographically or to provide historical background. Because this information is not really part of your specific topic, you get it out of the way briefly in the introduction, usually leading into the statement of focus:

> Four or five years ago our football team began to lose most of its home games. Gate receipts declined. Each year recently the Athletic Department has asked for a larger share of student activity fees to make up for the lack of paying customers. This year they want forty percent of the total activity fees, and our student government is resisting. I'm not taking sides. My purpose this morning is to explain objectively the arguments both for and against allocating forty percent of student fees to athletics.

State the Focus of the Speech   When the listeners know what to expect— where you're going in the speech—they are more easily able to follow you and are therefore more comfortable. The statement of focus is usually the last item in the introduction.

Sometimes a single sentence will make the topic of the speech clear to listeners: "I'm going to explain how to make ceramic coffee mugs in four steps." Sometimes you have to expand the statement of focus, for example, by defining key terms, by stating what you're *not* going to speak about, or by stating the main divisions of the speech. Though you would be unlikely to use all these devices to expand the statement of focus in any one speech, they are all illustrated in this example:

> How does white-collar crime operate? I intend to answer that question today. *I'm going to explain the techniques used by white-collar criminals.* By white-collar criminals I mean people in professional, managerial, and upper-level clerical positions who commit nonviolent theft of the property of others. I'm not going to deal with computer criminals, because they are a separate, specialized type of modern criminal. I will cover two main areas of white-collar crime: embezzlement and other theft committed against employers, and fraud committed against customers.

State the focus in direct oral style. Keep the key sentence simple. If you need to elaborate, do so in added sentences, rather than attempting to formulate one long, involved sentence that cannot be readily understood by a listener.

Be sure the statement of focus stands out *as such* in the presented speech. If the speaker on making ceramic mugs had said merely, "The fabrication of ceramic coffee mugs is a complex process involving four steps," the listener might nod in agreement . . . and wait to find out what this speech would be about. If necessary, use tip-off phrasing, such as "This morning I'll discuss . . ." or "That brings me to my subject . . ."

How to Plan an Introduction

As you did your brainstorming and research, you probably accumulated some ideas and materials for the introduction. It's a good idea, in fact, for a major speech or essay, to set aside a separate sheet of paper or some index cards for notes on possible content for the introduction and, separately, for the conclusion. Now you select, adapt, and add to this material to design the introduction.

Decide what is to be done in the introduction for this particular speech. Do you just need to get the speech off to a smooth start and state your focus? Or do you also need to arouse interest, provide background information, or demonstrate your competence or good will? Use only as much introduction as will help to make the audience receptive to the body of the speech and to you as speaker. This is rarely more than 10 percent, at most 15 percent, of the total speech.

With a little care and imagination, you can almost always plan your introductory material *to lead up to* the statement of focus. Usually, the first thing you need to do in the introduction is to create audience interest in the speech, unless circumstances guarantee that the interest is already there before you open your mouth. This is followed by whatever you intend to do to enhance your relationship with the audience and by any necessary background material. The full statement of focus comes last so that it will lead directly into the body of the speech.

The process of planning an introduction can perhaps be better understood by following the process through a specific case. In beginning to prepare her introduction for a speech on computer security, a speaker comes to three decisions: First, because she had in an earlier speech established herself as a computer science major and because her classmates seem generally to respect and like her, she decides that she need not now give particular attention to improving her relationship with her audience. Second, most of her classmates were likely to regard computers as a dull, technical subject that they probably couldn't understand anyway. Therefore, she decides to give particular attention to arousing their interest at the beginning of the speech. Third, though her speech deals with making the campus computer data bank secure, the topic will not have much meaning unless she establishes, in the background aspect of her introduction, that there is a problem of security to begin with. On the basis of these decisions as to what her introduction should do, she constructs this:

> Suppose all through college you got better grades than Joe Smith. When you graduate you both go after a great job. Smith gets the job. And he gets it because according to the records he has better grades than you do. You would smell something fishy wouldn't you? Is it even theoretically possible that someone could alter students' records stored in computers on college campuses? It's more than theoretically possible. In April 1982 a freshman student at one of the largest universities in Texas was arrested and accused of changing students' grades. He was working the university computer from a terminal in his dormitory room. Could this happen here? It is true that the central computer that stores our student records is also used by profs and students on campus. But it's also true that some pretty strong safeguards have been built into the whole record keeping system. I will explain the security devices built into computerized record keeping on this campus.

The speaker felt that for her speech class it was worth spending 10 to 15 percent of the total speech time on the introduction. For a report in her computer science class, however, she would have used a shorter introduction. Notice, however, that she would have added in a line suggesting her competence—her special research—on the topic:

> As you know, college students and even high school kids have been accessing college data bank records. I talked to people in the registrar's office and the computer center to see if we have a problem here. The answer is, possibly yes, but we also have some solutions. In the next few minutes I'm going to explain the security devices built into our computerized student record keeping system.

Plan the Conclusion

The conclusion is the final impression you leave with the audience, both of your ideas and of yourself as a person. It is worth preparing carefully.

In virtually any situation you want to appear in control, rather than careless, at the end of the speech. A speech that ends abruptly after the last point in the body almost always makes the speaker look awkward. Therefore use at least a brief summary or some other material to let the audience down with a sense of natural completeness in the speech. Even more unsatisfying to listeners than the abrupt ending is the conclusion that drags on and on. When you announce "In conclusion . . ." or otherwise telegraph that the end of the speech is near, accomplish what is needed efficiently, and end the speech crisply. Five percent of the total speech is a good rule of thumb for the length of the conclusion.

What a Conclusion Can Do

The following functions of a conclusion are alternate options:

> Summarize the main ideas.
> Make the central idea memorable.
> Suggest some action by the listeners.
> Tie back to the introduction.

You would usually select only one or a combination of two of these options—those that would best serve your purposes in the particular situation.

Summarize the Main Ideas Sometimes a speech that appears unclear, even chaotic, in the body can be saved in the conclusion by a summary that brings the key ideas into clear focus. Unless you have good reason for another order, summarize points in the same sequence in which they appeared in the body of the speech.

Summarize in terms of *ideas*, not just in terms of structure. This summary for a speech on tips for buying used cars is not really helpful: "First, I told you what to do before you go to the used car lots. Next, I gave you some tips about financing the car. Finally, I suggested some things to bear in mind when you are actually on the used car lots." A more useful summary would remind the audience of those tips and suggestions from the body of the speech:

> Before you go to the dealers, decide what sort of car you want and talk to friends who have bought used cars. In financing, decide your price range and stick to it, know in advance the best deal you can get on a bank loan, and be willing to bargain for a lower price. Finally, go to several lots before deciding, have your own mechanic test your choice before signing, and don't buy on the spot under pressure from a dealer.

Make the Central Idea Memorable Common ways to make your central idea memorable are by an example or an apt quote that captures the essence of the speech in a vivid way. For a speech that in a rather casual, entertaining tone urged the benefits of studying diligently during the term:

> Let me remind you of the final reward, with apologies to William Cullen Bryant's poem "Thanatopsis":
> > So study that when thy final examinations come,
> > Thou go not, like the quarry-slave at night,
> > Scourged to his dungeon, but sustained and soothed
> > By an unfaltering trust, approach thy exam
> > Like one who wraps the drapery of his learning
> > About him and goes on to pleasant grades.

You may simply state the central thought after a transitional phrase or sentence signaling the conclusion.

> Let me leave you with this thought. Don't assume the octopus is stupid just because it's a primitive life form. Scientists have shown that it's a lot smarter than most of us give it credit for being.

You may want to combine a brief summary with a final emphasis on the central idea, as in a speech dealing with the place of interpersonal oral communication in an age of electronic media:

> I think you will agree that even for practical communication within an organization, face-to-face talking has certain advantages. It permits flexible responses to immediate feedback. Vocal inflection and facial expression can permit subtle messages. And perhaps most important, people can lend emotional support to each other in a group. In the words of Earl Wilson, as quoted in *Omni* magazine, "Science may never come up with a better office-communication system than the coffee break."

Suggest Some Action by the Listeners   Even though an appeal for action technically makes a speech persuasive, mild suggestions for audience action can be used to conclude informative speeches without seeming inappropriate to listeners. After describing some major themes in current science fiction novels, the speaker could finish by naming three or four titles for listeners who might want to read for themselves novels dealing with those themes. A speech on various ways of customizing cars could conclude by giving the place and date for a forthcoming custom car show and suggesting that listeners might enjoy seeing elaborate examples of the speaker's topic now that they know about the labor and skill that go into these cars.

Tie Back to the Introduction   Tying the conclusion in with the introduction gives the speech a smooth finish and an appearance of overall unity. The conclusion may link to an example or promise made in the introduction, or to the title of the speech. In the sample speech on Hitchcock in Chapter 7, the speaker closes by restating her introductory assertion that Hitchcock is the master of the suspense movie. A speech might open by raising interest in and providing background material on Bigfoot and then promising listeners that by the end of the speech they would be better able to judge for themselves whether or not these large, hairy, manlike creatures exist in the Northwest wilderness. The conclusion could refer back to this promise and then summarize the two or three main arguments on each side of the issue developed in the body of the speech.

How to Plan a Conclusion

Begin by deciding what is needed in this particular speech to end smoothly and leave the right final impression with the audience. Do you need a summary? In an instructional speech or oral report, or in a persuasive speech based on a series of logical arguments, you would usually want the listeners to remember a list of major ideas. They are unlikely to remember the ideas unless you refresh their memories, so don't underestimate the value of a blunt, efficient summary. In some speeches, however, such a direct summary might appear overly "instructional." In a program speech, for example, you might want to leave the audience with only one central idea. In other speeches, you have impressed the central points on the audience, often through transitions in the body, and all you need do now is end the speech smoothly and efficiently.

In any case, avoid the temptation to use the conclusion as a catch-all for vaguely relevant ideas you could not work into the body of the speech. Such new ideas are likely only to confuse the audience and reduce the final effect of the speech. The conclusion should accomplish only the specific needed functions. It should avoid any impression of aimless rambling.

Once you have decided what needs to be done in the conclusion, you need to decide *how to meet those needs*. When using a summary, decide clearly what are the main ideas you want to leave in the listeners' minds. If the need is to impress the audience with the central idea, decide whether to use straight restatement or a more emphatic device such as an apt quote or a visual aid illustrating the central idea. A summary or a final focus on the central idea is often enough to give a sense of finish. If more is needed *or* if you need only to finish crisply without a summary, consider using a tie-in to the introduction or a suggestion for action.

Plan Transitions

A listener must follow the structure and spot the key ideas while the speech is presented. Unlike a reader, he cannot stop and go back if he becomes confused. Therefore, you as speaker need to add phrases, sentences, even paragraphs of transitional material to give the listener some sense of the overall structure of the speech, to tell him where you are in the structure, and to emphasize major ideas during the speech. These are in addition to your mainheads, your other idea headings, and your supporting materials. Transitions don't organize a speech, but they do make its organization clear.

Types of Transitions

You can use at least five major types of transitions: preoutlining, internal summary, connective, restatement, and key phrasing.

Preoutlining   In a preoutline, you tell an audience in advance the points you intend to cover so they will be oriented to your overall plan. You *preview* part of your *outline*. You may preoutline the main points of a speech (usually immediately after the key sentence in the statement of focus), or you may preoutline the major subheads in a section. The one-sentence paragraph that begins this section preoutlines the five "types of transitions" to be covered in this section.

Internal Summary   You know what a final summary in the conclusion does. It is also often useful to sum up, *within* the body of the speech ("internally"), either the major subheads within a main section you are just finishing or the main points you have made up to that place in the speech: "Thus far, I've suggested that before going to the car lots you decide what sort of used car you want, how much you plan to pay, and what reputations some of the dealers have." Internal summaries emphasize major ideas by restating them, and they bring any confused listeners back on track in following your organization.

Connective   Connective transitions let your listeners know clearly that you are moving from one section to another section, and how the sections are related. They may show your movement from a main idea to supporting ideas or materials, with such phrases as "For example, . . ." or "To illustrate, . . ." or "As proof of this, . . ." The shift to supporting ideas or materials can be made more emphatic by connective sentences, rather than phrases: "Let's see what the experts say." or "Let me give you some examples." Connective transitions can also clarify shifts from one main section to the next main section: "We have seen some causes of juvenile vandalism. Now let's look at proposed solutions." An elaborate connective transition may summarize preceding ideas and preoutline upcoming points:

> We have seen that there are several different theories for what causes juvenile vandalism. These include youths' economic frustrations, lack of healthy outlets for their time and energy, and lack of effective apprehension and punishment of the vandals. We turn now to solutions for juvenile vandalism. We will consider two general solutions: creating opportunities for more productive activity by these juveniles and increasing legal punishment for vandalism.

Restatement   Perhaps the simplest way to emphasize your shift to a new mainhead is to repeat the central idea two or three times, one time right after another, in different words: "There are several reasons why youths commit vandalism. Let's look at some of these causes for juvenile vandalism. I'm going to consider three main causes for this type of youth crime." One variation of restatement is the use of a question (transition) and answer (mainhead or subhead): "How can this type of juvenile crime be reduced? Experts have come up with two different solutions for juvenile vandalism."

Key Phrasing   When you have a series of sections that are parallel in nature and importance, you can repeat the same key phrase to let the audience know quickly and clearly that you are moving into the next section. Here the key phrase "solution for juvenile vandalism" is established in the mainhead and then used in each subhead:

>   I. Experts have offered several solutions for juvenile vandalism.
>   A. One solution for juvenile vandalism is . . . (and a section of the speech explains this solution).
>   B. Another solution for juvenile vandalism is . . .
>   C. Finally, a third possible solution for juvenile vandalism is . . .

Numbering the parallel points also helps to clarify the structure.

How to Plan Transitions

In a program speech, a ceremonial speech, or an emotional persuasive speech, transitional material is likely to be less elaborate and frequent. On the other hand, in most informative speaking and in persuasive speaking that depends on making lines of reasoning clear, you are likely to need more and blunter transitional material. To get some notion of how a speaker uses transitional material, look back at the speech on Hitchcock in Chapter 7 and at the sample outline for the speech "Succeeding with Essay Exams" later in this chapter. (Major transitions are shown in parentheses.)

Transitions that will be very helpful in the presented speech may not seem necessary or useful when you are writing the outline. Therefore, make an aggressive effort to discover points in the speech at which transitional material will help your listeners.

>   Can you use connective transitions at the major junctures, those shifts between the end of one main section and the mainhead for the next one?
>   Can you use a preoutlining transition immediately after the statement of focus or after a mainhead for a complicated section of the speech?
>   Can you use internal summaries at the end of one or more main sections?
>   Can you avoid indefinite phrases such as "Also, . . ." or "Another thing is . . ." by filling in key phrasing such as "A third standard for selecting movies is . . ."?

Try spotting transitions in material you hear or read. These transitions in a section of a textbook chapter or a lecture help you see what the major ideas are and how these ideas fit together. Seeing course material in patterns of ideas makes the material much easier to understand and remember. You also increase your own skill in using transitional material, in both speaking and writing, by learning from the examples of others.

Write Out Idea Headings

You have already planned your mainheads and probably one or two lower levels of idea headings—at least as topic headings and perhaps roughly as sentences. Now try revising them into better phrasing you could use in the presented speech. Begin by knowing clearly yourself the idea you want to convey with each heading. As you plan these idea headings on paper, try to think or say the idea aloud as you would say it face-to-face to a friend; then write down what you have said. This is a good way to begin, but it doesn't guarantee the best wording, so check what you have written for possible improvement.

Your basic aim is to enable your audience to understand your major ideas as you state them and to follow you through the plan for your speech. Although the degree to which you make the ideas bluntly clear varies in different situations, it is usually better to be blunt than to confuse the audience. Having ensured clarity of ideas, you can then aim for a more imaginative style that will make your ideas interesting and forceful.

Let's take as an example wording planned for the pattern of basic ideas on causes of the Wild West, from Chapter 6.

> **Statement of focus: Of the many theories offered by reputable historians for what caused the Wild West to be wild, at least three have gained a considerable degree of credence.**
>
> I. Many people who went West, whether of their own free will or because they were running from severe personal predicaments back home in the East or South, were characterized by a spirit of adventure and social irresponsibility.
>
> . . . .
>
> II. Often it was because duly constituted and enforceable legal jurisdictions were absent, or two jurisdictions would be in conflict, as in the Cochise County War.
>
> . . . .
>
> III. The social structure in boom towns was unstable.
>
> . . . .

These headings read well enough on paper, and they do state the purpose and main ideas quite accurately. But try reading them aloud. Some headings sound awkwardly stilted, and in some it's hard to grasp quickly the central idea. Also, if you imagine these sentences in six or eight minutes of continuous speech, it is unlikely that they would *stand out* as the *key* sentences stating the focus and main ideas.

Practicing a speech aloud helps you make sure your idea headings are as clear when spoken as they appear on paper. (Gale Zucker)

Therefore, in revising these sentences, a speaker would make them simpler, usually shorter, so the single, central idea in each heading would stand out clearly and be easy to understand. Secondary ideas would go into subheads or transitions. Pronouns with unclear referrents—such as "it" in II—would be changed, usually replaced with nouns, even if this looked repetitious on paper. In this series of similar headings, transitional devices such as key phrasing and enumeration, as well as parallelism in sentence structure, could be used to emphasize each heading. Finally, the style would show a person talking directly and naturally to other people, using a vocabulary normal for both speaker and listeners, and using words of direct address, such as "I," "we," and "you."

This is what the revised outline on the Wild West might look like—not perhaps as "well written" as the preceding version, but a good deal more functional for helping the audience understand the speaker.

> **Statement of focus: I'm going to explain three main reasons that made the Wild West wild.**

I. My first reason for this wildness is that many of the people who went West were not much concerned with society's rules.

. . . .

II. Another important reason for the wildness in the West is that sometimes no single authority was in charge of law and order.
   A. In the Cochise County War, for example, two opposing authorities claimed legal jurisdiction.

. . . .

III. A third reason the West was wild is that many new towns didn't have much social stability.

. . . .

Notice that the speaker has repeated in each mainhead the key word "reason" from the statement of focus. Enumeration is used with "first" and "third," although to keep the headings from appearing too mechanical "another" is used instead of "second." In addition, the central idea of the wildness of the West is repeated in roughly the same words in each mainhead to link the mainhead clearly to the statement of focus.

A speaker may want to go beyond simple clarity and use a more elaborate and imaginative style to make ideas interesting and memorable.

The following set of basic headings, for example, is not likely to stand out very clearly as main ideas or be very interesting, even though the headings state the speaker's ideas accurately enough.

> **Statement of focus: The history of computer technology may be divided into three stages.**

I. Computers were first developed by the military.

. . . .

II. Business and research made use of computer technology.

. . . .

III. Computers are being used more and more in everyday life.

. . . .

The speaker could simply add some key phrasing and enumeration to make the mainheads stand out clearly: "In the first stage, computers were developed by the military . . . In the second stage, business and research . . ." and so forth.

However, to make the main ideas more emphatic and vivid, the speaker might also plan some additional transitional material and use action words, metaphor and other language that creates mental images, and phrasing that suggests how the key ideas relate to the listeners' goals, fears, or other self-interest.

Statement of focus: We can better understand the subtle assault of computer technology on our lives if we see it as occurring in three waves.

(The first wave of attack was so specialized and remote that most people weren't even aware of it.)

  I. These first developments of practical computers were for military use in World War II.

. . . .

(In the next wave the developments were still so specialized that computers didn't seem significant to most people.)

  II. In this second wave the computers quietly pushed their way into being essential for some research and for the operation of large businesses.

. . . .

(Finally we come to the third wave of the computer assault, which now engulfs us.)

  III. Let's see how much computers are now influencing different aspects of our lives.

In sum, when you work on phrasing your mainheads and the most important subheads, keep the following suggestions in mind.

1. State the idea accurately in words the audience can understand.
2. Use short, simple, direct sentences.
3. Restate key nouns or concepts rather than using pronouns, which might be unclear, and use such restated words to link mainheads to statement of focus.
4. For a series of similar major points, repeat the same key phrase in each heading, and perhaps number the headings to make each heading stand out distinctly.
5. At important junctures in the speech, use both a heading and a major transition to ensure clarity.
6. Once clarity is assured you may use such stylistic devices as metaphors and action words to vivify main headings.

Prepare Final Outline

There comes a time when you pull all your preparation together into a final written form that will serve you in practicing and delivering the speech. You usually finish any major revision at this stage, so the speech will be "set" and you can begin to concentrate on effective and confident delivery.

This final revision overlaps your first rehearsals. Before writing the final draft of the outline, run through the speech two or three times with an open mind for making improvements. Can you simplify the basic structure or substitute clearer or more interesting items of supporting material? Do you have all the transitions you need? Do your introduction and conclusion do what you want them to do in this situation? After adding in the last parts of the speech and doing other revision, is the speech still within the time limit? Don't decide the outline is cast in stone before you have tried it aloud.

Use an Appropriate Outline Form

You want to use an outline form that enables you to prepare fully enough to meet the specific situation with confidence. Yet you also want to use your planning time efficiently and to have a plan that will encourage conversational spontaneity in delivery. These wants are usually best balanced by the full outline form for extemporaneous speaking shown below. Occasionally, however, in an unusually demanding situation, you may need even more detailed planning to be confident. Conversely, in a more relaxed situation, you may be comfortable with a briefer outline of topic headings.

Full Outline for Extemporaneous Speaking   The full outline form enables you to plan a complete structure of ideas, supporting materials, and transitions. Attention is given to specific choice of language only at such crucial points as major headings and transitions. This form also provides enough of a written plan to help you and your instructor analyze what worked well and what didn't in the presented speech. It's a good form for gaining experience in using transitions and oral language, as well as tight structure, so you can readily apply such skills even if much of your later speaking is from briefer topic outlines.

Succeeding with Essay Exams

Introduction

 I. Most of us would like to do better on essay exams we have to take in other courses.
  A. Typical specific courses using essay exams.
  B. Description of hypothetical confident student.
 II. Last year I took a short study skills course in how to handle essay exams.
  A. Covered both preparation and actual taking.
  B. Effects on my grades.

STATE-
MENT OF
FOCUS   III. Today I'd like to tell you how you can improve your
     performance on essay exams.

(Success occurs in three stages: what you do during the
course, what you do specifically preparing for the exam, and
what you do when you actually take the exam.)

Body

I. Solid preparation begins on the first day of class and
   extends through the whole course.
   A. The first advice during the course is to get complete
      lecture notes.
      1. Comparison of my sociology notes before and after
         the study skills course.
      2. Examples of specific details on sociology lecture to
         show that if you don't get it in class you won't
         have it for exams.

   B. The second advice during the course is to use reading
      assignments purposefully.
      1. Read assignments before they are covered in class
         lectures or discussions.
      2. Try to see how reading assignments and class ses-
         sions relate to each other.
         a. Example of Chapter 7 and class discussion on
            visual aids in speech.
         b. Chart: blowup of page of lecture notes with
            cross-referencing to textbook.

(If you have good lecture notes and have done the reading,
you are well prepared to move into the second stage of handling essay exams.)

II. Let me offer two main suggestions for that final prepara-
    tion before the exam.
    A. First, try to pull together course content from lectures,
       reading, and other sources in summary form under
       the topics you may be tested on.
       1. Example of four main topics in freshman history
          unit.
       2. Sample of materials on one topic in history unit,
          drawn from textbook, lectures, and class discus-
          sion.

B. A second suggestion for final preparation is that you test yourself in order to get actively involved in learning.
1. Contrast between student using active learning and one using passive learning.
2. Example explaining how to self-test, on lecture notes taken in speech class on April 28.

(If you have been working toward the exam during the term and have prepared for the specific exam by organizing the material and by testing yourself, you're ready to face the essay exam with some confidence.)

III. When taking the exam, keep three things in mind.
A. First, don't panic.
1. "The coward dies a thousand deaths."
2. My experience thinking I'd flunked and getting an A.

(Okay, so you're staying calm. What else can you keep in mind?)

B. You can remember to organize your answer.
1. History teacher's testimony on teachers' fondness for well-organized essay answers.
2. Use same skills in structure and transitions as in speech.

(You can use your speech skills not only in organization but also in supporting materials.)

C. When you take the essay exam remember to use specific detail in your answers.
1. Quick examples of types that can be used in a psychology course.
2. Comparison with use in speeches.

Conclusion

I. These then are three stages in handling essay exams successfully.
A. The first stage is, during the term get good lecture notes and understand the reading assignments.
B. The second stage is, in the preparation time before the exam get actively involved by pulling course content together under main topics and by testing your knowledge.

C. In the final stage, when you take the exam, be optimistic and use your skills with organization and supporting material.

II. The method produces results.
   A. It can make you more successful and more confident when you take exams.
   B. It worked for me.

Statement of Sources

1. Walter Pauk, *How to Study in College*, 2nd ed. (Boston: Houghton-Mifflin, 1974), Chapter 12: "How to Study for Exams," and Chapter 13, pp. 176–182, on essay exams.
2. Ralph C. Preston and Morton Botel, *How to Study*, 4th ed. (Chicago: Science Research Associates, 1981), Chapter 7: "How to Prepare for Examinations," and Chapter 8, pp. 99–113, on taking essay exams.
3. Alton L. Raynor and David M. Wark, *Systems for Study*, 2nd ed. (New York: McGraw-Hill, 1980), Chapter 6: "Preparing for Examinations," and Chapter 7: "Taking Essay-Type Examinations."
4. Nancy V. Wood, *College Reading and Study Skills*, 2nd ed. (New York: Holt, Rinehart and Winston, 1982), Part 4: "Taking Exams."
5. Took four-session course on handling essay exams, at Study Skills Center, March 1986.
6. Interview with Prof. Carl Jackson, April 19, 1986.

Rules for Full Outline Form. The following ten "rules" will help you use the full outline form to advantage as a visual picture and tool in planning structure. Rules 9 and 10 are actually additions to your speech plan, but they are often required by special circumstances. The reasons for each rule are given so you will understand *why* the rule is helpful.

1. Use *one side* of full-size sheets of paper. Thus you, or another reader, can see the entire outline, perhaps three or four pages, in one panoramic view. Incidentally, it's handier to do your notes and work sheets also on only one side of sheets of paper.
2. Use a *consistent symbol system*: I, II, etc., for mainheads; A, B, etc., for the next level; 1, 2, etc.; a, b, etc.; (1), (2), etc.; (a), (b), etc. You can then tell the relative importance of a heading just by the symbol.
3. When a heading is two or more lines long, *indent all lines* of the heading at least as far as the symbol for that heading. This produces a clearer visual picture of the structure than if you ran subsequent lines out to the left margin.
4. Divide the outline into *three separate parts*: introduction, body, and conclusion. Begin the introduction with I, begin the body with I, and begin the conclusion with I. This emphasizes visually that the introduction and conclusion perform functions different from those of the body of the speech.

5. *Label your statement of focus* in the margin of the outline. This tells you that you have a statement making clear to the listener the central focus of your speech and dominating the structure of the speech, and it enables your instructor or other reader to locate that key statement quickly on the outline.

6. Plan the *idea headings* (usually at least the first two levels—I, II, etc. and A, B, etc.—on the outline) *as complete sentences* in *oral* style you could actually use in the presented speech. This will help ensure clarity and interest in the particular speech, and will improve your general sense of oral style.

7. Plan which *items of supporting material*, including visual aids, you will use where in the speech, but show them on the outline only by phrases or other brief topic headings. This permits tight planning of the speech yet leaves some room for spontaneity in delivery.

8. *Plan major transitions* fully in oral style (and show they are transitions by putting them in parentheses), and work key phrasing and other transitional material into idea headings. In a speech of any complexity, good transitional material is too important for clarity to be left to chance.

9. Put a *title* at the beginning of the outline. The title may indicate the topic quite clearly or it may be cleverly ambiguous to arouse curiosity before you state your focus. Titles are useful if a chairperson is to introduce you, if advance publicity is to be released about the speech, or if the speech is to be reported or recorded in print.

10. Put a *statement of sources* at the end of the outline. Cite printed sources fully enough so they could be readily located from your citations. Include such sources as particular personal experiences, observations, and interviews. This shows your instructor where the material for the speech came from, and it is especially satisfying for a student who has used a good range of sources.

Understanding why you follow these rules for a full outline will help you decide when it is really to your advantage to switch either to more detailed outlining or to a briefer topic outline.

More Detailed Outlining   The speaker on preparing for essay exams is sure that after some rehearsal he will be able to make most of the points in his outline clear to the listeners without further written planning. But a few points give him trouble. He wants to list the four topics in his example of the freshman history unit, but not being very familiar with ancient history, he can never remember what they are unless he refers back to his original notes. His contrast of the active learner with the passive learner depends on fairly close phrasing, and he suspects he will never get it phrased very well unless he really focuses on the details of that example during written planning. He can ad-lib specific phrasing and detail in the other items of supporting material from the headings now in his outline; and he certainly doesn't intend to consume his preparation time dealing with all the special problems of a word-for-word complete manuscript. So he does the sensible thing. He plans in greater detail only those parts of the outline where such planning will really help his presentation. This is how section II of his outline looks:

II. Let me offer two main suggestions for that final preparation before the exam.
   A. First, try to pull together course content from lectures, reading, and other sources in summary form under the topics you may be tested on.
      1. For example, first six-weeks unit in world history was divided into four main topics:
        Greek democracy, to 338 B.C.
        Rome to domination over Greek East, about 160 B.C.
        Rome dominant and republic, to 27 A.D.
        Rome empire to collapse, to 455 B.C.
      2. Explain with sample materials on first unit (Greek democracy), drawn from textbook, lectures, and class discussion.
   B. A second suggestion for final preparation is that you test yourself in order to get actively involved in learning.
      1. Difference between active and passive listener? Passive lets eyes go over book or notes with no real engagement, like a car rolling along in neutral gear. Active is engaged, in gear, using energy to think about what material means and if knows detail. Neutral is OK for going downhill. But learning material is an uphill climb to get somewhere.
      2. Example explaining how to self-test, on lecture notes taken in speech class on April 28.

Two suggestions will help you use detailed outlining effectively. First, use it only when it will really help you. Unfamiliar material and points at which you need just the right detail or wording are the most common reasons for using such detailed outlining. Only unusually challenging situations are likely to profit from an entire outline done in this much detail, so don't make an entire outline detailed just to be consistent.

Second, use sections of detailed outlining as a planning device rather than as a text for delivery. Try to avoid writing complete, exact phrasing of your own examples. Then you won't be tempted simply to read the items of supporting material to your listeners. Work on getting your planned detail and phrasing in mind during rehearsal so that in delivery it will come naturally as you talk to your listeners.

Briefer Topic Outline   Perhaps you have relatively little time to prepare, the topic is familiar, and the situation—audience, occasion, time limit—is informal and low-pressure. In these circumstances, a topic outline may produce better returns for the time you can invest in planning than would a more complete outline form. In a topic outline you use just a few words for each heading. The outline for the speech on criticism in Chapter 1, (page 15) illustrates the use of a topic outline.

A topic outline is a very efficient way to plan what you will say in a particular situation, providing you apply what you know about the anatomy of an effective speech. As a minimum, plan the structure of main ideas and subideas, the important items of supporting material where they will be needed, and some way of opening and closing the speech smoothly. Attention to major transitions is also often useful. Unless you have already presented each chunk of material to other audiences several times, you will do well to rehearse at least a couple of times to be sure the speech will flow smoothly and you are comfortable with the plan.

Speaking Notes

In some situations you will find it advantageous to reduce a detailed outline to much briefer speaking notes. Such notes are likely to increase spontaneity and direct contact with the audience in delivery because you are less tempted to depend on reading your notes as you go along. Also, the notes can be put on 3 × 5 or 4 × 6 cards, which makes them less obtrusive and more easily managed, especially if you don't have a lectern on which to lay your outline. A final advantage is that by reducing the outline to one page or a few cards, you may actually have a sharper sense of the structure of the speech than when it was spread over several sheets, and this can improve confidence and natural vocal variation in delivery.

Using speaking notes is something of a skill in itself, and the following suggestions, plus practice, will improve your skill:

1. Indicate each idea heading, transition, and item of supporting material by a word or phrase.
2. Keep the appearance of structure by using levels of indentation and numbering the headings.
3. Write out quotes, statistics, and other material that must be stated precisely, even if you didn't write it out fully on your planning outline.
4. Avoid the temptation to write out the introduction or conclusion fully on your speaking notes. You especially want to speak directly to your audience, rather than reading at them, in those parts of your speech.
5. Run through a few initial rehearsals with your detailed outline before you write the speaking notes, but be sure your final rehearsals are with the notes you will actually use in delivery.

The speaker on handling essay exams reduced his outline to five 3 ×

5 cards. Each card contained one segment of the speech, so shifting cards during delivery helped emphasize the move from one main part of the speech to the next. Using five cards also gave him room for easily visible words and structure, rather than cramming a lot of words into a small space. If he were sure he would be speaking with a lectern, he might have decided to put the entire set of notes neatly on one sheet of paper.

```
                          Intro.
    I. Like to do better on exams.
       A. Courses using: psych. lit. history. soc.
       B. Confident student.

   II. My course in S.S.
       A. Studying and taking
       B. My grades

  III. I'D LIKE TO TELL YOU HOW TO IMPROVE ON ESSAY EXAMS

  (Success in three stages:  during course
                             just before exam
                             when taking)
```

```
    I. FROM FIRST DAY THRU WHOLE COURSE

       A. Complete lecture notes.
          1. Soc. notes before and after.
          2. Soc. details: ''groups''/uses of/types defined

       B. Read assignments.
          1. Before class.
          2. Relate to class.
             a. E.g. Chap. 7 - Visual aids.
             b. // CHART //

  (If have notes and reading — second stage.)
```

Summary

The process of moving from a rough plan for the body of the speech to a
final detailed outline can be roughly divided into six parts.

1. Check over the body of the speech to be sure that you have a simple,

---

II. FINAL PREPARATION JUST BEFORE

   A. Pull from all sources.
      1. Four topics in world history:
         Greek demo – 338. / Rome over Greece – 160.
         Rome republic – 27. / Empire-collapse – 455.
      2. Greek demo: book, lecture, disc.

   B. Test yourself.
      1. Active –– passive: Neutral – downhill
                  Uphill – engaged.
      2. Self-test on lect. sup. mat. Speech Apr. 28.

(During course plus before exam = confidence now.)

III. WHEN TAKING EXAM

   A. Don't panic.
      1. ''Coward dies a thousand deaths.''
      2. My econ. exam.

   B. Organize.
      1.Jackson: easy to read; student smart.
      2. As in speech: structure, transitions.

(Also as in speech...)

   C. Use supporting material.
      1. Psych exam: contrast/two sources/real
                example/hypo. example.
      2. Like list of types in speech.

```
                    Conclusion
    I. Summarize:
       A. First stage: lectures and reading.
       B. Second stage: pull together; self-test.
       C. Third stage: optimistic; organize;
                       supporting material.
   II. Results:
       A. You.
       B. Me.
```

logical pattern of ideas that can be covered in the assigned time limit and to discover what can be done in the introduction, conclusion, and transitions.

2. Plan an introduction that will provide the audience with a clear focus on what the speech is about and will perform any other useful functions—such as arouse interest in the topic, establish your credibility and friendship with the audience, and provide the audience with any needed background information on the topic.

3. Plan a conclusion that will end the speech smoothly and leave the audience with a favorable impression of you. The conclusion may focus on any main idea or ideas you want the listeners to remember from the speech, may suggest some action for the listeners to take, or may tie back to the introduction.

4. Plan major transitions in the speech and add transitional phrasing in major headings, so the audience can follow you easily through the speech and can see clearly what the main ideas are.

5. Work over the wording of the mainheads and a level or two of subheads so they will state your ideas accurately, clearly, and interestingly in oral style. (This step and to some extent step 4 are usually omitted if you are using a briefer topic outline.)

6. Do final revision to produce a finished copy of your outline to use in rehearsal. The degree of detail in which the outline is planned should be appropriate to the demands of the situation. You may reduce the outline to briefer speaking notes to use in final rehearsals and delivery.

Exercises

1. Present a four- to six-minute informative speech on a topic of your choice. Major emphasis in this assignment is on, first, using the introduction to make the audience receptive to speaker and topic and, second, using transitions and final conclusion to be sure the audience can follow the organization and see clearly the main points you want to make about the topic. In this speech, transitional material should be used to the point of "overkill." Class members in critiquing the speech should be able to explain the devices used in the introduction and conclusion and to point out the various sorts of transitional material used.

2. Bring to class a rough full draft of the outline for a major speech you are working on. Unless your instructor specifies otherwise, follow the ten requirements for form on pages 169–170. Students will work in teams of three, spending one-third of the class period on each team member's outline, suggesting improvements in structure, transitions, introduction, and conclusion. (This is a continuation of exercise 2 in Chapter 7.)

CHAPTER NINE

Presenting the Speech

"**P**rojecting confidence and general poise, even if you're scared, does as much for your speech as its content." This modern student's insight echoes an emphasis on delivery by the two most powerful orators of classical history, Demosthenes and Cicero. Skillful planning lays the foundation for an effective speech, but that speech comes into being only when it is presented to an audience. And whether justly or not, exceptional skill in presentation can often make even mediocre speech content seem impressive.

Effective presentation combines style and delivery. *Style* is the *choice and combination of words* with which you express the ideas in the speech. The style would be there even in a printed version of the speech. *Delivery* is the *vocal inflection* with which the words are uttered and the *facial expression, gestures, and other physical aspects* accompanying the words. In the preceding chapter, the section on phrasing idea headings in final planning was concerned mainly with style. Some further suggestions on style are included in this chapter because you can continue to improve choice of language, as well as vocal inflection and gesture, during rehearsal.

Confident and forceful presentation depends as much on a foundation of the speaker's attitudes as it does on specific techniques. We will look first at this foundation and then at rehearsal method and the specific techniques.

Foundations of Effective Presentation

The most important foundation for a speaker is the *desire to communicate* his or her ideas. You think about your purpose all through preparation of the speech, but this attitude comes to full fruition when you face the audience and recharge your earnest desire to have the listeners experience what you have experienced, understand what you now understand, believe what you believe.

This desire is the key to the attribute of speakers that is perhaps most respected by audiences: sincerity. In fact, most audiences will tolerate, often not even notice, many technical defects in delivery if they believe you to be sincere in your intention to communicate a message you think is worthwhile.

A second foundation of effective presentation is *commitment of physical energy* to the task. Normally your body will generate plenty of nervous energy to meet a speaking situation. So commit yourself to use this energy for firm posture, good vocal volume, and a lively awareness of your own ideas as you move through the speech. Don't imitate those speakers who retreat into low volume, total communion with their notes rather than with the listeners, self-conscious apologies, or the fake hyperrelaxation of draping oneself on the lectern and lethargically plodding through the speech. This commitment of physical energy often requires practicing energetic delivery during rehearsal, and it may require a conscious decision to take physical charge in the situation and to put some force behind the effort to communicate. When this commitment begins to pay off in speeches, even when you feel nervous inside, you will show the poise, alertness, and energy needed to keep your audience attentive.

Third, effective presentation depends on a *natural, conversational directness* with the listeners. As one student put it, "Be yourself when you give your speech." Natural gesturing, smiling when you feel like it, genuine eye contact, and the sorts of vocal inflection you would use in conversation with a friend—all these increase conversational directness in delivery. The use of "I," "we," and "you" and less formal sentence structure seem natural in style. Ad-libbing responses to audience feedback or making minor changes in your outline plan as you speak may provide welcome spontaneity. An audience finds a fellow human being—even one who may stumble and fumble occasionally, but is really conversing with them—much easier to listen to with interest and to relate to personally than a speaker who rants at them or, worse yet, simply stands in front of them and moves like a machine through a preprogrammed exercise.

Self-Confidence in Presentation

How can you channel nervous energy in ways that will help rather than hinder you in this creative act of presenting a speech? In Chapter 1, the two most useful suggestions are explained: Prepare fully, by developing a plan for the speech and especially by rehearsing. And second, concentrate on getting your ideas across to your audience rather than on yourself. Even with just a little experience following these suggestions, many beginning speech students learn to welcome the surge of nervous energy that will make them more alert and forceful in presentation.

What other suggestions will help you increase confidence and use nervous energy to your advantage? Insofar as you have a choice, pick topics in which you have good background knowledge and genuine interest. It's much easier to talk to people about what interests you. And if you know a good deal about the topic, through experience or through research, you have something to fall back on if your prepared plan begins to fall apart during presentation.

Careful preparation, especially rehearsing, can help you appear more confident in front of an audience. (Elyse Rieder for Random House, courtesy of Pace University Speech and Drama Department)

It's also helpful to remind yourself of just what sort of situation you do face. Basically you are talking (a normal activity) about a subject you know at least something about to a group of people who are, usually, much like yourself. The effects of the speech are likely to be quite good, possibly great, and in any case you'll survive to speak again. One successful speaker has commented that she finds it helpful to think of her audience as individual people who are almost always friendly and favorably disposed toward her. Similar advice was given by a speech student who was very shy and self-conscious early in the course but by the end became, somewhat to her surprise, quite relaxed and able to relate very effectively to her listeners: "An audience is not something that will hurt you. Therefore, why worry yourself and get nervous over nothing?"

As the time draws near for presentation, emphasize the stronger aspects of your speech in your own mind. Especially, resist any temptation to make drastic changes at the last minute. If you have some good specific examples or visual aids, stay aware of those strengths. If you have special experience or thorough research on this topic, dwell on that in your own mind. In any case, you probably know more about your topic than do your listeners. If the speech is particularly novel or useful to your listeners, remind yourself of that. If you are well rehearsed, let that be a source of confidence. At this late stage of preparation, recall the good things said about your earlier speeches rather than the negative criticism. There is no way to predict your degree of success, but positive feelings toward both yourself and your listeners increase the odds in your favor—and at this point you have nothing to lose by modest confidence.

Finally, here are some further quick suggestions made by students, and each seems to work for some people but not for others. Allow yourself time for a good night's sleep before a major speech. Move around some when giving the speech; using visual aids will help you do this. Wear something in which you feel especially good. Know your introduction cold so you can get off to a good start.

In a group of student speeches, one speaker managed to hold his listeners' rapt attention with a speech on marble as a building material whereas another speaker managed to lose her audience's interest with a speech on the sexual harassment of students. What was the essential difference between the two speeches? Enthusiasm. The first speaker was energized by a desire to share his own fascination and experience working with marble. The second speaker seemed to have little interest in either her topic or her listeners. Enthusiasm can manifest itself in many different sorts of delivery, from intimately conversational to physically vigorous. It rests on the foundations discussed earlier: desire to communicate, commitment of physical energy, and conversational directness. Although enthusiasm begins in the first steps of preparation with selection of topic and awareness of particular audience, it is practice in rehearsal that finally paves the way for an enthusiastic presentation.

Practicing for Presentation

The Importance of Rehearsal

Rehearsal can do a great deal more than just give you the confidence to get through the speech. On a final exam in speech, students were asked what advice they would give beginning speakers. The most common single item was, as one honors student put it, "Rehearse, rehearse, and then rehearse some more." Another student—an A average major in math and computer science—said that it was during rehearsal that he worked in his most effective transitions, improved key headings, substituted better items of supporting material, and especially developed the confidence to depart from his outline and return to it without losing control of the speech. It is in rehearsal that a speaker develops eye contact, spontaneity, freedom to gesture and move, fluency of ideas, and vocal variation to be used in the actual presentation. Thoroughly practicing each speech also improves your general skills in style and delivery—useful later when you have to give speeches with little or no rehearsal.

How many times should you rehearse a speech? That varies, of course, with how important you regard the occasion, how familiar you are with the topic, and how much time you can spend preparing for the speech. An experienced speaker can smooth a lot of kinks out of a speech in a couple of rehearsals and may often speak on a familiar topic with little or no rehearsal. Any speaker facing an unusually important and unfamiliar situation is, however, better off to rehearse as much as he possibly can, as many as ten to fifteen times. Is there such a thing as too much rehearsal? Probably not. But there is such a thing as rehearsing in an unproductive way until the speech becomes a mechanical exercise. You avoid this by keeping in mind the pattern of ideas and supporting materials you want to get across to the audience, rather than letting yourself learn the speech as a memorized performance. The best answer to "How much to rehearse?" is to practice at least until you really want to give the speech.

Method for Rehearsal

The following method, divided into three stages, will give you a way of using your rehearsal time profitably, rather than just reading the outline over and over or trying to memorize strings of words. You have time to discover improvements if you spread these practice sessions over several days. Your pattern of ideas also has time to sink in and become your natural way of thinking about the topic, so you are more confident.

In the *first stage*, you make final improvements in the outline and become confidently familiar with your plan. The first rehearsals often overlap final planning of the outline and are best done from a rough draft. After you have the outline in final shape, read or scan it silently a few times to refresh your memory on the logic behind the organization and supporting materials you plan to use. Then go through the entire speech aloud from beginning to end until you get the plan comfortably in mind and feel you can present the speech with reasonable fluency and eye contact.

Many student speakers either stop here or at most keep repeating the speech from time to time to increase their confidence. Actually, they have just reached the point at which they can begin to make significant gains in presentation skills.

In the *second stage*, you experiment with choice of language and with conscious delivery techniques. You have already planned phrasing of major ideas and transitions that will work well enough, but there may be ways of stating these ideas in more interesting and memorable language. There is much other content that you would not write out word for word (unless you were preparing the speech in manuscript form). You can now try out different ways of saying this material more appropriately, clearly, and vividly. Later in this chapter we will look at some ways to improve choice of language that can be applied in rehearsal. You do not necessarily memorize your more careful or creative phrasing, but some of it will stick with you in delivery.

In order to work on delivery, you have to duplicate as closely as possible the physical circumstances of the actual presentation: at least standing up, giving the speech aloud, and imagining yourself in the room in which the speech is to be given. If you have been validly criticized for poor posture, speaking too softly, or other flaws in delivery in earlier speeches, now is the time to concentrate specifically on eliminating those flaws. Beyond just over-coming flaws, however, experiment to develop the positive techniques in delivery to be discussed later in this chapter. In rehearsal, why not loosen up and try some of the more emphatic and dramatic uses of these techniques? This sort of experimentation and practice will make your voice and body a more flexible and forceful instrument for expressing your ideas and feelings in any speaking situation.

In the *third stage*, final rehearsal, you go through the speech from beginning to end and think of the whole as an organized unit for accomplishing a real purpose with your listeners. Insofar as you think of technique at all, think in larger terms: Does your delivery show an easy familiarity with the material and an enthusiastic desire to get it across to your listeners? Do the style and delivery reflect a sense of directly conversing with your audience? Is your manner of presentation appropriate to the degree of casualness or formality and other expectations in the situation? Reinforce your urge to communicate and your confidence by reminding yourself of why this speech will be worthwhile and interesting to your audience. If no notes will be used, don't use notes in the final rehearsals. If you can spread these final rehearsals over a few days, you have shown great self-discipline in pacing your earlier steps in preparation, and it will pay off in greater polish and confidence in delivery.

Aids to Rehearsal

Different speakers, both student and professional, profit from different aids in rehearsal. Perhaps the only aid that will work for virtually any speaker is a trial audience of one or more gentle but perceptive and honest critics. When using untrained critics you may have to ask them, before the practice run-through, to watch for specific matters—such as distracting gestures or repeated phrases (e.g., "you know") that you are trying to change. Other matters are better raised after the practice delivery: Was the speech interesting? Did the critic-listener get confused at any point in the speech? Your friendly critic won't be able to answer all your questions, so settle tactfully for a few clues to strong points and to possible improvements.

If you use a tape recorder, be sure that some of your recorded rehearsals are done standing up and envisioning your audience: possibly have one or two friends present, so your delivery is for presentation rather than just being recorded. Don't judge your fluency too harshly: what may sound like a rather slow, uneven rate on tape *may* work much better when the physical dimension is added in actual delivery. Some students are relieved to discover from the tape that they have a plan that makes sense, and that some pauses, shifts in volume, or other dramatic delivery techniques are really working. If they listen critically, they are likely also to spot unclearly phrased idea headings, weak or missing transitions, slow-moving or unclear supporting material, or overuse of "okay" or other filler phrases, all of which can then be improved.

A number of students recommend practicing a speech in front of a mirror. Some of them are relieved to discover that they really do look like public speakers when they give their speeches. A mirror causes some students to realize the possible value of firm posture and pleasant and responsive facial expression. Some students also find that a mirror gives a sort of immediate feedback that helps them experiment with a greater range of movement and gesture.

Video recording during rehearsal can combine and extend all these uses of aural tape and mirror, but note two words of caution: First, avoid the temptation to be solely concerned with delivery techniques. Don't neglect to critique your content, organization, and style, all of which are also revealed by the video recording. Second, avoid seeing the speech as a "performance" for a video camera rather than as an act of communication with a live audience.

You can use rehearsal to better advantage if you understand what choice of language can do for you and what techniques contribute to effective delivery.

Improving Choice of Language: Style

Improving your choice of language can make your ideas more credible, clearer, and more interesting to your listeners. Let's look at some ways to obtain each of these three advantages.

Language Choice Can Increase Your Credibility

Precision in language helps credibility. An audience is less likely to trust the competence of a speaker who ends every third sentence with "and stuff like that" or "and so forth," or who relies on vague, all-purpose words such as "thing." So in rehearsal, try to recast sentences in ways that avoid such fuzziness. Change "Out in these hills you can find agate, petrified wood, and stuff like that" to "Out in these hills you can find several types of collector's rocks, including agate and petrified wood." Change "There are four things about psychopathic killers" to "Psychopathic killers usually have four characteristic tendencies."

Use restraint and a sense of your audience in the language you use to express your opinions and ideas. Avoid highly opinionated language or sweeping generalizations that your listeners are likely to find unacceptable. If you refer to all lawyers as "shysters" or all new weapon developments as "plots of the military-industrial complex" or all advocates of space exploration as "nuts way out in science fiction land," you had best be sure your audience shares your view. We tend to trust a speaker who uses language that to us reflects a fair-minded and accurate view of reality—and to mistrust one who seems blindly or stubbornly biased.

You can also avoid several simple sorts of errors that damage your image as a credible source. Be sure you know how to pronounce the words you are using, such as place names and technical terms you encounter in your research. Don't use obscenity, profanity, or unnecessarily repugnant descriptions even with an audience who would accept that language in private conversation. As much as possible, avoid technical jargon that will be unfamiliar to your audience and may seem used to make you appear "superior" to them. Eliminate slang that is inappropriate for the topic or the occasion, or that merely covers up sloppy thinking.

Language Choice Can Make Your Ideas Clearer

Know clearly what you want to say. Then say it as simply and directly as you can. The speaker who says, "After suitable deliberation, the dean was of the opinion that the students were deserving of suspension," is so much concerned with words that she has lost sight of the idea. When she returns to the idea, she will probably say, "After considering the case, the dean suspended the students."

Break complex, convoluted sentences into simpler, usually shorter ones. "The space-age technology, despite some doubts that many people have because of various failures and high costs, still represents, if we take a long view of the human race's destiny, at present our most challenging and exciting frontier for exploration," would be clearer as "Space technology is costly and has had some failures. Yet in the long view of human destiny, space exploration is now our most exciting frontier."

Choose words that will have your intended meaning for your listeners. As explained in Chapter 2, your words create meaning in a listener's mind by triggering off what the listener already associates with the words. If you refer to a book as a junk novel and "junk novel" means the same thing to both you and your listeners, your meaning will be clear. However, if to you "junk novel" means "worthless" but to your listeners it means "fun reading," you had better find a different phrase to convey your meaning. Perhaps "trite, boring piece of drivel" would create in the listeners' minds the meaning you intend.

Style is improved when you replace vague, repetitious language with more specific explanation or other supporting material. In the following example, the speaker dwells on the point because he thinks it is important, but he doesn't dwell on it effectively:

> Movies don't like television. For whatever reason there are a lot of attacks in movies on the whole idea of television. Movies seem to think that television does some bad things to people. If you try, you can probably remember some of them in which people who watched television weren't shown in a very good light, nor are the people who make television shows shown to be high-minded people. Television just isn't shown in a very good light by movies.

Even if the speaker does not need to cite illustrative movies to prove his point, he can make the point clearer by being more specific:

> Movie makers don't seem to like television. Movies like "Network" have shown TV manipulating news events to increase ratings. Movies have also shown TV viewers confusing fiction with reality and TV addicts as almost like zombies. Movies like "Looker" depict TV commercials that no one's mental defenses can guard against. Movies have thus attacked both the television producers and the viewers.

Language Choice Can Make Your Ideas More Interesting and Memorable

Efficiency itself increases interest: the more crisply the ideas and items of supporting material flow, so long as they are clear, the greater is the audience's interest. Thus, in rehearsal, paring out excess verbiage and perhaps replacing it with more specific detail will increase interest as well as clarity. Concrete imagery that sets the object or event vividly before the mind's eye of the listener also creates interest and emotional impact.

In addition, when rehearsing (or when writing a manuscript speech), seek places where you can use the following specific techniques to make ideas more interesting, forceful, and memorable:

1. *Ellipsis.* In giving a series of details, you can produce a greater sense of energy or urgency by leaving out "and" or other grammatically normal words. "The abandoned dog was starved, flea-ridden, scared." "He had a quick, sarcastic mind; a master of the put-down." The audience partici-

pates by mentally filling in the missing words, such as "he was" in the middle of the latter sentence.

2. *Short climax sentence.* After describing some examples of modern business-persons who worked hard and made a lot of money, the speaker clinches the point: "Hard work pays off." The short sentence makes the major point easy to remember, and it also subtly suggests that the idea has a simple, perfect truth.

3. *Parallelism.* You begin or end a series of clauses or sentences with the same words, in order to emphasize a similarity or parallelism in the ideas being stated. "With calm confidence we began the speech course. With calm confidence we did each exercise, gave each speech, took each exam. With calm confidence we await our final grades."

4. *Antithesis.* This can be used when you want to stress the contrast or opposition between two ideas. The clauses or sentences in which the opposing ideas are stated are similar to each other in structure. This similarity in structure focuses the listener's attention on the direct contrast in ideas. "Dumb car buyers look at the paint job. Smart car buyers look at the power train." Antithesis may be used in parallel series to state a series of contrasts, sometimes as an emphatic summary device.

> The speaker meets his audience face-to-face; the writer is only a printed name. The speaker speaks with his whole mind and body; the writer writes with detached intelligence. The speaker speaks and stands ready to defend his ideas against immediate attack; the writer having written, moves on and leaves his ideas to fend for themselves.

5. *Alliteration.* Beginning two or more words in a series with the same sound is a novelty that has mild interest effect. "We began our trip in a car that was a rusty, rattling wreck." Heavy use of alliteration calls attention to itself, but can, like a catchy jingle, help make an idea memorable: "My opponent for office is a cornered, conniving, con-artist."

6. *Rhetorical question.* The speaker in the preceding example might have asked, "Do you want to elect a cowardly con-artist?" to which presumably the listeners mentally answer, no. When a question is used as a transitional device, the speaker usually also provides the answer. In the use of a rhetorical question, however, the audience is expected to supply, mentally, the fairly obvious answer. The listeners become actively involved, and thus more interested, in a sort of mental dialogue with the speaker. By mentally supplying the anticipated answers to the speaker's questions, audiences also may help persuade themselves. Are you not more easily convinced if you think you are deciding the answers yourself?

7. *Periodic sentence.* When a speaker wants to arouse mild curiosity and then satisfy it with a sense of natural finish within a sentence, he can make the climax of meaning and the end of the sentence coincide. This is the opposite of the loose sentence, in which we have first the main idea and then, after we know that, the speaker continues to add on clauses, which

occur to him as he goes, and which may be interesting, but we can sort of lose interest as the sentence goes on and on, like this one, even if we find that the sentence had an originally interesting idea, which we have almost forgotten. To impart an impression of crisp control in speaking use periodic sentences. In any case, avoid the indefinite loose sentence, in which even shifts in thinking are connected by "and uh"—as if the speaker feared his life must end with the end of the sentence. At the end of the sentence, stop. Then start the next sentence.

8. *Metaphor.* When you use the words for thing A (e.g., rose-colored glasses) to mean thing B (an optimism that distorts reality), as in "She looks at the world through rose-colored glasses," you are speaking metaphorically. Why not just say, "She looks at the world too optimistically"? Why use metaphor? One reason is that the listener enjoys his successful discovery of your meaning, especially if the metaphor is novel or striking but not so far-fetched as to be difficult to figure out. This keeps the listener actively involved and interested in the message. Another reason is that most metaphors are tangible, concrete terms for vague or abstract ideas, and this makes the ideas more vivid and thus more interesting and memorable. "Will power resisting temptation" is not as vivid as "Slamming and bolting the iron door of will power against the slimy demons of temptation." The selection of metaphor can also, often subtly, influence how an audience sees and evaluates the thing we are talking about. It makes a difference, for example, whether we refer to college life as "a jungle" or "a workshop" or "an amusement park." You can use with good effect metaphors that are already in public use, such as "a tidal wave of public resistance." But when you have an important idea that you want your audience to sense more vividly, why not invent your own metaphor?

The interest value and other effects of these stylistic devices depend on how they *sound* in context. Thus although you may have jotted down some creative phrasing earlier, rehearsal is an especially good time to experiment with style. Recall that you can emphasize different sorts of ideas by different sorts of stylistic treatment: a series of similar ideas invites parallelism or ellipsis, for example, whereas contrasting ideas invite antithesis.

You may be better able to develop your own fresh, forceful phrasing if you realize that the effects of most of these devices are based on a few principles:

Novelty: whatever differs from the ordinary, obvious way of saying it
Compactness: saying it in relatively few words
Concreteness: making the idea physically tangible, vivid to the senses
Repetition: a sort of refrain in sounds, words, or sentence structure.
Audience involvement: leading listeners to a sense of discovery or mental response

Improving Delivery

Techniques in delivery vary widely among effective speakers. One speaker may move around a lot, whereas another will be relatively stationary. One speaker may seem to converse quietly with her listeners, whereas another will appear highly energetic. Although there is no one "right" way to present a speech, almost any speaker has within his or her own delivery some weaknesses that could be eliminated and some strengths that could be added. Also, most speakers would gain by increasing the range of techniques they can use in delivery to influence both what the audience *sees* physically and how they *hear* the words presented.

We will approach the technical aspects of delivery first in terms of what you can do with posture, movement, and other physical channels of expression, and second in terms of what you can do with vocal channels of expression. (You just read a blunt preoutlining transition.)

Physical Channels

The first impression you make on an audience, even before you utter a word, is physical: how you are dressed and groomed, and how you approach the lectern. In dress, appropriateness to the occasion and to audience expectations is more important than formality for its own sake; but if you are in doubt, it is usually safer to lean toward the more formal. In any case, avoid distracting the audience by what you wear or by sparkling or clanking jewelry. When your time comes to speak, walk to the lectern firmly, pause a few seconds to remind yourself who is in control, thank your chairperson if you had one to introduce you, smile slightly at the audience if that seems natural, and begin. When you end your speech, finish at the lectern and then depart, leaving a final impression of poise; don't trail off the conclusion as you start back to your seat.

The four types of physical channel we will consider next have a significant effect, especially on how the listeners *feel* toward speaker and message and therefore on how receptive they are. Unnoticed physical cues are often more potent than those the audience is aware of.

Posture   Your posture tells your audience whether or not you are in control of the situation. The safest stance for good effect is to stand firmly on both feet. Don't sag on one leg, or cock one foot toe-down behind you, or lean on the lectern. Firm posture and vibrant muscle tone not only suggest strength and control but also give you maximum freedom for moving about at the lectern and gesturing. Avoid crossing your arms, as this connotes aloofness from your audience. If you must clasp your hands together, behind your back is better than the "fig leaf" stance in front. One or both hands resting lightly on the lectern or at your side, with some frequency of gesturing, is the best way to handle hands. One hand in pocket, with the other free to gesture, is at least better than both hands in pockets. If you tend to jingle coins or other debris in your pockets, remove the stuff before you speak if you can't break the habit any other way. Leaning slightly forward is a subtle way of emphasizing the intensity of whatever you are saying at that moment.

Movement and Gestures   Effective movement and gestures, regardless of any specific meanings the gestures may have, can reduce your nervous tension by draining it off in useful ways. They can also increase the audience's attention by the energy and variety of your movement, and can enhance your image as a sincere and confident speaker.

In the actual presentation, your gestures and movements should flow from natural impulses. During rehearsal, however, you can deliberately experiment in order to reduce inhibitions and to develop a variety of gesturing and movement. You can take a couple of steps to emphasize a shift from one main section to the next, for example. You can use hand gestures to show size and shape of objects, numbering, or other description, or just to emphasize an idea. You may also during rehearsal have to work on eliminating distracting movement, such as too much nervous pacing about or repetitious, meaningless gestures (e.g., rubbing your nose or playing with a pencil). Often you solve these defects by substituting effective gestures for the distracting ones during rehearsal.

Gestures should be firm and definite rather than incomplete or feeble. For instance, when a speaker's hands twitch upward at the sides of the lectern we know he has the impulse to gesture but is too unsure or inhibited to do so forcefully. In rehearsal, he could consciously practice forceful hand gestures so as to loosen up and have that capacity when he actually gives the speech.

Facial Expression   Although speakers and audiences are often not consciously aware of it, facial expressions—jovial, friendly, frowning, intense, sorrowful, optimistic—influence listeners' attitudes toward a speaker and what she is saying, sometimes a great deal. For example, if you appear bored, the audience is likely to return the feeling, so generate some interest or enthusiasm and let it show through your face. It's usually a mistake to fake smiles or other expressions that you do not really feel. However, you can at least be vigorously enough aware of your own ideas so that your face is responsive to much of what you say, and your expression can reflect a friendly attitude toward your audience. Close attention in a mirror or by a critic can help you avoid unknowingly having harmful facial expressions, such as a cheerful smile when discussing tragic events or a habitual frown that may not accurately reflect what you really feel.

Effective gestures and facial expressions influence listeners' reactions to a speech. (Alan Carey/The Image Works)

Eye Contact Maintain genuine and consistent eye contact with your audience. This means really looking individual listeners momentarily in the eye, at least in small audiences; and it means looking primarily at the audience, with only occasional glances at notes if any are used. Of all physical channels, eye contact is, for most speakers, the most important for establishing a close link between speaker and listeners. Freedom from notes also suggests that you have a confident knowledge of your subject. You get a lot of feedback from eye contact, and positive feedback is much more inspiring than looks of disagreement or disinterest; so, although you should cover all the audience occasionally, maintain your most frequent and genuine eye contact with those listeners who are giving you the most positive and encouraging feedback.

Vocal Channels

Your voice is a very flexible instrument for refining the meanings of words and for showing your feelings toward the audience. Four important elements of vocal inflection are pitch, volume (loudness or softness), rate of words per minute, and pauses. You can deliberately experiment with these elements during rehearsal in order to affect the clarity, interest, emphasis, and credibility of your presentation.

Clarity   If the audience doesn't hear the words, none of your other speech skills counts for anything. Therefore, the first rule in delivery is to speak loudly enough to be heard by all the audience. Don't drop your volume at the ends of sentences. If you have trouble speaking loudly enough, practice projecting your voice to the back of a large, real or imagined, room. When giving the speech, talk at times directly to the people in the back of the room. Articulate words clearly; don't mumble. Don't rush your delivery so much that you slur words together unintelligibly. If you are criticized for speaking too rapidly, select portions of your next speech— often main headings and key transitions—and practice a slower rate in those portions. This can help you get control over your rate.

Interest   Variation in volume, rate, and pitch increases audience interest. You may not be able to change your basic rate greatly, but at least you can break it up by deliberately practicing to move more rapidly through supporting detail and slow down for some key ideas. If you tend to speak in an intense, relatively strident, high-pitched tone, spot places in the speech where you will, in rehearsal, pause a couple of seconds, back off mentally, and start in on the next section with a lower, more normal tone. A speaker, perhaps closely tied to notes, may be accused of relatively dull, monotone delivery, and may reply by arguing validly that he used a lot of changes in volume, rate, and pitch. His defense misses the important point that the *range*—the extremes—of variation is the key to maintaining audience interest. Also, the variation should reflect what is being said, rather than following some regular sing-song pattern or the consistently strident intensity of the "debater's delivery." Observe closely the wide range of vocal inflections used by a speaker who seems alive with his ideas and with the desire to impart them to the audience.

Emphasis   When we hear a speaker, our level of attention constantly shifts in intensity. The speaker wants our maximum level of attention at certain places, usually when she is stating or summarizing main ideas or is making a strong emotional appeal. Vocal variation is used—sometimes subtly, sometimes dramatically—to maximize our attention level at the appropriate points. Devices used include (1) a pause before or after a key statement, (2) a dramatic pause and shift into lower pitch when going into an emotional point, (3) a shift to a slower rate when stating a main idea, (4) an increase in volume to heighten attention, or (5) a dramatic lowering of volume almost to the point at which the audience has to strain to hear for an especially intense sentence or two.

Credibility   Vocal tone and inflection influence the listeners' trust in you as a person and therefore in your ideas. A wide range of natural, spontaneous variation signifies that the speaker is strongly interested in both his ideas and his audience. If the speaker believes in his ideas so strongly, will not the audience also? The speaker should also be fluent if he is to show a command of his material. Fluency does *not* mean rushing rapidly through the speech, fearfully avoiding any pauses as if these might ruin the "performance." True fluency is more a matter of energy and of readiness of ideas; you obtain it by having your plan well in mind and intending seriously to get it across to the audience. In rare cases, a speaker may have such a problem with habitual slow rate that he must deliberately practice, during rehearsal, increasing his rate more or less constantly throughout the entire speech. Perhaps the most frequent defect in fluency, however, is the repeated use of filler phrases—"okay," "you know," "all right," "and like that." To cure this habit, the speaker first has to become aware that he or she is using these filler phrases, and this can come from class criticism, a friend as critic, or a tape recorder during rehearsal. Then the speaker must consciously combine elimination of the offensive phrases with acceptance of pauses as useful. Incidentally, some of the most effective pauses in student speeches probably occur when the speaker momentarily forgets what comes next.

Most speakers experiment with these various techniques of delivery during rehearsal. When actually presenting the ideas to an audience, they concentrate on getting the ideas across rather than on the mechanics of voice and gesture.

Adapting Delivery to the Specific Situation

The size of the room and audience, and the nature of the topic and occasion should have some influence on delivery. One would not normally address five or six members of a hobby club with sweeping arm gestures, a loud and strident voice, or a general formality of presentation. However, on a serious topic, even an audience of twenty fellow students seems to require a firmness of posture and an efficient use of language at least a cut or two above casual conversation.

Should you use a lectern? Sure, if one is available, as long as you use it to put your notes on, and not as something to lean on or hide behind. However brief your speaking notes, you can prepare them on full-size sheets of paper, rather than cards, so as to be able to see more of the speech structure at one glance. Use sheets that are unattached, rather than stapled or clipped together, so you don't have to fold them over. Don't fiddle with your notes. If you won't have the use of a lectern, prepare your notes on stiff index cards, and make a special effort to rehearse enough to be able to depend on only brief notes.

In any speaking situation be prepared for the unexpected. If the microphone fails to work, raise your volume and perhaps move closer to the audience. If a visual aid becomes unworkable, do the best you can without it. If you can make a quick response to some crash or other noise, do so and move on in your speech; otherwise just ignore it. If the audience is much smaller than expected or several people walk out for no apparent reason during your speech, focus your thinking on those who have come and are staying. Give them your best effort. The key notion in all this adaptation to the unexpected is to remember that you have come into the situation with a job to do. Never lose sight of that guiding purpose.

Don't exceed the maximum time limit imposed by the situation. The downtown civic club is just as sensitive to the end of the twenty-minute limit for their luncheon speaker as you are to the end of your fifty-minute class period. To fit a tight time limit, plan and rehearse tightly. If you don't have someone to give you time signals or a wall clock in view, you can at least glance at your watch. If nothing else, listeners' glances at watches and other restlessness can tell you that it is time to wrap up your speech briskly and sit down.

To prepare for the physical situation and boost your own confidence, a few hours or days in advance look over the room in which you will be giving the speech. Will you have a lectern? A microphone? A place to display visual aids? How loudly will you have to project your voice to be heard easily? Are there likely to be noises or other distractions from outside the room? Where will you sit before speaking? You may discover that you are expected to give your presentation sitting at a table.

Arrive at a speaking engagement several minutes early. Check final arrangements with your chairperson and, if you are on a panel, meet the other panel members informally for a few minutes. Some speakers give themselves just enough time to check in with the chairperson and get the physical feel of the situation. Others are more comfortable if they can chat a bit with audience members to establish some person-to-person relationship before the speech.

Other Modes of Presentation

Thus far we have dealt mainly with the extemporaneous mode of speech-making: the speaker outlines and rehearses the speech quite carefully in advance and then delivers it from notes while ad-libbing at least some of the phrasing. It is a flexible method that allows efficient preparation of content, and it encourages conversational directness and spontaneity in delivery. It is the best single method to learn. But it doesn't work well in all situations. You may want to speak from memory, either ad-libbing from a *memorized outline* or delivering a scriptlike *memorized manuscript*. You may need to speak *impromptu*, with little or no advance preparation. Or you may *read from a manuscript* you have prepared.

All these modes rely on the same basic principles of having a distinct purpose, sound and clear organization, specific supporting materials, and direct and energetic delivery. Thus the skills you learn and practice in extemporaneous speaking can serve you well when you are in a situation calling for one of these other modes.

Speaking from Memory

When might you want to deliver a speech without notes, from memory? It would be most likely when you want to plan carefully in advance what you intend to say but want to give the impression either of spontaneous, sincere feeling or of relaxed expertise on the subject. So plan a detailed outline, as you would for an extemporaneous speech.

In most of these situations, you need to be concerned with memorizing the pattern of ideas and supporting detail rather than the word-for-word phrasing. First learn the mainheads as a basic framework, then learn the major subheads under each mainhead, and so on down to the items of supporting material under each subhead. Spread your rehearsals over several days. Occasionally question yourself on the speech content: What are your four main ideas? How do you develop the second main section? Though you may remember some phrasing, don't start trying to memorize the exact words. Learning the speech primarily as a logically organized *pattern of ideas* you want to get across makes the speech easier to remember; it also makes your delivery more conversational and varied.

There are a few situations, such as some eulogies or emotional persuasive speeches, in which you may want to plan and memorize a short speech word for word. Unless you have unusual talent in memorizing material, you probably do best to avoid this mode whenever possible, especially for longer speeches: the hazards of forgetting or of monotonous "tape recorder" delivery are not worth risking. Both these hazards are reduced if you think first in terms of structure and ideas and second in terms of exact language—both in preparing the manuscript and in learning the speech. Some speakers also, once they have the content well in mind, find it useful to plan deliberately some use of pause, change in volume, or other techniques of delivery.

You may be more confident if you prepare a complete set of speaking notes on cards to keep in your pocket or unobtrusively on a table or lectern near you. If worst comes to worst, refer to them—with complete composure—and continue. An audience assumes you know what you're doing up there, and they will go along with just about anything if you remain reasonably cool. Incidentally, you can practice this "emergency" reference to notes a time or two during rehearsals. Finally, remember that your audience won't know if you jump around in your plan or find yourself ad-libbing.

Speaking Impromptu

You are at a meeting and an issue is raised about which you feel strongly. You had not planned to speak at the meeting, but now it appears that some important things will not be said unless you say them. So you speak for two or three minutes. You give an impromptu speech. Most of us can speak impromptu if the spirit moves us enough, especially if we are with a familiar group. So the challenge is to do it well whenever we really want to secure an effect. Developing skill and confidence in impromptu speaking is not a trivial matter: many people give short impromptu speeches more frequently than they give long, carefully prepared speeches.

One source of power in impromptu speaking is to use whatever time you can get for preparation. If you are going to a meeting or a class at which an issue important to you is going to be discussed, think through your position, reasons you could use to support it, opposing arguments that you might need to counter, other contributions you might make to the discussion, and examples and other supporting materials you could use. You must, of course, stay flexible and adapt to the flow of discussion at the meeting. But some great "impromptu" speeches have been prepared in advance, even to the point of rehearsal.

The other sort of preparation time is those few minutes between your decision to speak and your contribution. In a situation in which you must adapt to the ongoing flow of discussion, this may be very little time indeed; but often you can see the drift of an exchange between other speakers and wait for an opportune moment for your contribution, or after listening to a formal speech and some discussion, you can set your own time for introducing your line of thought. Use this time to apply what you have learned from doing more fully prepared speeches:

> Get clearly in mind your central point of information or argument, as well as any supporting ideas.
> What examples or other supporting detail can you quickly recall or create?
> Do you need an opening transition to show explicitly how your contribution is related to other points in the discussion?
> If your contribution is at all complex, you should probably use a brief summary or final sentence to bring your central point into clear focus.

If you have a choice, stand rather than sit when you deliver your impromptu remarks. You have better control over the situation and an opportunity for more forceful delivery. Use what you already know about delivery, such as the importance of firm posture and a voice that can be easily heard. As much as possible, maintain eye contact with your listeners. In a situation where opinions differ, remember that your real audience is the neutrals, whose opinions can be swayed, rather than your opponents. End crisply and in control. If you feel yourself becoming flustered, restate your central point firmly and stop.

Three further suggestions will increase your effectiveness in impromptu speaking. First, keep your speech within a *length* appropriate to the situation. Contributions from the floor that turn into full-blown speeches are especially annoying, as are responses that digress from the immediate point. Examples, explanations, and other supporting details are appropriate and useful when a short speech is called for, but stop when you have finished your point. Conciseness counts toward effect. Second, *focus* your contribution on a single central point. When you cover two or three completely separate points in one short speech, you usually dissipate the effect of all the points. Third, exercise *self-control* both in what you say and in your delivery. Many of the situations in which impromptu speaking is used tend to be emotionally charged. Tact and respect for other people almost always create a better impression and sway more neutral opinions than does personal attack or uncontrolled anger.

Using a Manuscript

A manuscript is a word-for-word plan of the entire speech. It is best used when exact phrasing throughout the speech is really an advantage—as, for example, in a complex technical oral report or in a speech depending on precise logical argument and evidence. Manuscript preparation is also common when the speech must fit a precise time frame or when the speech content must also be submitted as a written paper. In other situations the manuscript may be used as only a tool in preparation, to let the speaker experiment closely with language choice, even though the final presentation is done extemporaneously from an outline. A speaker facing an unusually threatening situation may write out a manuscript simply to relieve his anxiety; but in this situation a manuscript does not usually produce results as good as would the same time spent on thorough extemporaneous preparation.

A well-done manuscript speech differs from a well-written essay read aloud as a speech. "Speeches of the literary men sound thin in the actual contests; while those of the orators sound well, but look crude when you have them in your hands," Aristotle remarked in the *Rhetoric*. The speech manuscript will tend to have a simpler and more obvious pattern of major ideas, a more distinct introduction and conclusion, more supporting material per idea, more frequent and blunter transitions to make sure the major ideas stand out clearly, shorter and less formal sentences, more repetition of key nouns rather than pronouns or synonyms, and frequent use of "we," "I," "you," and other marks of direct address to the audience. The manuscript is written to be interpreted and enlivened by vocal variation and gesture in delivery. If the speaker simply writes a good essay and then reads it flatly, she is very likely to be unclear and to bore her listeners. Special care in both preparation and delivery produces an effective manuscript speech.

Preparing a Manuscript Speech   Begin preparing a manuscript speech the same way you would an extemporaneous speech: after researching and brainstorming, plan your pattern of main ideas, then subheads, and finally items of supporting material. Then phrase the idea headings and plan major transitions. Think in terms of *oral* presentation to listeners. Rough out a plan for the introduction and conclusion, probably a combination of outlining and fully written out blocks. By now, much of the manuscript, except for supporting material, is already written out—and it is organized and written for a *speech*. Now pull all this together, phrasing the supporting material as you go, preparing a complete written version from beginning to end. You have a rough draft of the manuscript.

In revision, first read the speech aloud *at your normal speech-delivery rate* to check the length against the required time frame. As you read it aloud two or three times, try ad-libbing different phrasing at various places in the speech. If the ad-libbing sounds better, write it in. Review and apply the section "Improving Choice of Language" earlier in this chapter. Check to be sure that the statement of focus will stand out clearly as such, that main ideas and other sentences can be easily read and understood, that you have enough transitional material for the audience to follow the organization, and that the introduction establishes a direct speaker-listener contact, rather than the impersonal tone of an essay.

On the final version, double- or triple-space between lines for easy reading and for any last-minute minor improvements in phrasing. You may also write the manuscript in outline blocks: each subsection as a block indented a little from the main section under which it falls, each item of supporting material as a block indented a little more than the subsection, and so forth. You will then have both exact language and a visual picture of the structure to help you keep in mind what the *main* ideas are.

If you are reading a manuscript that is prepared primarily for written submission, you can at least run through a photocopy of the manuscript aloud a few times and pencil in some adaptations for oral delivery. Break up sentences that don't work orally. Add some preoutlining, internal summary, or other transitional material that will bring organization and key ideas into sharp focus. Insert some brief personal asides or supporting detail. A more radical way to handle the problem of two versions is to write the paper first, and then prepare an outline for an extemporaneous speech, using the written paper as the main source of material.

Delivering a Manuscript Speech   Working with a manuscript can be deceptive for the speaker because when he gets it written he is likely to think he has finished his preparation. Many inexperienced speakers, however, read a manuscript with so little liveliness and vocal variation that it is almost impossible for listeners to follow the line of thought or pay attention. When you use a manuscript, your delivery must still help maintain audience interest and refine the meanings of the words. Think of the rehearsal stage as preparation to use voice and body *to interpret* the written words for the listeners.

When you rehearse reading the speech, remind yourself of what your main ideas are, to whom you are giving the speech, and for what intended effect. If you don't write the speech in outline blocks, it may help to star or underline key ideas. Keep alive your feelings about the speech as ideas and items of supporting material rather than just strings of words. Practice reading and thinking through the speech enough times so you can maintain frequent eye contact with your listeners. Develop some freedom to use hand gestures.

The preceding paragraphs suggest ways to increase your natural purpose and sense of communication in delivery. You may also approach delivery techniques more mechanically by deliberately planning, for example, to use pauses or a slower rate for emphasis at certain important points in the speech. Use no more of this deliberate planning than you can make appear natural, however, lest the speech appear to be an artificial performance rather than sincere communication.

Finally, as with extemporaneous rehearsal, don't overlook the value of giving the speech before a friendly critic or two, both to check delivery and clarity of content and to become more comfortable with the feel of actually delivering the manuscript speech to an audience.

With this preparation, you can read the speech with a conversational directness of style and eye contact, a broad range of vocal variation that reflects your feelings about the ideas, and some gesturing. And unless you are held to a very strict time limit or a need for very precise planning, you still may digress *briefly* from your manuscript a few times, if for no other reason than to make your presentation more lively and personal.

Summary

A speaker with a strong desire to communicate, physical energy and poise, and a sense of conversing directly with listeners has the foundations for effective presentation. Skills in presentation include both the choice of language, or *style*, and the use of vocal and physical channels in *delivery*.

A speaker can increase confidence and enthusiasm by rehearsing the speech. Rehearsals can also improve specific technical skills in style and delivery.

In style, choice of language should promote respect for the speaker and should convey ideas clearly and efficiently. Various stylistic devices—such as parallelism and antithesis, rhetorical questions and metaphors—can increase audience interest and emphasize main ideas.

In delivery, the speaker should aim for firm posture, varied and definite movement and gestures, facial expression consistent with the ideas being uttered, and genuine eye contact. Vocal delivery should be varied and fluent, and should use pauses and changes in rate or volume to emphasize main ideas; vocal variation should reflect the speaker's active feelings about the ideas being uttered.

Although the extemporaneous mode of speech preparation and presentation is the most commonly used, other modes may better serve a speaker in some situations. Speaking from a memorized outline, rather than notes, can enable a speaker to prepare carefully while appearing spontaneous or casually confident. Skill in impromptu speaking can enable a speaker to give coherent, effective speeches in response to unexpected or changing situations. Manuscript speaking permits close attention to style and very tight advance planning, but the speaker must be especially careful that style and delivery show a speaker talking to audience members in a lively and direct way, rather than flatly reading an essay to them.

Exercises

1. Prepare and present a three- to five-minute manuscript speech. Plan at least five distinct stylistic devices for interest and emphasis, and label them on the manuscript (see pp. 184–186). Turn in a planning outline with the manuscript.

2. Present a seven- to ten-minute speech that has been put through the full extemporaneous method of preparation. Turn in a detailed outline of the speech. (This is a continuation of exercise 2 in Chapter 8). The class will critique each speech, both on content and on delivery. Partly from this feedback, try to determine which stages in preparation you handled well and which might have been done more effectively. (Your instructor may ask you to turn in your notes on this self-analysis and response to feedback.)

PART III

Further Development of Speech-Communication Skills

PART III

CHAPTER TEN

Speaking Persuasively

Two speakers attempt to persuade listeners to get more exercise. One has assembled many statistics and statements by experts showing that exercise increases the likelihood of good physical and mental health. The audience respects the speech, but no one really decides to exercise more. The other speaker uses some of the same expert testimony; but he describes in addition a friend who was often anxious and tired, and he points out some of the pressures that reduce the energy level of many college students. He asks the listeners if they wouldn't like being more consistently energetic and optimistic. He describes the dramatic change in his friend's mental attitude and physical well-being after she began exercising regularly. Finally he briefly explains a variety of convenient ways to exercise regularly. Several listeners, including the instructor in the class, resolve to get more exercise.

Two speakers before a city council argue against a change in city zoning that would permit developers to build a huge discount store in the middle of their residential area. The first speaker gives an angry speech attacking the greed of land developers and hinting darkly at bribes or other corruption of the city council members he is addressing. He also explains in some detail why he finds large discount stores offensive. The council members decide to vote in favor of the land developer's request. But wait.

Another speaker rises to oppose the developer. She reminds the council members of their key role in making decisions that will benefit the whole community, and she praises them for some past decisions. She then reasons that allowing the discount store will increase noise and traffic, thus reducing the quality of life in the surrounding residential area and discouraging further home building. She reinforces this line of reasoning by citing a neighboring community in which such commercial development turned a pleasant neighborhood into a blighted area. She asks if the council members would not better serve their role of representing the community by refusing the request. The council agrees and denies the developer's application.

Definition of Persuasion

Persuasion is the attempt to influence the beliefs, attitudes, or behavior of a target audience. As the preceding examples illustrate, neither masses of evidence nor an unleashing of personal emotions will necessarily persuade—though both evidence and emotion are used in persuasion. What then does persuade?

The fundamental rule for success in persuasion is this: Adapt your persuasive efforts to the target audience to bring these particular listeners to accept your purpose. A student probably already knows that exercise is good for his health, but he is unlikely to change unless he is motivated enough to improve. So the speaker concentrates on making listeners want to change, as well as showing how relatively easy it will be. A city council is not much interested in one resident's feelings about developers and discount stores, but the council members do want to fulfill their duty as civic leaders. So the speaker shows them logically how the only decision consistent with their duty is against the developer.

Basis for Techniques of Persuasion

Successful techniques of persuasion are based on the ways people normally think when facing choices and making decisions. A person usually decides a certain way for one or more of three reasons. She may be convinced that the decision is rationally consistent with the facts, her beliefs, and her real self-interest. Or she may be so overcome by an emotion—such as anger, anxiety, pity, or strong desire (e.g., for the gooey dessert, although she is on a diet)—that she makes a decision without weighing the consequences rationally. Or she may decide a certain way because someone she trusts recommends that particular decision. Thus the persuader has three main modes of appeal: to convince the listeners through appeals based on real or apparent *logic*; to disturb them through appeals based on arousing *emotion*; to develop their trust in the speaker's *ethos*, or image as a reliable person.

Often a persuader must lead his listeners step by step through a line of reasoning, rather than simply throwing out arguments in random order. Thus the organization, or *structural strategy*, of the speech is also an important area of technique.

To use persuasive techniques effectively, the persuader begins by analyzing his audience and then shaping his general intent into a specific purpose that is appropriate for that audience and situation. This analysis of audience and clear definition of purpose then guide the speaker's use of modes of appeal and structural strategy.

Analyzing Audiences for Persuasion

You begin with the listeners where they are mentally in order to move them to where you want them. Your chances of consistent success in persuasion are greater if all through preparation you give considerable thought to three audience factors: the listeners' attitudes toward your topic, their motives that might be affected by the topic, and their beliefs in relation to the topic.

Audience Attitudes Toward Topic

You have a topic and a general position on it. Your topic is required attendance in all classes and you favor it. Or you favor greatly increased federal funds for space research. Or you are opposed to the use of credit cards. An initial step is to determine as well as you can your audience's attitude toward your position on the topic: Are they favorable to your position, neutral, or opposed? Often the simplest way is, when you begin preparing the speech, to ask some members of your future audience casually what they think about your topic, *and why*. This assumes that you can get to some prospective audience members days or weeks before you give the speech. Such is the case in your speech class and will be in many situations in later life. You may also try to guess listeners' attitudes from the groups to which they belong or because you are already familiar with similar audiences. If the audience is very mixed or unknown, then you may have to construct in your own mind an image of the target audience— those neutral or those mildly opposed, for example—on whom you will concentrate your persuasive efforts.

Favorable Audiences If you know *why* a favorable audience agrees with your position, you know what particular reasons to reinforce. If, for example, audience members are reluctant to use credit cards because they fear getting into debt, you can expand on the harms of too much debt and provide vivid examples of people who got too far in debt. You can also bring fresh arguments to provide listeners with even more reasons for their position. If you know *how strongly* the audience agrees with your position, you have some idea as to how much further you can push them. If the audience is only slightly reluctant to use the credit cards they own, it may be enough to firm up that reluctance. If, however, they already agree quite strongly with you in theory, you may be able to persuade some of them to destroy their credit cards.

Neutral Audiences Listeners may be neutral for several different reasons, and each reason suggests a somewhat different strategy for the persuader. If they are *unconcerned* about a topic, they may not be persuaded until you show how the topic affects their values or self-interest. Other audiences may be well informed and concerned but still *doubtful*, waiting to be convinced one way or the other. Because these listeners usually know both sides of the topic, the persuader must provide arguments that satisfy their specific doubts or objections to his position. To do that, he needs to know what those doubts or objections are.

Opposed Audiences   Are the opposed listeners personally involved and well informed on the topic? If so, their opposition to your position may be too firm to change very far, and you may have to settle for a specific purpose in the speech that is a compromise between your real position and theirs. For an audience strongly opposed to the required class attendance that the speaker favors, it may be enough in one speech to convince them that some students in some classes might have gotten better grades if they had been required to come to class. If the audience is less informed or concerned about the topic, you may be able to swing them all the way to your position.

Audience Motives

When listeners are asked to do something, they want to know what is in it for them. What motives of theirs will be satisfied if they accept your proposal? This applies whether they are asked to perform an action individually or to favor a particular course of action by some group—club, nation—of which they are a part.

Some of these motives—reasons we do the things we do—are crass and selfish; but many are also admirable, even idealistic. People, for example, are motivated by a desire to be good parents or to fulfill their responsibilities as employees or to demonstrate their courage or honesty.

To aid you in discovering audience motives that might be used in a particular speech, a list is provided—largely an expansion of a hierarchy of motives developed by Abraham H. Maslow in his book *Motivation and Personality*. Maslow's hierarchy suggests a useful notion for the persuasive speaker: a person is not very responsive to higher-level motives, such as esteem and self-actualization, as long as important lower-level motives, such as survival and security, are frustrated or threatened. It's hard to persuade a man to make his house an attractive part of the neighborhood if he is wondering how to feed his family. If you are urging students to take a particular course, you might appeal to academically confident listeners on the basis of new experience and self-actualization. However, for listeners who are worried about surviving in school you would do better to explain how with moderate effort one is almost sure of getting a good grade in that particular course.

When preparing a persuasive speech, you can scan this list, asking yourself which of these motives might yield reasons for listeners to accept the course of action you advocate.

1. Survival needs: food, warmth, and shelter; physical safety
2. Health: physical well-being, strength, endurance, energy; mental stability, optimism
3. Financial well-being: accumulation of wealth; increased earning capacity; lower costs and expenses; financial security

4. Affection and friendship: identification in a group; being accepted, liked, loved; being attractive to others; having others as friends or objects of affection
5. Respect and esteem of others: having the approval of others, having status in a group, being admired, fame
6. Self-esteem: meeting one's own standards in such virtues as courage, fairness, honesty, generosity, good judgment, and compassion; meeting self-accepted obligations of one's role as employee, child or parent, citizen, member of an organization
7. New experience: travel; change in employment or location; new hobbies or leisure activities; new food or consumer products; variety in friends and acquaintances
8. Self-actualization: developing one's potential in skills and abilities; achieving ambitions; being creative; gaining the power to influence events and other people
9. Convenience: conserving time or energy; the ease with which the other motives can be satisfied

To illustrate how this list of motives can be used, let's assume a speaker is attempting to convince listeners to buy a used large American-built car rather than a new smaller foreign import. A quick scan of the list might yield the following possible motive appeals: a larger, heavier car is safer (motive 1 on the list); the cost of the used car will be lower (motive 3) and replacement parts are usually cheaper (motive 3); buying an American car shows support for the nation (motive 6); the greater comfort of the car will be appreciated by the purchaser's family (motive 4); within a year or two, when both cars are used, the larger car will be more prestigious (motive 5); if one hasn't owned a large car, it's time to try out this luxury (motive 7); it is easier to get a common American-made car maintained and repaired (motive 9). Some of these appeals would be rejected as either too hard to prove or inappropriate for the particular audience, but the speaker has at least rather quickly discovered eight possible motive appeals from which to select.

Now try scanning motives 4 through 8 for arguments you might use to persuade listeners to undertake some volunteer work, such as being aides in a children's hospital. And an unusually resourceful discoverer of motive appeals might also argue that such volunteer work could pave the way for a good job later (motive 3) or provide access to some medical knowledge or advice (motive 2).

Audience Beliefs

You are sure you can persuade your friend to go to a public lecture by Kurt Vonnegut. After all, Vonnegut is certainly one of America's leading novelists. You are astonished by her response. She believes that Vonnegut is a minor writer who happens to be in vogue with a few weird college students. Your persuasion fails because the belief on which it rested was not present in your receiver's mind.

On almost any topic of which listeners have any knowledge, they will have certain beliefs, and the persuader must adapt his or her reasoning to those beliefs. Beliefs may be about *relatively specific facts*: Lawyer X was reported in the press to have defrauded his client of money won in a lawsuit. Student Y refused to cheat on the math exam when she could do so without fear of being caught. Beliefs may also be *broad generalizations*: Most lawyers are corrupt—or, conversely, most lawyers have high ethical standards. Students can be trusted to make an honor system work. Some of these beliefs are so broad and vague that they seem to bear little relation to verifiable facts. Yet they may represent an important part of reality to the believers: Hard work pays off. Or it's not what you do but who you know that gets you ahead in life. Finally, some beliefs are personal *value judgments* about what is good and true and important: Reading serious novels is good for one's personal development. Getting a higher salary is more important than liking the job. Tough competition is good for a society. Fairness is an important human virtue.

When a responsible persuader works out her own position on a topic, she bases that position on what *to her* are the verifiable facts and the generalizations reliably based on those facts. But when she turns to persuade members of an audience, she must begin with the ways *they* perceive and evaluate reality. She needs to know the audience's beliefs relevant to her topic for two main reasons.

First, some beliefs can be used directly to support her position. If the audience believes that most politicians are dishonest, this can be used to support the speaker's assertion that candidate Rinkle has no intention of keeping his campaign promises. If the audience members know of particular unemployed people who want to work, this can support the speaker's argument that most unemployed people would rather be at work.

Second, if the audience does not hold beliefs that are crucial to the speaker's position, then the speaker must provide arguments and evidence to develop those beliefs. In a speech urging aid for the jobless, if the listeners do not believe that people who lose their jobs really suffer, the speaker should provide evidence of such suffering. You might even try to convince your friend that Vonnegut is indeed a major author and therefore worth hearing.

Your understanding of the audience guides you in shaping your specific purpose as well as in devising the means for appealing to the audience.

Types of Persuasive Purposes

A speaker asks you to believe that there are prehistoric monsters swimming in Loch Ness in Scotland. What would cause you to accept this proposition?

You would probably want evidence. But if a speaker asks you to join the army, you are more likely to ask how it would satisfy your motives to do so. If a speaker asked you to believe that acid rock is good music, he would probably not be able to prove this in any objective sense nor would he find appeals to your motives very relevant. Rather he would have to discover some of your standards for good music—perhaps that it's inventive, lively, emotional, and so forth—and then show how acid rock meets these standards.

The point here is that in persuasion, specific purposes—stated as propositions—fall into different categories. Furthermore, the category into which a specific purpose falls tends to determine what sorts of appeals, support, and strategy are needed to get an audience to accept the proposition. One common set of categories is type of issue: *fact* (a monster in Loch Ness); *evaluative* (acid rock is good music); *policy* (join the army).

Propositions of Fact

Speeches urging propositions of fact attempt to persuade listeners that a central assertion about reality is true, or probably true, regardless of how the speaker or audience feels about it. Intelligent beings from outer space are flying around our planet. There are mysterious monsters in Loch Ness. Large federal budget deficits do cause higher interest rates. Smoking does greatly increase chances of cancer and heart disease. Such propositions are proved mainly by reasoning from real examples, expert testimony, statistics, and other evidence that is acceptable and significant to the audience.

With a proposition of fact, consider what *level of probability* you intend to prove. Often this is largely a matter of how you phrase your proposition in the speech. It is much easier to convince an audience that there *might* be a monster in Loch Ness than that there *is for sure*. It is easier to convince an audience that *most* doctors are ethical than to convince them that *all* are.

Propositions of Evaluation

Speeches urging propositions of evaluation attempt to persuade the audience to make a positive or negative *value judgment* about something. Intercollegiate athletic programs are good. Capital punishment is bad. Camping trips are fun. Camping trips are a boring waste of time. Ingmar Bergman is a great film director. Such propositions are proved mainly by showing how the subject in question meets listeners' standards for such a thing being good or fun or worthwhile or admirable. Conversely, if the speaker's purpose is to show that the subject is bad, harmful, evil, worthless, or otherwise inferior, he has to show how it falls far short or is the reverse of their standards. The Soviet Union's invasion of Afghanistan was an evil international act. It violated our standards for "good international acts"—that is, acts which promote rather than threaten world peace, which serve human interests rather than destroy people, which show restraint in the exercise of superior military force, which respect the sovereignty of nations. The speaker assumes that the audience accepts these as standards for good international acts, at least as applied to the case at issue. In order to prove that Kurt Vonnegut is a skillful novelist or that Federico Fellini is a great film maker you have to apply standards for "skillful novelist" or "great film maker" that your audience will accept.

Propositions of Policy

Propositions of policy almost always concern the future: what should we do or support others in doing. (Deciding whether something we have already done was good or bad is an issue of evaluation.) In a *public issue* we are asked to support, or oppose, a course of action by a group of which we are a member: increase local taxes; give our club's surplus money to charity; put federal money into military defense rather than space exploration; urge our college to establish free day-care centers for student parents. In a *private issue* we are asked to favor a personal policy: love our fellow persons; resolve to maintain regular study habits; decide to get more physical exercise.

We can make a further distinction between propositions that merely ask us to be in favor of a policy in *theory* and those that ask us to perform some *action* in support of that policy. We may favor in theory a policy of having fire detectors in our home, but this is not the same as our action in signing a contract to purchase them. We may favor the work of the Salvation Army (theory) but this is not the same thing as contributing money (action). The television commercial is not successful unless we eventually buy the brand of toothpaste being huckstered (action). And as you probably know, being in favor of diligent study hours (theory) is not the same thing as going to the books (action) when tempted to stay in conversation with friends. As a general rule, the need for strong motivational appeals is greatest when you ask people actually to do something.

As you may have guessed, on many topics it is easier to persuade the audience to accept the probability of an alleged fact, harder to persuade them genuinely to make an evaluative judgment or a policy decision in theory, and hardest to persuade them to action. A smoker may perhaps accept the speaker's proposition that smoking creates health hazards, and he may even be persuaded to favor a personal policy to stop smoking; but it is much harder to persuade him to throw the cigarettes away permanently. You may persuade your listeners that there could be some mysterious monster swimming around in Loch Ness. You may even get them to agree that expeditions about such phenomena are worthwhile. Now try to get them to act by contributing money to an expedition to Loch Ness! After the speaker has selected a topic, her decision on type of specific purpose is often influenced by her intended listeners' attitudes toward the topic. In this one speech can she move them only to belief or can she move them all the way to action?

After deciding on a specific purpose and framing a proposition, the speaker must then apply creativity and research to discover possible appeals to use in the speech.

Modes of Appeal

We have noted three main ways in which you bring an audience to accept your proposition: through logical reasoning, through arousing them emotionally, and through their faith in you as a reliable person. Different situations call for different types of appeals or combinations of appeals.

Logical Appeal

You use logical appeal in most cases to convince your audience that assertions in your speech are true in objective reality. Such assertions may deal with *past fact*: Vikings landed in America before Columbus. Or *present fact*: These artifacts found in New England are pre-Columbian Viking implements. Poor management is causing Exel Industry to lose customers. Or *future fact*: Earth will experience another ice age within the next seven thousand years. Or the assertion may be that a particular *action will satisfy rational motives*: Eating this sort of food will give you more energy.

Four Forms of Logical Proof   Whenever you must convince your audience of an assertion made in the speech, you have four main ways to do it. All four are simply ways of guiding the listeners in the reasoning processes we normally, though often subconsciously, use when we make decisions rationally.

Generalization.   If you broke out in a rash the last three or four times you ate strawberries you will probably decide that strawberries cause you to have a rash. We generalize from a few examples. Sometimes only one clearly valid and significant example will lead us to a conclusion: the auto mechanic charged us for new brake linings and never touched the brakes; we decide he is dishonest.

Similarly, a speaker can use *examples* to prove an asserted generalization. The number of examples needed depends on the particular assertion and the particular audience. Cynical listeners might require only one or two

Logical appeals can be persuasive because they show how your assertions are based on facts.
(Anna Kaufman Moon/Stock, Boston)

examples to convince them that Peace Corps members had been used as government agents. Those listeners with more faith in the ideals of the Peace Corps might require a dozen examples from reliable sources involving a wide variety of cases before they would accept the asserted generalization. Audiences are more likely to be convinced by examples they believe to be valid, significant, and typical cases of the generalization being asserted.

Statistics are a sort of shorthand method for stating large numbers of examples. Percentage statistics can also tell us how typical the examples are. A speaker asserts that many older citizens do not have the average income needed to pay major medical costs. He supports this by stating that 87 percent of the retired elderly live on incomes of $15,000 a year or less. This 87 percent not only covers millions of examples, it also states the proportion of examples—87 out of every 100—covered by the generalization. See Chapter 7, pages 121–123 for suggestions for using statistics effectively.

A speaker may also prove a generalized assertion by reasoning from *signs*. Blood on his face and clothes is a sign that Don has been in a fight. China's oil exploration agreement with U.S. firms is a sign that China desires friendly relations with the United States. Mary's frequent presence in the library with her books is a sign that she is a good student. As with examples, the audience must believe that there is a valid connection between the sign and the assertion it supports: only good students spend time in the library.

The essential notion in generalization is that you support your assertion with more specific data—such as examples, statistics, and signs.

Deduction.   The essential notion in deduction is that you support your assertion with a broader idea, or *premise*. This premise is usually a belief or value that the audience already accepts, and you apply this belief or value to the case at hand to draw a conclusion about that case. This conclusion is the assertion you are trying to prove.

> *Premise:* Dishonest mechanics are to be avoided.
> *Case at hand:* mechanic A is dishonest.
> *Conclusion* (the point you are asserting): Therefore, mechanic A should be avoided.

For a deductive argument to work effectively it should meet three standards. First, the audience must agree with the premise (dishonest mechanics are to be avoided). Second, they must believe what you say about the case at hand. If they do not believe that mechanic A is dishonest, your argument won't work. (You might set out to prove that mechanic A *is* dishonest, but that would require an additional, supporting argument, quite likely an argument by generalization from examples.) Third, they must believe that the premise does in fact apply to the case at hand. When all three requirements are met, deductive arguments are usually the most convincing proof you can offer for an assertion.

We rarely spell out deductive arguments fully and formally when we use them in speaking or writing, and the assertion (the "conclusion" part of the argument) often comes first in order when it is stated. If you were trying to persuade your friend, for example, you would probably say, "Avoid mechanic A. He's dishonest." Your friend subconsciously fills in the premise, "dishonest mechanics are to be avoided," and thus himself contributes part of the argument by which he is convinced to avoid mechanic A.

When you develop deductive arguments, you know the case at hand and what you intend to assert about it. Therefore, the challenge is to discover the premise, preferably in the listeners' minds already, that will lead them to the assertion you want them to accept. On almost any assertion you can discover some premise that will provide support. If you are against required attendance in freshman classes, you could argue from a premise of freedom of choice. If you favor such required attendance you could argue from a premise that the school has a responsibility to help students adjust to college.

Analogy.   What you assert about the case at hand is true because it is already known to be true in a similar case. This watch is reliable—because a similar watch purchased by a friend two years ago proved to be reliable. Assertions about what will happen in the future are often supported by *analogous cases* of what did happen in the past or is happening now in similar cases. If we don't stop this powerful nation in its small aggressions now, we will end up by fighting a major war to stop it—just as our failure to stop Hitler's Germany in its small aggressions in the late 1930s resulted in World War II. Close federal control over handguns will reduce murders and fatal gun accidents in this country—because nations, such as Great Britain and Japan, with close control over handguns have a much lower death rate from guns.

As this last instance suggests, argument by analogy is often the strongest support for the workability of a policy or solution you are proposing: it will work because it has already worked somewhere else. An honor system will work in the College of Arts and Sciences because it is already working in the College of Engineering.

Usually the existence of the analogous case itself is not likely to be questioned by the audience. Appeasement of Hitler did end in World War II. The honor system does work well enough in the Engineering College. What is likely to be questioned is that the two cases are similar enough to warrant believing that what happened in the analogous case will necessarily be true for the case at hand. Are there crucial differences between the two cases? "Gun control" in Great Britain consists of denying handgun ownership to most citizens; what is usually proposed in this country is registration of guns. The law in Britain was instituted when few guns were in private hands; in the United States there are millions of untraceable handguns owned by private individuals.

Often a persuader will strengthen the argument by explaining how the two cases are essentially similar, at least in regard to the point asserted about the case at hand. Or she will bring two or three analogous cases, rather than just one, to bear on the case at hand.

Expert Testimony.   Expert testimony is the most direct form of logical support for an assertion. The audience accepts your assertion because you cite an expert source who backs up your position on the particular point. Heavy smoking is a frequent cause of cancer and other illnesses because the Surgeon General's office says so. Such expert sources may be newspapers or magazines, government agencies, private organizations, and other impersonal groups, as well as individuals whose statements you have read or whom you have interviewed. Their reputation as experts may be nationwide or may not extend beyond your school. It may even be a fellow student who has had a special opportunity to observe whatever you are talking about.

Expert testimony is effective proof if the audience (1) has faith in the source's judgment and knowledge on this topic, (2) believes that you are stating the source's opinions accurately, and (3) believes that what the source said really does apply to your specific point.

The easiest way to use sources your audience will trust is to select ones they already know and respect. If your sources are unknown to the audience, briefly explain their credentials to show why they deserve trust on this particular subject. At the very least, you can avoid using sources that your audience is likely to reject as being incompetent on the subject, biased, outdated, or of poor character. And a source—a conservative economist, for example—that will seem highly competent and objective to one audience may seem to another audience to lack good judgment and be biased.

If the audience is likely to question the accuracy with which you represent the source's opinions, take special pains to quote the source word for word, in full context, and with a complete reference as to where the information came from.

If you find a reliable and esteemed source who says exactly what your major assertion says, you are lucky. More frequently, the support is less direct, on a subpoint perhaps, or agreeing that you might be right. Did astronomer Carl Sagan really say, with the speaker, that Earth is being visited by aliens from outer space? Probably not. Probably what he actually said is that there may be life in other solar systems. Speakers who value their own ethics as well as their reputation with the audience will distinguish clearly between what the source said and their own line of reasoning. It is also sometimes necessary to explain clearly how what a source said does support a key assertion of the speaker.

Using Logical Appeal in a Speech   A speaker wants to convince his student audience that gaining a knowledge of computer science will help them succeed professionally. From his brainstorming and audience analysis he finds two factors that his audience believes are marks of professional success. Thus for his main deductive arguments he has two premises:

> To have a lot of job opportunities is a mark of professional success.
> To be able to advance into a top-paying position is a mark of professional success.

Recall that when arguments are stated in the speech, the conclusion of the argument—the assertion to be proved—is often stated first. The central assertion of the speech is stated as the proposition. In each mainhead this speaker will make a statement about the case at hand—that is, about having a knowledge of computers. The audience will, presumably, mentally fill in the appropriate premise to complete the argument linking the mainhead as a reason to accept the proposition. So the speaker's basic outline for his speech will look like this:

> **Statement of proposition (assertion to be proved): A knowledge of computer science will help you succeed professionally.**
>
> I. A working knowledge of computers will give you more job opportunities.
> II. Computer knowledge qualifies a person to advance more rapidly into a top-paying position.

This speaker is sure that in the first argument his audience will mentally provide the premise, that having more job opportunities is a mark of professional success. He is, however, not at all sure they will accept his statement about the case at hand: that "a working knowledge of computers will give you more job opportunities."

Therefore for his first main argument to work, he must drop down one level in his outline and regard this first mainhead as itself an assertion requiring logical proof. Because it seems a very important point for his purpose, he uses four different items of logical proof:

I. A working knowledge of computers will give you more job opportunities when you graduate.
  A. As you know, any commonly used technical skill you can pick up on the side qualifies you for that many more jobs. And computers are certainly a commonly used skill. (Deductive argument.)
  B. Let me tell you about four specific students from fields as diverse as history and electrical engineering who were able to get the jobs they now hold because they had at least a couple of courses in computer science. (Argument by generalization.)
  C. Understanding computer programming is like being fluent in a foreign language: when a prospective employer needs that specific kind of communication and you are one of the few people available who can do it, you are likely to get the job. (Argument by analogy.)
  D. The manager of DeWitt employment agency tells me that the greatest single demand by employers is for people who are proficient in computer data base design and management. (Expert testimony.)

Through carefully considering both subject and audience, a speaker can become very shrewd in discovering relevant audience premises to apply in her arguments and in bringing strong supporting arguments and evidence to bear on exactly those steps where the audience might be doubtful. Such a speaker is indeed a formidably convincing persuader.

Emotional Appeal

A friend on her way to a party invites you to come along and have some fun. Having fun is a good idea, but you think you had better stay home and study for two exams coming up. The friend persists, reminding you how much fun you had at a similar party a couple of weeks earlier, pointing out how some relaxation this evening will make you more efficient tomorrow, mentioning some old friends who will be at the party, and describing a couple of interesting new people who will be there. You become increasingly dissatisfied with your decision to stay home and study, and finally you say, "Oh heck, tomorrow is another day. Let's go." You have been persuaded, primarily by emotional appeal. Thus one function of emotional appeal is *to intensify motives*—to make listeners want to have or do something more than they ordinarily would.

A second function of emotional appeal is *to create in listeners a strong emotional state*, such as anger, friendship, anxiety, optimism, guilt, or pity. This heightened emotional state will influence how the listeners interpret the evidence and other material offered in persuasion. As Aristotle noted, "The same thing does not appear the same to men when they are friendly and when they hate, nor when they are angry and when they are in gentle mood." Good trial lawyers understand Aristotle's point very well. A prosecuting attorney will try to make jury members angry about or fearful of the sort of person the defendant is. The jury members will then be in a mood to see feeble evidence as clear signs of guilt and to deal harshly with the defendant. The defense attorney will attempt to arouse pity for the defendant so that the jury members will be almost seeking reasons to find the defendant innocent or at least guilty of no great crime.

Both functions of emotional appeal may operate together in persuasive messages that rely heavily on emotional appeal. In addressing homeowners, a door-to-door salesperson for smoke detector alarms can intensify motives of self-preservation and meeting parental responsibility to protect their children. Through building on these motives and in addition vividly describing the disaster of undetected fire, the salesperson can create an emotional state of anxiety. The motives can be satisfied and the disturbing emotional state can be reduced only by signing a contract for immediate installation of smoke detectors. If things go well for the salesperson, the homeowners will be too disturbed to realize rationally that they could buy adequate smoke detectors in a store for a fraction of the price they are paying this salesperson.

Despite what the preceding examples may suggest, emotional appeals may be used for ethical purposes. Let's assume that just as you are about to go out the door to that party a true friend shows up. He points out that if you stay home and study you will go to sleep with a clear conscience and will do better on the exams, and he vividly describes how satisfying it is for you when you feel confident and get good grades. You decide to stay home and study after all. The friend has appealed to your more genuine and long-term motives, but he still had to intensify those motives to persuade you. A highly ethical and challenging use of emotional appeal is to persuade people to act in their own genuine, long-term interests rather than according to their short-term, more pleasurable inclinations.

Techniques for Developing Emotional Appeal   How can you intensify an audience's motives or move them into an emotional state? Of the many techniques for emotional appeal, we will look at three main sorts.

Amplify a Key Motive.   Seek out one or more key motives of your listeners that would be satisfied if they accepted your purpose. Often these are motives that your audience agrees with but doesn't feel strongly enough to act on. "Yes, I suppose I would be healthier if I stopped smoking." Or "It would be nice to have more money to spend rather than use it to pay interest on credit accounts." Your job is to make them feel that desire for good health so strongly that they will quit smoking or feel that desire for more spending money so strongly that they will make a temporary sacrifice in order to pay off their credit accounts.

To amplify a motive, provide several reasons for having or applying the motive. Often, you can think of these reasons as more specific motives and they can be supported by evidence and vivid description.

The speaker against smoking amplifies the key motive of appeal to good health: Heavy smoking tends to cause heart attacks; statistics are given in support. Heavy smoking tends to cause emphysema; would the listener want to spend the last several years of his life as a semi-invalid in pain? Heavy smoking causes lung cancer; the listener is reminded of three or four famous movie actors who were victims of lung cancer. Heavy smoking causes shortness of breath and lack of energy; doesn't the listener want to feel more vigorous?

Create Vivid Experience.   Motive appeals can be intensified by describing in specific detail how the motives will be satisfied if the listeners do what the persuader wants them to—*positive visualization.* In the following case the motives are security and self-esteem.

> You are in your kitchen when you notice across the street a van you haven't seen before. A few weeks earlier at a neighborhood get-acquainted party you learned at least the name and appearance of your neighbor. You don't recognize anyone in the van. Of course it could be relatives. Then again, it might not be. You act fast, first noting the license number and description of the van, then dialing the neighbor's telephone number. No one answers. You hang up and dial the emergency police number and report the occurrence and description. As you return to the kitchen your heart sinks because the van is backing out of the driveway. But halfway up the block it is intercepted by a police cruiser. Stolen property is identified. Not only have you saved the property of a neighbor but you have also caused the apprehension of a pair of burglars who might have hit your home next. Your participation in your neighborhood Crime Watch program paid off.

Although positive visualization often uses hypothetical examples, it may also use real examples from your research or personal experience.

Negative visualization can be used to describe in detail what will happen or continue if the audience does not accept the persuader's purpose. Such threat appeals can range from the frustrations of inefficiently cramming for exams (unless one accepts the speaker's proposition, to learn time management) to detailed examples of violent unexpected death (if one does not use seat belts).

A speaker can also use the vividly described scene or real or hypothetical example to arouse pity, indignation, or other emotional states. If we are emotionally disturbed by vivid description of tortures inflicted on helpless civilians by a foreign government, we may be predisposed to accept almost any arguments for cutting off aid to that government. For other suggestions, go back to the discussion of supporting material used for emotional impact in Chapter 7 (pp. 113–115).

Control Interpretation.   How we interpret and evaluate a person, organization, or event will often determine how we react to it emotionally or how we see it as affecting our motives. Some students might stay away from a "mean" teacher who "bosses the class like he thought he was Attila the Hun," but they might be attracted to a "firm" teacher who "runs a tight ship." It could be, of course, that two different speakers have simply described the same teacher.

A persuader can control her audience's view of some item in reality by her choice of language and detail when she refers to it, describes it, or explains it. An audience gets one sort of predisposition toward a child molester if during the speech the molester is referred to as "gravely ill," "a helpless victim of his own impulses," "a pathetic misfit in society." This predisposition is reinforced if the speaker emphasizes the molester's remorse and attempts to reform. The audience gets a very different emotional predisposition if the speaker refers to the child molester as "a moral degenerate," "a criminal attacking the most innocent and vulnerable of victims," "an uncontrollable pervert," and emphasizes the psychological damage done to the victims.

Appeal Through Ethos, or Personal Credibility

Audiences for persuasive speeches often do not have enough information to judge the content of the arguments. Thus the degree of faith listeners have in the speaker's personal credibility—or *ethos*—becomes a crucial factor in whether or not they are persuaded. Listeners' trust in a speaker is largely based on three things: Does the speaker seem knowledgeable and competent enough to form reliable judgments on this subject? Does the speaker seem to have good intentions toward us? Does the speaker seem to have honesty and other qualities of good character?

Your ethos comes from two sources: external and internal. *External sources* are those that operate before you rise to speak. *Internal sources* are those within the speech, both content and delivery.

External sources include the speaker's reputation, the organizations he is associated with or represents as far as the audience knows these, and the chairperson's introduction. External sources are important for two reasons. First, they can often be controlled to some extent by advance publicity and by the information the speaker provides for a chairperson's introduction. Second, the speaker may have to adapt during the speech to overcome weaknesses in external ethos. A student speaker who has so far given superficial speeches now really wants to persuade the audience on a topic that is important to him. He may make a special point to use in-depth factual information and to mention a variety of research sources and his personal connection with the topic to show that on this speech he is competent.

Internal ethos is a result of virtually everything a speaker does in the speech. Occasionally a listener will consciously think, "Yes, this speaker has the same beliefs that I do, and therefore I trust her opinion on this matter," or "I know those facts to be wrong; I don't trust this speaker," or "Anyone whose line of thinking is as garbled and rambling as that can't know what he is talking about," or "If he doesn't even look at me when speaking to me, I can't trust him." More commonly, however, the speaker's ethos comes from qualities in the speech that are recognized only subconsciously by the listeners. A skillful speaker can consciously plan ways to improve ethos during the speech.

How to Improve Internal Ethos   If you are well prepared and sincerely believe that your proposition is the best choice for your audience, you are more likely to appear credible even without giving special attention to ethos. You want, however, to avoid carelessly harming your ethos, and in some situations you face special challenges to demonstrate your competence or good intentions or good character.

Competence.   Almost any personal experience or training that is somehow related to the topic area can be tactfully mentioned. A student arguing against use of a particular food preservative, for example, should mention his premed major, preferably in the introduction or early in the body of the speech. Demonstrate knowledge of your specific topic also by abundant use of recent and accurate factual information from a variety of sources. Cite your sources briefly but explicitly. Interviews and direct observation especially should be mentioned.

An audience is more likely to trust your judgment if you avoid extreme assertions that you can't support very well and if you organize your material logically so that the audience can follow it easily. Also, the impression created by confident, fluent delivery is worth some extra rehearsal in situations in which demonstrating competence is especially important. For some audiences apt quotes, allusions to literature, and historical analogies indicate a breadth of background that the listeners subconsciously associate with intelligence. Avoid errors of fact and mispronounced names and terms.

Good Intentions.   You demonstrate good intentions when you take your listeners' motives and beliefs seriously. Show how your specific purpose is consistent with beliefs of the audience. Don't unnecessarily attack strongly held attitudes. For example, a speaker who makes a cynical remark about religion to a strongly religious audience, even just in passing, has made a costly and pointless mistake. Don't criticize the audience without including yourself in the criticism or at least seeming reluctant to think badly of the audience.

Listeners are much more likely to trust the intentions of a person with whom they can *identify*—that is, with whom they have much in common. How can you get your audience to identify with you? You can show that you have the same motives and the same values. "None of us trusts the Communists, but we still have to survive with them without blowing each other up." You increase identification by mentioning any points of background you have in common with the audience: age, sex, vocation or profession, ethnic or geographical origin, socioeconomic level, political or religious beliefs, schools or clubs, friends and enemies, and past experiences. Avoid mentioning points of background that will separate you from your target audience.

Audiences also trust the intentions of a speaker they like. They like a speaker who likes them. When you can do so honestly and appropriately, tell the audience you feel pleased or honored to be with them or tactfully praise them for their judgments or achievements. A bit of relevant humor or a pleasant facial expression helps.

As with most devices for enhancing ethos, these signs of good intentions should be made quickly, in passing. If the signs of good intentions or liking for the audience are labored so they become obvious, the audience may distrust you.

Good Character.   If an audience values compassionate concern for the welfare of others, then the speaker who shows herself as compassionate will be respected by that audience. Good character in this context means showing the traits of character that the audience in the particular situation values. One audience may admire a lofty, even impractical idealism in a speaker, but another audience may admire an almost cynical practicality.

One quality, however, seems almost universally respected in a speaker: sincere belief in what he or she is advocating. A wide, natural range of vocal variation and general intensity in delivery suggest sincerity, but these are hard to develop unless you really have convinced yourself of the truth and importance of your purpose. Fluency and other marks of careful preparation, including such small things as neatness in visual aids, suggest sincere concern with the topic. Perhaps the most direct and effective way to show sincerity is to explain why you are concerned with this topic and purpose.

When you face listeners who are doubtful or opposed to your position on the topic, take special care to seem fair-minded. Show you realize that reasonable people might hold positions other than your own. If you

Sincerity is a quality most audiences respect in a speaker. (Adolahe/Southern Light)

consider those positions in order to refute them, state the positions accurately and fairly. Avoid dogmatic, extreme statements. Restraint in choice of language and in delivery mark the speaker who is objective and thoughtful, qualities that are respected by informed neutral or doubtful listeners.

Structural Strategy in Persuasion

An airline executive announces to his pilots that they will have to take a cut in pay. Then he gives reasons, attempting to convince the pilots that the cut is just and necessary. He faces an uphill battle because the pilots are hostile from the initial announcement. A shrewder airline executive begins by explaining that the company is facing some financial difficulties. She explains that management has had to take some cuts in pay. Now, for the company to survive and everybody to keep their jobs, she must ask the pilots also to take a cut in pay. Both speakers have the same proposition: pilots, be willing to take a cut in pay. And both might use generally the same arguments. But the second speaker stands a much better chance of getting the pilots to cooperate with the pay cut *because of the structural strategy she used*. In this case, she paved the way for a proposition her audience would find unattractive by *first* making them aware of the problem that necessitated the pay cut, by getting on common ground (showing that management also was willing to take a pay cut), and by gently reminding the pilots that their own self-interest was tied to the existence of the company. As in this case, success in persuasion may depend on the sequence, or pattern, of ideas through which the speaker leads the audience step by step to the desired conclusion.

Stating the Proposition

In informative speeches, you typically reveal your specific purpose in a statement of focus in the introduction of your speech. Yet the second airline executive in the preceding example shrewdly did not reveal her purpose until late in the speech. Unlike what is typical in informative speeches, the speaker's real purpose in many persuasive strategies is not stated until late in the body of the speech or in the conclusion, and in some persuasive strategies the real purpose may not be stated at all. In persuasion, this statement to the audience of the speaker's real purpose is called the *statement of proposition*.

When the statement of proposition comes late in the speech, the persuasive speaker still needs to give the listeners some sense of what the speech is about, the focus, usually at the end of the introduction. The second airline executive, for example, after a few introductory remarks, might have stated the focus of her speech: "I intend to explain some of the steps the company has taken and must take to maintain financial stability." This *statement of focus* is not the same as her *statement of proposition*, which will occur late in the body of the speech: "Now, difficult as it is, I must request that you pilots take an average fifteen percent reduction in pay."

The persuasive speaker has three options in stating the proposition. First, for a direct, straightforward organizational strategy the speaker states his real purpose at the end of the introduction as a statement of proposition. Since this also establishes the focus for the speech, there is no additional statement of focus. Second, when the statement of proposition is delayed until later in the speech, the speaker needs *also* to use a statement of focus in the introduction; *both* are used in the speech. Finally, if the real purpose is never stated, the speaker will use a statement of focus in the introduction but no statement of proposition in the speech.

Adapting Strategy to Purpose and Audience Attitudes

How do you decide which pattern, or strategy, to use? One important consideration is the type of specific purpose you have. A proposition of fact may be most efficiently proved by a list of three or four main arguments each supported by evidence, much like the structure of a typical informative speech. A proposition of policy, on the other hand, may profit by a more subtle structure, in which listeners' motives or values are first aroused and then later in the speech linked to the proposed policy.

Often, the most important factor when you decide on your organization is the listeners' attitude toward your specific purpose. The following are general suggestions for adapting to each audience type.

Favorable to Speaker's Purpose   If the speaker elects merely to reinforce the audience's present views, his chief challenge is to make the familiar position more interesting, vivid, and compelling. He does this mainly by bringing up new reasons and by using detailed examples, imaginative comparisons, visual aids, and other supporting materials with high interest value to support both the new and the familiar reasons.

A common pattern for this sort of speech is, after the introduction and statement of proposition, simply to give one reason and develop it, then to give a second reason and develop it, and so forth. This *list of reasons* pattern has the advantage of being clear, and the speaker usually has no reason to be subtle.

Interested in the Topic but Somewhat Doubtful About Your Purpose
Listeners in an audience may be interested in the topic and range from tending in your direction to being mildly opposed. They are open-minded enough at least to consider your position. Because they are seeking a decision, you do best to get to the point quickly and provide reasons for your position clearly and efficiently. Some of these reasons may be selected to overcome the audience's particular objections to acceptance of your position, such as their doubts about the workability of your plan. You may also want early in the speech to establish grounds of common agreement between you and the audience.

Unconcerned and Neutral Toward Your Purpose   When an audience is unconcerned and neutral toward your purpose, your first task as speaker is to penetrate their wall of indifference. If a speaker begins by stating that she will advocate low-interest, guaranteed loans to farmers, most listeners are likely to start thinking about something else more interesting. If she first explains that large-scale farm failures will drastically increase the prices her listeners pay for food, and *then* tells them of her proposal to avoid this, she will probably have a more interested audience.

As this example suggests, one common way to get an audience interested is to show how their important motives are affected by the situation under discussion. It is sometimes possible to move an audience all the way from initial indifference to final action by emphasizing strong appeals to motives throughout the sequence of the speech.

With propositions of fact and value, it may not be possible to appeal to audience motives; but a speaker can often arouse interest and create a favorable understanding of the topic by giving background information before going into arguments that may be relatively technical. Before presenting arguments that the Shroud of Turin is the burial cloth of Christ, for example, a speaker should provide some explanation of what the shroud is alleged to be, its significance if it is authentic, and serious scientific investigation conducted on it so far. The audience is then more likely to be interested in the speaker's reasons for the shroud's authenticity.

Opposed to Your Purpose   In planning structural strategy in a situation where the audience is opposed to your purpose, your foremost aim is to avoid crystallizing the audience's opposition before they have heard at least part of your reasoning. The young woman says to her parents, "You have urged me to become self-reliant and to face up to how the real world is." The parents nod in agreement. She continues, "I'm sure, then, you will agree with my plan to move into an apartment, drop out of college, and take a job in a fast-food restaurant."

When facing an opposed audience, you are likely to delay stating your proposition until the middle or end of the speech. And in some situations you may be able to provide information supporting your position on the topic without ever stating your proposition.

Patterns of Organization for Persuasive Speeches

How can you work out a plan of organization to fit your specific purpose and target audience? One way is to work intuitively from scratch, following some of the general suggestions given earlier. In many situations, however, you can use a shortcut: Mold your material to fit a conventional pattern that has already been shown to work in that particular sort of situation. Before we consider some of the most frequently used patterns, let's look at a table that suggests how each pattern may be particularly appropriate for certain purposes and audience types. The table is meant to be *only suggestive*. It's a place to start when you are searching for a way to organize your material, but you may modify one of these patterns or even work out a plan that isn't on this list.

The "favorable audience" is not included in the table; the "list of reasons" pattern will almost always work well for any sort of purpose with favorable listeners, although you might want to use some other patterns just for variety or interest.

Purpose	Audience Interested, Doubtful	Audience Unconcerned, Neutral	Audience Opposed
Fact	List of reasons	Information-proof	Apparent speech of information
Evaluation	Applied criteria— direct	Information-proof	Apparent speech of information
Policy-theory	List of reasons, or problem-solution, or applied criteria	Problem-solution	Applied criteria— delayed
Policy-action	List of reasons (focus on removing objections or on motives)	Motivated sequence	Applied criteria— delayed

Introductory material and a conclusion would be added to any pattern described here except the motivated sequence. (In the motivated sequence the special functions of the introduction and conclusion are built into the pattern itself.)

In the discussion that follows, the patterns are arranged roughly in order from most direct to most subtle.

List of Reasons Pattern   In the list of reasons pattern, the specific purpose is stated clearly as a proposition at the end of the introduction. Each main section in the body of the speech develops a reason for that proposition. The reasons may be blocks of argument proving the proposition, ways in which acceptance of the proposition would satisfy audience motives or values, or points of refutation. Support for each reason may range from vivid examples for a favorable audience to evidence and logical argument for a more doubtful audience. The pattern is direct, clear, and efficient.

The parent-teachers association is debating the value of routinely teaching competitive sports in grades four through eight. Most of the parents are interested and reasonably open-minded. They have been swayed somewhat by a preceding speaker who argued that teaching competitive sports would make less athletically talented students feel inferior. Smith is in favor of the competitive sports. After an introduction in which he reminds the audience that he is as interested as anyone in the feelings of his children and that he can be objective because his children have not demonstrated any particular athletic talent, he states his purpose:

Statement of proposition (and of focus)	I think we should support teaching competitive sports to all students regularly in grades four through eight.
First reason, as defense against preceding speaker	I. In this program no student would have to feel inferior, because a great range of types of sports would provide something for everyone.
Second reason, appeal to ambition of some parents for their children	II. This program would enable students with unusual physical talent to gain self-confidence and begin to develop their special abilities.
Third reason, appeal to motive of children's physical well-being	III. This program would guarantee that every one of our children would get at least some healthy physical exercise.

Each point would be explained more fully. For example, in section II the speaker would appeal to fairness by pointing out that students with unusual talent in music and academic subjects have opportunities to excel in the lower grades. The speaker might conclude by summarizing his main points. Note that Smith begins by refuting the preceding speaker's argument. As long as the audience is swayed by that argument they are less likely to be open to Smith's other arguments, so he refutes it first. When you don't have to worry about refutation, you generally want to begin and end with your strongest arguments. Smith's last argument (section III) is likely to register with more of his listeners than is his middle argument (section II).

Problem-Solution Pattern   In the problem-solution pattern, your specific purpose—the solution—may be announced at the end of the introduction, but usually you announce it at the beginning of the solution section. You begin by focusing the audience's concern on the problem, often by emotional appeal or by showing how it affects their motives and values. If necessary, explain why the problem exists or how significant it is in scope. Make the audience want a solution. Then give them the solution, which is your proposition. A speaker advocating state-funded shelters for abused wives might spend two-thirds of her speech proving with statistics and vivid examples that a serious problem exists, before stating her proposition.

In the following example, the speaker began by knowing her specific purpose: to bring the audience to favor a joint U.S.-U.S.S.R. manned space flight to Mars. After discovering possible appeals in support of this policy, she decided on one major argument: such a cooperative endeavor would reduce tension between the United States and the Soviet Union, tension that she would describe as a dangerous problem. She also decided that she would stand a better chance with doubtful listeners if she laid some groundwork of argument before stating her proposition. She decided to use a problem-solution pattern.

Statement of focus.	Today, let's think about relations between the United States and the Soviet Union. (Do we have a problem?)
Problem	I. I submit that we do have a serious problem in the extreme tensions between the United States and the Soviet Union. A. These tensions affect all of us.
Effects of problem explained as harms and threats to audience motives.	1. The cost of increasing military preparedness comes out of our own taxes. 2. We face the psychological stress of threats to our oil supply and other vital imports. 3. Over all is the danger of ultimate devastation in nuclear war. B. One cause of these tensions is the feeling that we are inevitable enemies, incapable of true cooperation. C. Without some dramatic change in relations between our two countries it appears that these conditions will only get worse.
	(Therefore I propose such a dramatic change in order to reduce this problem.)
Statement of proposition, as solution.	II. I propose that the United States and the Soviet Union jointly conduct a manned space flight to Mars.

Refutation of possible listeners' objections to cost and plausibility of solution.	A. With a commitment of thirty billion dollars, a small fraction of our military budget, it is technologically feasible. B. The 1975 link-up of the *Apollo* and *Soyuz* spacecraft showed that it is politically feasible.
Confirmation that solution will reduce (or eliminate) problem.	C. Cooperation between our two nations in the greatest endeavor of the century would reduce the feeling of inevitable enmity and the resulting costs and dangers.

Normally the conclusion summarizes the problem and the solution, and it may end with a final plea for commitment to the proposed policy.

In problem-solution speeches, more frequently than in other persuasive speeches, you are likely to make assertions about cause-effect relationships that are debatable. You may assert, for example, that certain harmful conditions are the effects of causes which your proposed solution would eliminate. In a speech proposing legalization and medical treatment of drug addicts, the speaker might assert, in the problem section, that much burglary is caused by drug addicts supporting their illegal habit. If such asserted cause-effect relationships are likely to be questioned by the audience they must be proved just like any other assertions, using the forms of logical proof discussed earlier in this chapter. For example, the speaker asserting that much burglary is caused by illegal drug addiction might cite examples or statistics showing that burglars are often drug addicts and he might cite expert testimony from law enforcement officials.

In cause-effect assertions, the speaker should avoid overly simplistic reasoning that the audience will find unacceptable. A listener might reasonably ask: "Can the asserted cause alone be sufficient to produce the observed effect?" or: "Will the policy or action proposed be sufficient to produce the alleged desired effects?" In addition to using logical proof to fortify soft spots in causal reasoning, the speaker may have to qualify the assertion to make it more realistic. In the speech urging a joint U.S.-U.S.S.R. space flight to Mars, the speaker asserted only that *one* cause of tension between the two nations was a feeling that we are inevitable enemies (I.B.); and she asserted only that her proposal would *reduce*, not eliminate, this feeling (II.C.).

Motivated Sequence Pattern   The motivated sequence pattern is designed primarily to lead a relatively unconcerned listener all the way to action. When a door-to-door salesman tells you that you have been selected to receive a free gift, he gets your attention; and if you end up buying a vacuum cleaner or some magazines that you didn't really need, you have probably been persuaded by something close to this pattern. The complete pattern as popularized by Alan Monroe follows a rather rigid five-step sequence: First, get the listener's *attention*. Second, make him feel that strong motives are being or will be frustrated if a particular *need* is not met. Third, propose a policy as *satisfaction* for that need. Fourth, *visualize* the listener in a happy state of affairs if he will act on that policy. Fifth, urge him to take *action*.

A basic outline for a motivated sequence follows. Like most uses of this pattern, it divides the entire speech into five main sections corresponding to the five steps in the sequence. The "attention" step is the introduction, the "action" step is the conclusion.

Attention	I. Are you being cheated out of several hours of your life every week by an addiction that seems harmless?
Need (statement of focus)	II. Many of us are heavily addicted to watching television—lots of it—for entertainment.
(need amplified by showing harms to motives and values of listeners)	A. This addiction does some bad things to us. 1. It wastes a lot of time. 2. According to some experts it increases stress rather than relaxing us. 3. We lose some freedom and individuality because we have to watch the same sorts of things everyone else watches. B. We often allow this addiction because television is the only convenient recreation.
	(How can we replace this addiction?)
Satisfaction	III. We could choose to read something instead of watch television. A. We just need to have something interesting at hand to begin to switch our habit to reading. B. With a bookstore or library available, we have literally thousands of choices.

Visualization	IV. When you feel like relaxing, instead of switching on the boob tube hoping to find something watchable, sit down with a magazine, or a book.

Visualization

IV. When you feel like relaxing, instead of switching on the boob tube hoping to find something watchable, sit down with a magazine, or a book.

A. You feel in charge because you are choosing what interests you personally.

1. Maybe it's escapist fun: examples of escapist sorts of reading.

2. Maybe you are following up on something you have always wanted to know about: examples of some classmates' personal interests.

B. You also choose when to read, and after you have relaxed you can put the book aside knowing that your choice will be waiting for you tomorrow.

Action (statement of proposition)

V. So today pick out a book or magazine to read the next time you need convenient, relaxing entertainment.

On some topics, the pattern may require logical evidence, as in step II of this example; but the pattern operates primarily by keeping a high level of interest and by triggering motives as strongly as possible, especially in the "need" and "visualization" steps. The primary function of the first step is to capture the listeners' attention, usually by citing a threat to their motives or values, providing surprising information that relates to them personally, or arousing curiosity. Although a focus on some "need" is established in the second step, the statement of focus is likely to be less obvious than in most other patterns. The third step, "satisfaction," provides any necessary explanation of how the proposed policy would work in theory. The "action" step, or proposition, may call for only a strong mental commitment; but often, as in the speech on reading for recreation, the speech will be fully effective only if some of the listeners actually carry out the action being urged.

Applied Criteria Pattern   Although there are several variations on the applied criterion pattern, they all operate basically by first setting forth the criteria, or standards, for an ideal choice among alternatives and then showing how the speaker's proposal meets these criteria—if not perfectly, at least better than any other alternative. This proposal may be a policy to be accepted or to be acted on. Or it may be a proposition of value: to prove that *Apocalypse Now* is a great film by first setting forth the criteria for "greatness" in a film and then showing how *Apocalypse Now* meets these criteria. The pattern can also be used for a proposition of fact: to explain what climatological factors would indicate a significant warming trend in Earth's climate, and then show that those factors are now present.

The persuader has to do two things if the pattern is to be fully effective. First, he must select criteria that his audience will accept as the most appropriate ones for judging the item or policy at issue. For policy or action issues, these criteria are often motives or values: What investment will give me the greatest profit and security? Second, the speaker, must demonstrate that his proposal meets the criteria at least better than any other choice would.

The pattern may be used as a *direct* strategy with a favorable or neutral audience. The statement of proposition appears at the end of the introduction: "I'm going to show why Bergman is a great film director." The first main section of the body explains the criteria for greatness, the second main section shows how Bergman meets these criteria.

Or the pattern may be used as a *delayed proposition* strategy with a doubtful or opposed audience. At the end of the introduction, the issue at hand is stated as a focus for the speech; but not until the conclusion of the speech, after the criteria have been laid out and applied, does the proposition appear. Here is the framework for a speech urging students to vote for an increase in activity fees that they now oppose.

Introduction

I. The administration should hardly be surprised that we students are angry over the proposed forty dollar a year increase in student activity fees.

II. Many of us feel we aren't getting much for our money now.

Statement of focus   III. I propose that we resolve this fee increase issue in a way that is best for most students.

Body

Explain proposal at issue   I. The proposed increase would add about a third to the fees we now pay.

A. Present fees go mostly for big-cost items like health facilities and intercollegiate athletics.

B. Added fees would go for a bigger range of relatively low-cost items like movies, concerts, speakers, and intramural sports.

Criteria (should be accepted by and important to audience)

II. Our decision should be based on three aims.

A. We should do what is *fairest* for all students.

B. We should recognize students' right to *freedom of choice*.

C. We should ensure that each student gets *the most for his or her money*.

Show how proposal meets criteria

III. Let's look at the fee increase in relation to our three aims of fairness, freedom of choice, and most value for our money.

A. Because the increase would provide a broader range of activities, students who don't like to watch major sports would be more likely to get at least something for their money. This is fairer for all students.

B. It would provide each of us more choices among the entertainment and cultural events we could attend free.

C. The combined buying power of all our students times forty dollars would bring in so many events that anyone who really took advantage could get several times forty dollars worth of free entertainment alone.

Conclusion

I. I admit that the fee increase is not a welcome addition to college cost.

Summary of ways in which proposal meets criteria	II. But if you think about it objectively, it will mean that more students will get something for their fee money, and any one of us will have a greater choice and a chance to get much more for the money, most of which we would have to pay anyway.
Statement of proposition	III. So let's support the fee increase.

Section I of the body, explanation of the proposal at issue, may be omitted if the issue is simple and is already understood by the audience. In many cases, however, especially if the policy or other item being evaluated is complicated, explaining the issue before you evaluate it increases your apparent objectivity and knowledge of the topic.

An applied criteria pattern may also be used to compare two policies or other items. In the first main section of the body of the speech, for example, a speaker might set up criteria for an ideal way to handle juvenile offenders: it would change the offenders into good citizens; it would protect society; and it would be cheap and efficient. In the last main section of the body two solutions—closely supervised probation versus training in a detention facility—would be compared in relation to each criterion, with one solution clearly meeting the criteria better than the other solution. Or the criteria for a public office could be set forth and then two candidates evaluated against the criteria.

Apparent Speech of Information Pattern   A persuasive speech may provide information about the topic from which the listeners appear to draw their own conclusions. The speaker's persuasive purpose, or proposition, is never stated. Examples, statistics, and other data are grouped into three or four sections under appropriate main headings. The speech resembles an ordinary informative speech. However, the main points and supporting materials are selected by the speaker to lead the listeners to the conclusion he desires. If the strategy works successfully, the listeners feel more confident of their decision because they feel they have made it themselves.

The following sample outline deals with a proposition of fact. If the speaker had announced, "I'm going to convince you that huge prehistoric beasts are living in a lake in Scotland," she would probably get a very cynical response from most of her audience. Who, however, can object to a speaker who simply wants to tell about the curious phenomenon of people thinking they see a monster out in a lake? After an introduction that establishes some background information, the speaker says:

Statement of focus

This morning I'd like to describe attempts to explain this alleged monster in Loch Ness.

I. The history of sightings and attempted explanations goes back at least fifteen hundred years.
II. In recent times, serious scientific expeditions have investigated the alleged monster.
III. Photographs, sonar records, and other secondary physical evidence have accumulated.
IV. Two main theories have been advanced to explain where such animals might have come from.

The conclusion of the speech does *not* state the speaker's real purpose: to convince the audience that large beasts probably live in Loch Ness. Rather, she simply states that it is an interesting phenomenon and then summarizes her main points: there have been alleged sightings by responsible people for centuries, serious scientists have assumed the creatures might exist, and so forth.

Similarly, a speaker dealing with a proposition of evaluation might never state his real purpose: to increase respect for police officers.

Statement of focus

Let me describe a typical career in the city police force.

I. The rookie has to pass a rigorous six-month training program.
II. The routine duties require a wide range of skills.

Especially in this section specific examples are used to make points vivid.

III. A police officer faces special challenges.
    A. The officer must deal with some very unpleasant situations such as bad car accidents.
    B. The officer risks being killed on duty.

Such speeches are sometimes given for purposes of public relations by representatives of a company or other organization. While apparently informing listeners of some facet of the company, the speaker's real purpose is to produce a positive evaluation of the company. A spokesperson for an electric company, for example, may explain how the company's investment in nuclear generating capacity will help it meet future needs of the community. The real but unstated purpose is to demonstrate the company's wisdom and concern for its customers.

For a policy purpose, the speaker may describe a general type of situation with the intention that the listener will apply the content of the speech to his or her own situation. For example, a speaker may give an "informative" speech describing how a group of students profited by getting involved in local politics. The unstated intent of the speech is to persuade each audience member to become involved in local political campaigns. The general situation may be a negative one—for example, a speech describing the life style of a "typical" hard-drug addict, with the intent that each listener will choose to avoid that life style.

Information-Proof Pattern   In the information-proof pattern, what begins as an apparent speech of information may have the persuasive purpose stated explicitly in the body of the speech, and the last parts of the speech may develop persuasive proofs more directly. For example, the speaker on the Loch Ness monster could have followed the first three main sections with a major transition plus statement of proposition asserting that all these sightings, interested scientists, and other evidence are proof of the probable existence of creatures in the lake. She might have added a fourth main section refuting the listeners' likely objection: if the monsters exist why have no physical remains been found?

Planning a Persuasive Speech

In a successful persuasive speech the specific purpose, modes of appeal, and organizational strategy are selected and adapted to persuade the particular audience. How do you put such a speech together? The six-step process described in Chapters 4 through 9 can be adapted to the needs of the persuasive speaker.

Step 1: Decide on a Specific Purpose   Decide clearly what you want the audience to believe or do as a result of this particular speech. As with informative speeches, you often begin by deciding on, or being assigned, a topic area and then from that topic area shaping a specific purpose for the particular speech.

In this step also begin the analysis of your audience's attitudes, motives, and beliefs in relation to your topic. Analysis and adaptation to the audience will continue throughout preparation. At this point you especially want to form some idea of the attitude of the listeners on your topic, so you will know how far you may be able to persuade them in one speech.

As you reduce your topic to a more precisely focused purpose, you may want to take only a narrow part of your original topic. For example, a general purpose urging increased space exploration might be narrowed to a specific purpose urging that money be committed to a full-scale unmanned probe of Venus. You may want to reduce your general purpose in another way: try to move your audience, in one speech, only part of the way to your ultimate purpose. An audience strongly committed to the other candidate is not likely to be persuaded to switch to your candidate in one speech; but you could at least inform them of some of the accomplishments of your candidate in order to soften up their resistance to him.

Attempt to prove only what is needed to accomplish your ultimate purpose. Don't try to convince a doubtful audience that utility companies are entirely evil when all you need to do is convince them that a particular rate increase should not be granted.

Step 2: Discover Ideas and Materials to Use   As you search your mind, jot down notes for these sorts of material: arguments and other appeals you could base on audience beliefs and values, examples from your personal experience and marks of your personal credibility, sources you could go to, and any other ideas that might make your speech interesting or convincing to these particular listeners. The arguments and other reasons that convince you may not necessarily convince your audience, but they are one place to start. Use audience analysis and a list of general motives, such as those given earlier in this chapter (pp. 203–204), to discover audience motives to which you can appeal. Can you determine specific objections your listeners have that must be overcome if they are to accept your specific purpose? Are they, for example, likely to think your plan wouldn't work, or would cost too much, or would be unethical? How might you overcome these objections?

Use research to suggest ideas and to provide support for your major appeals. Although the library is often your quickest source of evidence, interviews may produce more interesting expert testimony and more recent other evidence. Observations, interviews, and such chance sources as newspaper stories and conversations may produce dramatic real-life examples for purposes of interest and emotional appeal.

Step 3: Plan the Basic Strategy of the Speech   In this step you *select the major arguments and other appeals* you will use, and you decide on the *pattern of organization* for the speech. Selection and patterning are interwoven processes, but you can usually start by isolating in your notes what seem to be the strongest reasons for the audience to accept your specific purpose and by considering the audience's attitudes toward that purpose. Can you, for example, simply state your proposed policy and then give reasons why it will work and has advantages, or must you first intensify the listeners' concern with the problem and then lead them to your solution.

The earlier section "Structural Strategy in Persuasion" provides you options and guidelines for deciding on a pattern.

Within this pattern, select major points that will be persuasive with your particular audience. A speaker decides to use a problem-solution pattern to persuade an audience that stronger laws are needed against the sale of child pornography. In the problem section, the speaker knows she must show that the child pornography is significantly harmful. To an investigative committee she can show how large a problem it is—that is, how many children are involved and how large the volume of such material is. She may also prove that there are psychological harms to children, to consumers of the material, or to both. This would be primarily a logical approach, relying on expert testimony, statistics, and other evidence. If the speaker, however, faced a strongly moralistic audience, she might take a different approach to arousing concern with the problem: Arouse emotions of pity and indignation with vivid descriptions of individual victims of child pornography rings, and emphasize how offensive the whole business is to strongly held audience values. To parents of young children she might in her problem section emphasize the dangers of children being abducted or tricked into such activities.

From such decisions emerges the pattern of mainheads and major subheads for the body of your speech.

Step 4: Fill in the Supporting Detail   Set in place the detailed examples, analogies, statistics, expert testimony, and other support needed to make each major point in the speech work effectively with your particular audience. Do you have evidence to convince your listeners at each point requiring logical proof in the speech? At what points in the speech do you want to intensify motives or arouse emotions? As you fill in detail, look for opportunities to improve your ethos by mentioning your sources or personal connections with the topic.

Step 5: Final Planning   For most of the organizational patterns described earlier in this chapter, you need to add an introduction and a conclusion. In persuasion, the most important introductory functions are usually to arouse audience interest in the topic and to develop your ethos with the audience. Most commonly, the conclusion will summarize the main arguments from the speech, make the central idea of the speech memorable by a vivid example or apt quote, or urge action or commitment to action.

To increase clarity and force in the body of the speech, work on transitions and on phrasing key headings. The importance of using transitions to make the organization clear to the audience varies according to the type of speech. A speaker relying mainly on impassioned emotional material may shrewdly calculate the organization of the speech but want to conceal that planning from the audience. On the other hand, in speeches depending mainly on logical appeals it is usually important that the listeners see and remember your key arguments for the proposition and that they follow your line of reasoning clearly. To emphasize main ideas and clarify organization, you use the sorts of transitions described in Chapter 8.

Before turning your working notes and drafts into a final outline, go through the speech aloud to check length and to see if you can improve structure or supporting material, as you would for an informative speech.

Step 6: Rehearsal and Delivery   The lively, confident, conversational delivery described in Chapter 9 is a good standard to start with in persuasive speaking, and the suggestions for rehearsal given there are also serviceable. But in persuasion you often have a greater opportunity to affect your audience through delivery. Also, different situations call for different sorts of delivery and style of language. The impassioned, aggressive delivery and style that would inspire a favorable audience might further antagonize an opposed audience in a tense situation. With a doubtful or opposed audience you often get further by using a restrained, reasonable tone in submitting your case for their consideration, rather than by dogmatically asserting your arguments.

Whether your mode of delivery is reasonable or impassioned, mean what you say. Remind yourself of your own belief in your purpose during rehearsals and when you give the speech. Rethinking the arguments, the vivid examples, and the other appeals with which you intend to persuade the audience can also persuade you anew.

Experiment with language. Earlier in this book it was explained that the words you select can influence how your audience sees and evaluates the reality you are talking about and that such devices as parallelism, rhetorical questions, and metaphor can make ideas more interesting, forceful, and memorable. This is also true of the rhythms into which you break sentences and groups of sentences. A speaker who had planned to say, "Interfering in that country's internal war will make us look bad to our allies and it will waste money for no good reason," found herself saying, "If we interfere in this country we become aggressors. We anger our friends. We waste tax dollars. We risk our soldiers. And what do we gain?"

In some speaking situations you will face the possibility of questions from the audience. An experienced speaker welcomes such question periods and may leave openings in her speech that invite questions for which she has carefully prepared "spontaneous" answers. In any case, try to anticipate and prepare replies to questions you might get, especially on the most vulnerable points of your speech. When answering questions, whether anticipated or not, keep a cool perspective on the situation. Don't be angered or drawn into a foolish debate with an audience member. Try to make your own case stronger with each answer. Be brief in each response.

Summary

Effective persuasion is guided by adaptation to the listeners' attitudes concerning your topic, to their motives, and to their beliefs related to your topic. Persuasive techniques should also be appropriate to the type of proposition urged by your speech: fact, evaluation, policy-theory, or policy-action.

Audiences are persuaded through three modes of appeal. Logical appeals convince listeners of the speakers' assertions by using generalizations from more specific information, deductions from general premises, analogies with known cases, and expert testimony. Emotional appeals intensify motives and influence emotional states by amplifying key motives, by creating vivid experience, and by controlling the interpretation of reality through choice of language and detail. Ethos appeals promote the listeners' faith in the speaker's competence, good intentions, and good character.

Structural strategy for a speech is determined partly by the type of proposition and partly by audience attitude toward your purpose: favorable, interested but doubtful, unconcerned, or opposed. Common organizational patterns include: list of reasons, problem-solution, motivated sequence, applied criteria, apparent speech of information, and information-proof. The proposition of the speech may be stated directly at the end of the introduction, delayed until the middle or end of the speech, or never stated at all.

The six-step process for creating and presenting a speech, as described in Chapters 4 through 9, may be adapted to the needs of the persuader.

Exercises

1. Prepare and present a four- to six-minute persuasive speech on a topic of your choice. Be prepared to meet audience objections and questions on the content of your speech. In your preparation, apply both the general techniques for speech preparation from earlier chapters and the special techniques for persuasion described in this chapter. Turn in an outline of the speech.

2. Prepare and present a five- to eight-minute persuasive speech on a topic of your choice. Along with a detailed outline, turn in a two- or three-page essay explaining your analysis of the audience, selection of specific purpose and structural strategy, and use of some of the logical or emotional appeals in the speech. Why, for example, did you use the particular organizational pattern? In what ways are your appeals based on audience motives or beliefs?

CHAPTER ELEVEN

Speeches for Specially Defined Situations

The secretary who never sought the spotlight finds herself dubbed the one to honor the boss's promotion with a speech and gift from the employees. The treasurer of the parents' association is regarded, despite his protestations, as the very one to introduce this month's featured speaker. An engineer is expected to give a short speech accepting an award for his division's contribution to marketing designs. You are unlikely to get through life without being called on to give speeches, or at least "say a few words," in such highly defined situations. These speeches, often called "ceremonial," perform a variety of useful and often important functions.

Another sort of special situation is one in which you can usually choose whether or not to speak; but groups that are important to you may suffer unless you or someone else can ease a tense situation. Members of an employee association, for example, are strongly split over whether to accept computerized evaluation of their work. The association itself seems likely to collapse unless someone can resolve the conflict within the group or at least reduce the tension between the two factions, and this may require a special sort of speech.

Although many speeches in such special situations look spontaneous, the shrewd speaker knows that most successful ones—whether ceremonial or to reduce conflict—are carefully prepared. The six-step process already described in Chapters 4 through 9 is a good basic framework for preparation. However, the peculiar nature of each of these different situations poses special challenges. This chapter provides suggestions for meeting these special challenges.

Ceremonial Speeches

We will consider three of the most common sorts of ceremonial speeches: introducing another speaker; praising a person or group, as when giving a eulogy or presenting an award; and accepting an award or other recognition. There are many other sorts of ceremonial speeches: welcoming an individual or group to a community, dedicating a building or major work of art, reporting on the activities of a part of an organization to the general membership. For the most part the following three qualities of good ceremonial speeches would apply to those situations as well.

Qualities of Effective Ceremonial Speeches

To speak effectively in a ceremonial situation aim to be sincere, appropriate, and fully prepared.

Be Sincere Lack of sincerity often occurs simply because the speaker forgets to be sincere. Either she takes her task—introducing a main speaker, for example—so casually that she doesn't really think much about what could be said in his favor in her introduction, or she becomes so concerned with meeting the formal requirements of the situation—of "doing a good job"—that she forgets about the substance. The solution: When you are planning the content of the speech, ask yourself what points are really relevant and significant for your purpose. Why should this audience want to hear this speaker? Why does this person really deserve this award? In a farewell speech, what happy memories and momentary regrets do you really feel leaving this company or this community? For one accepting an award, three sentences of sincere appreciation are superior to five minutes of rambling thoughts and platitudes.

In delivery, be natural and sincerely responsive to what you are saying; don't rush through with mechanical glibness or, at the opposite extreme, overemphasize everything with majestic pomposity.

Be Appropriate Except for such speeches as funeral eulogies and inaugural addresses, which are centerpieces in ceremonies, ceremonial speeches should seldom take more than three or four minutes, often less. The effective ceremonial speaker is modest enough to accept what is usually only a supporting role. He does not try to show off his own talents as a speaker, nor does he express his own opinions and knowledge except as they directly support his task in the particular situation. The most effective presenter of an award, for example, will say only what is needed for the audience to appreciate the purpose of the award and the worth of the one receiving it. He will leave the recipient in the limelight.

The ceremonial speaker also tries to adapt to the emotional anticipations of the listeners: serious and formal or relaxed and jovial, as seems suitable to the situation. Be conservative in such adaptation. If you're not sure whether humor is appropriate or whether you can handle it, don't try it. If your parallelism and metaphor in language seem strained and too elaborate, settle for more ordinary language.

Ceremonial speeches also require careful preparation and adaptation to the situation. (Robert Kalman/The Image Works)

Be Fully Prepared Gathering material may take only twenty minutes of brainstorming for ideas for an acceptance speech, or it may take several hours of interviews, research in print sources, and reflection for a eulogy or an important introduction. Manuscript planning is sometimes wise for more demanding ceremonial speeches; otherwise, plan at least to the detailed outline level.

Because most ceremonial speeches are short, you can work carefully on your supporting detail and choice of language. Spot triteness in your rough draft and replace it with fresh, sincere language. Spot vague generalities and add or replace them with specific detail. "Smith has worked for our company with unfailing loyalty" by itself probably says nothing except that the speaker doesn't really know or care much about what Smith has done for the company. A speaker who does know and care will develop two or three selected points in praise of Smith with enough detail to make them meaningful: "Twelve years ago when half our account executives switched to other companies Smith stayed. He believed this company would outlast most of those others. He was right. I guess he was smarter than those other fellows. But more important, he understood what loyalty means. He showed this on another occasion when . . ."

Effective delivery almost always requires some rehearsal, even for a manuscript speech or a one-minute introduction. Speaking from memory, providing it can be done with full confidence and feeling, may be best for a short speech. For any ceremonial speech, careful advance planning plus rehearsal should give you the confidence to speak loudly enough and to articulate clearly when you face the audience.

Let's turn now to some specific suggestions for three of the most common sorts of ceremonial speeches.

Speech of Introduction

A speech of introduction is a short speech given by a chairperson to pave the way for a featured speaker. The speech may be as casual as a few sentences introducing a familiar guest speaker at a hobby club meeting or as formal as a three- or four-minute introduction of a distinguished speaker whom listeners have each paid several dollars to hear. Such introductions are given for speakers at high school and college assemblies, at civic and professional organizations, and at almost any other form of organization or assembly—and just about any member of the organization may at one time or another be selected to provide the introduction.

Your primary task as a chairperson is to arouse or increase the audience's favorable feeling toward the speaker and their interest in what he or she has to say. With a speaker "who needs no introduction," courtesy usually requires at least four or five sentences acknowledging the speaker's distinctions and breaking the ice between speaker and audience. For a speaker who is less well known by at least part of the audience, you make a major contribution by taking two or three minutes to inform those listeners why this speaker is worth listening to on this topic and by otherwise creating a friendly atmosphere between audience and speaker.

Gathering Material for a Speech of Introduction   When gathering possible ideas for the introduction consider four aspects of the situation.

1. What are the *speaker's* general distinctions and achievements, and what experiences and training especially qualify him to speak on this topic?
2. Why is the *topic* itself timely, significant, unusual, or otherwise interesting?
3. Does the *audience* have any unusual distinctions, anything in common with the speaker, any special relationship to the topic or special profit to be derived from the speech?
4. Should the *occasion* be noted, perhaps as one in a distinguished lecture series or as having special relevance for the speaker or topic?

Where do you get this information? Apply your own creativity to your general knowledge of the speaker, topic, audience, and occasion. The best additional source, when available, is the speaker himself. (And, incidentally, when you are a main speaker you do well to cooperate fully by giving a chairperson both general information about yourself and your topic and specific suggestions for the introduction. Remember that a chairperson can do a great deal to initiate a favorable relationship between you and your audience.) Printed information you receive from a speaker or sponsoring agency may be supplemented by information you gain by visiting or calling the speaker or agency. For more famous speakers, you may also obtain information from various reference sources in a library.

Processing and Presenting Material for a Speech of Introduction From the material you have gathered, *select* only what will help to pave the way for the speaker *with this audience*. If you simply read off a standard list of biographical facts and achievements you obtained from a sponsor or reference source, you will probably bore the audience, and this hardly paves the way for the speaker.

Often you will meet the speaker, perhaps for the first time, shortly before the speech—at the airport, for lunch or dinner, or at the auditorium as the audience is gathering. Check the information in your planned introduction with the speaker, both for accuracy and for any deletions or additions he may suggest. Do this briefly, and do not press the main speaker on this matter; he has his own speech to worry about.

Don't apologize to the audience for the speaker or topic, except perhaps to explain a legitimate delay if the program is starting late; and don't apologize for the size of the audience. You hardly create a positive atmosphere for speaker and audience by such statements as, "Mr. Smith's topic is so deep I'm sure I'll never understand it but I hope you will," or "I can't understand why so few people turned out this evening; usually we have a much larger crowd." Don't praise the person's speaking ability excessively; you simply put the speaker on the spot by doing so. You might, however, mention other distinguished audiences he has addressed recently on this topic.

Sample Speech of Introduction In the sample that follows, Mike Haggerty, an unsuccessful local candidate for U.S. Congress, is to address the party workers in his county. The occasion is a dinner kicking off the campaign for county and state offices. Because Haggerty's own recent campaign was unsuccessful, the chairperson gives particular attention to the speaker's distinctions and achievements, and spends less time reminding the listeners of the fairly obvious relevance of the topic to this audience and occasion.

Our speaker this evening has had experience at just about every level of political campaigning. He twice won election to city council and twice to the state legislature. In the only campaign he ever lost, for U.S. Congress, he was narrowly defeated. In fact, he came closer to carrying this district for our party than any other Republican candidate in nearly a century. He remembers with deep gratitude how many of you worked with him in that campaign. As we begin anew a tough four months of campaigning for local and state offices we can use all the ideas we can get. Our guest tonight understands from his own experience the challenges and problems we face, and he has a winning record in the very sorts of campaigns we will be waging to win. So let's hear from our fellow Republican Mike Haggerty speaking on "Campaign Strategies to Win."

Speech of Praise

A variety of ceremonial occasions call for speeches of praise. One form, so common that it is often regarded as itself a major type of ceremonial speech, occurs when we praise the recipient of an award. We also praise our nation and people on the Fourth of July; we praise our business organization at an annual meeting; we praise our city at ceremonies on its hundredth anniversary. We may praise new members as we welcome them to our organization or community. We praise the candidate when placing her name in nomination. And perhaps the most challenging speech of praise is the funeral eulogy. The length of a speech of praise may vary from three or four sentences in the presentation of an award to a half hour or more for a major eulogy or commemorative speech.

Speeches of praise are similar to persuasive speeches dealing with evaluative issues, in that both sorts show how the subject fits the listeners' criteria for excellence. The crucial difference, however, is that the ceremonial speech is not usually intended to convince the listeners. The assumption on most ceremonial occasions is that the subject deserves the award or other honor (even if some listeners might privately disagree), and the speaker's task is to provide the praise in an appropriately polished speech. The best speeches of praise do often inspire in listeners at least a temporary urge to imitate the person being praised or a loyalty to the community or organization being praised. Thus there may be a secondary persuasive effect of some importance.

Gathering Material for a Speech of Praise   If you are familiar with the subject of the speech, you may be able to depend just on your own creativity to generate a stock of material. It may also be useful, and sometimes necessary, to interview friends, relatives, and associates of the person being praised or members familiar with the institution being praised. Interviews provide not only basic factual information about distinctions and achievements, but also anecdotes and other detailed examples and quotes with which you can increase the interest and emotional force of the speech.

Although you would not use all these sorts of ideas in any one speech of praise, the following are three categories within which to look for material:

1. What *personal attributes* does the subject seem to possess? Possible virtues that are likely to be admired by an audience include fairness, courage, honesty, sense of duty, compassion, generosity with time or money,

friendliness, reliability, modesty, restraint or self-control, enthusiasm, and wisdom. Other attributes include wit, intelligence, talent, experience, leadership ability, and power and influence over others. Audiences tend to admire more those attributes that the subject had to earn and those that are used to benefit other people such as the audience members.

2. What distinguished *acts and achievements* has the subject performed? Seek not only the most obvious and important actions but also the less well known achievements. A eulogy for the athlete Jesse Owens would recognize, of course, his achievements at the 1936 Olympics, but it might also recognize his life of public service and the fact that he was an important black orator in the generation before Dr. Martin Luther King, Jr. Also seek the minor actions that represent major character traits and abilities—for example, Lincoln's pardoning of a soldier sentenced to death for sleeping while on sentry duty, as a sign of his great compassion.

3. What *honors and other recognition* have already been given the subject? These, especially if from sources that are varied and are respected by the audience, serve as signs of the subject's worth.

You are looking for attributes, achievements, or honors that will seem positive and significant *to this audience*. Particular types of speeches of praise suggest additional guides to gathering material. When presenting an award, the nature of the award, the sponsor, the criteria for earning it, and the worthy competition all may provide material to amplify the subject's achievement. In fact, if the listeners are unfamiliar with the award, some of this information may be necessary. In a nominating speech, criteria for the office itself and characteristics of past respected holders of the office suggest merits that should be attributed to the subject of the speech.

Processing and Presenting Material for a Speech of Praise   Your task is not to cover every possible merit of your subject. Usually you would focus mainly on a few of the subject's virtues, accomplishments, or other general points that are appropriate for the occasion and consistent with the audience's values.

Much of the technique in a speech of praise depends on interpreting or enhancing the facts. The speaker interprets the facts, for example, by *assigning good motives* to known actions. An honored football lineman made his outstanding tackles and blocks "for the good of the team." Attributes and achievements can be enhanced by showing how they are *unusual* or by *comparing* them with esteemed persons or acts. "There she was, always in the classroom faithfully day after day. No other teacher equaled her record of four years without a day lost from work." And the student receiving the local science fair grand prize for his project in astronomy "is carrying on in the great tradition of wonder and determined inquiry of Copernicus, Galileo, Hubble, and Sagan." Actions can be described as detailed examples and can be enhanced by showing that they were performed under *difficult circumstances* or that they had large or long-term *benefits for other people*.

The recipient and usually the audience like to feel that the occasion for praise is significant. The speaker can make it more significant by using metaphor, parallelism, short emphatic sentences, and other stylistic devices described in Chapter 9.

Sample Speech of Praise   At an awards banquet the following speech is given to honor one of five college students receiving the highest award bestowed on graduating seniors. Because these presentations are the high point of the award ceremonies, more is expected than just a sentence or two. Yet because this is only one in a long list of awards to be presented this evening, a lengthy eulogy would be inappropriate. The length here is fairly common for presentation of a significant award. The speaker has done some research, for example by interviewing a couple of the recipient's professors and the director of a tutoring service in which the recipient worked. Since the audience was well aware of criteria for the awards, the speaker does not describe the award but rather concentrates on showing how the recipient merited it.

> Our next Top Senior has maintained a 3.8 grade point average in engineering while taking course overloads in liberal arts electives every semester. She has gone beyond the required courses in history, political science, and sociology because she believes technical people should have a broad perspective on the social implications of their work. Her advanced literature instructor, Dr. Burling, says that she is the most thoroughly prepared student he has had this year. She is truly a Top Senior academically.
>
> She is also a Top Senior in leadership and service. As an elected member of the publications board, this senior showed great courage in defending our school newspaper editor when his job was at stake for his strong attacks on the administration. Dean of Students Atwater credits the compromise which resolved that difficult situation largely to the fairness and judgment of our award recipient. Even though she held various high offices in student government, she was modest and willing to work on jobs such as putting up posters for the forum speakers program. With her challenging schedule she still found time to volunteer as a free tutor for freshmen in both math and composition. For meeting all criteria for this award in outstanding ways, I'm proud to present our third Top Senior award to Marsha Green.

Speech of Acceptance

When you are given an award or other recognition or are welcomed into a community or organization you may be expected to respond to the honor with a short speech of your own. Such speeches should be very easy: They are usually brief and come entirely from your own mind; all that is expected is that you be sincere and appreciative. Often, however, the right "brief remarks" do not seem so easy—unless one prepares in advance.

Gathering Material for a Speech of Acceptance   In a speech of acceptance you would be likely to develop two or three points from among the following four sorts. Brainstorming with these suggestions should produce the necessary stock of ideas for the speech.

1. Your own pleasure in receiving the award or recognition, joining the company, or accepting the nomination. You may also express your gratitude; remember that someone has gone to the trouble of providing this recognition. You may also explain the importance of the recognition to you personally.
2. The social value of the award and the worth of those who sponsor it. "By sponsoring these oratory contests the Optimist Clubs help to keep vigorous a long tradition of public speaking. I feel privileged to be among the hundreds of students that Optimist Clubs nationally have encouraged."
3. Those who helped you achieve the award or recognition, especially if they are in the audience. Single out two or three people, often only one, who were really important, and perhaps make an interesting and specific comment about them. Avoid the tedious long listing of everyone who ever contributed to your development.
4. Your respect for your competitors if the award is based on competition and if you can sincerely acknowledge the worth of your competitors without appearing either arrogant or falsely modest.

Processing and Presenting Material for a Speech of Acceptance   Preparation for an acceptance speech may mean thinking up two or three quick remarks for a relatively informal situation, or it may mean writing and memorizing a short speech. Plan to accept praise gracefully, but don't be so self-effacing that you seem to reduce the worth of the award or competition or to question the judgment of those who decided to give you the award.

In presentation, don't let the effort to remember exactly a prepared speech interfere with your expression of genuine emotion. If in the excitement of the moment you forget part of your prepared remarks or you feel emotion more strongly than you expected, your preparation still gives you a good base of material from which to say something that both is appropriate and expresses your immediate emotion. And be flexible enough to adapt to the situation. If other people receiving awards on this occasion say only a few words of thanks, perhaps you had better reduce your brilliantly prepared five-minute acceptance speech to three or four sentences.

Sample Speech of Acceptance   The following speech is Marsha Green's acceptance of the Top Senior award. The importance of the award calls for more than a one-sentence thank you, but the schedule for the evening requires that her remarks be brief and efficient. She wants to express her genuine appreciation for the honor in a personal and honest way while still being appropriate to the situation.

> I am excited! I am really grateful to the committee to be chosen for this award.
>
> I must thank my older brother who is in the audience tonight. Before I left to begin college he told me that college was not just a process I would go through for a degree, but that it could also open opportunities to develop as many facets of myself as I had the time and energy to pursue. Thank you, Dan, for starting me on the right path.
>
> It was not until my sophomore year that I began to hope I might achieve this award. I'm not sure I ever really deep down expected it, but the requirements for Top Senior set a model and a challenge toward which I worked. The people who established and maintain these awards help many of us to remember all that is truly worthwhile as we go through college.
>
> This is the greatest honor I have ever achieved. I will treasure both it and the wonderful friends I have made in school, always.

Speeches to Reduce Conflict

The school administration intends to shorten the time the library is open at night, and students oppose this policy. Feelings are strong. The administration refuses to discuss the matter. Angry students threaten to demonstrate. Rather than take a stand for one side or the other, a speaker might instead focus on trying to reduce the feelings of hostility and bring the two sides together to cooperate in solving the dilemma.

As this example illustrates, some speeches are intended to reduce or resolve conflicts among groups of people. In a broad sense, these speeches are persuasive because they urge cooperation, but they avoid supporting one side or the other on the sorts of issues described in Chapter 10. Such speeches may be given at all political levels, from a city government to the United Nations; at meetings of other sorts of organizations; in attempts to resolve labor-management disputes; and in other situations in which groups of people verbally confront each other. And the techniques of such speeches are used in less formal situations, such as personnel counseling in a business organization and in marriage and family counseling. Some rhetorical theorists believe that such speeches are not given well enough or often enough—that in fact the most valuable effect a public speaker can achieve in our stress-filled, strife-ridden world is to cause people to overcome short-term hostilities in order to pursue together their common long-term goals.

Situation and Purpose

We should note three common sorts of purposes in conflict reduction speeches.

To Confirm Unity   When a threat to unity of the group looms on the horizon, a speaker may be able to eliminate or at least reduce the threat by confirming unity within the group. Often such speeches emphasize areas of commonality among members of the group. Keynote speeches at political or union conventions, for example, often aim to establish overall unity that will endure through the inevitable struggles among different factions at the convention.

To Reduce Tension   A situation calling for a speech to reduce tension occurs when a distinct issue has shaped up between factions, such as labor and management in a contract dispute, and emotions are aroused. The speaker tries to reduce hostility or pave the way for cooperation by causing the opponents at least to see each other as reasonable fellow human beings rather than as evil or stubborn enemies.

To Achieve Compromise   The speaker proposes a compromise or other solution to a conflict between factions and urges one or both sides to accept it. The speaker has succeeded if the compromise is accepted grudgingly. But perhaps the highest achievement in conflict reduction speaking occurs when the opposing parties become genuinely reconciled, even to the point of identifying with each other's interests.

When facing an audience composed of one or more factions on an issue, the speaker's choice of specific purpose should be adapted to the state of the audience. Calm listeners who see little self-interest at stake in their positions may readily be brought to a reasonable compromise by a skillful speaker. But with an intensely angry and committed audience, the speaker may aim only to reduce tensions so that more reasonable discussion can ensue.

After a speaker has decided on a specific purpose adapted to the situation he must discover appeals and other techniques that can be used in the speech and then select and weave these into an appropriate organizational strategy. For this discovery he relies mainly on close audience analysis and his own creativity.

Analyzing Audience and Developing Materials

The audience to be analyzed includes all the major factions in the dispute—actually two or more different audiences. The speaker must understand each faction's reasons, both those announced and those unannounced, for its position. When he addresses only one faction as the immediate audience, the speaker needs to be able to explain the other faction's position accurately and fairly as well as to appeal to motives and beliefs of his immediate audience. Audience analysis for this sort of speech has to be unusually objective and open-minded. The speaker should remember that usually both sides in a conflict believe sincerely that they are right, often for highly idealistic and important reasons. Knowledge of the audience can be expanded by interviewing and by reading and listening to persuasive messages from both sides.

Audience analysis paves the way for the following main sorts of techniques used in conflict reduction speeches.

Emphasize Areas of Commonality   People are more willing to negotiate, compromise, and cooperate if they believe that their similarities with each other outweigh their differences. Therefore, the speaker seeks to discover, make explicit, and amplify with examples points that the opposing factions have in common. The following are five places to look for possible points of similarity:

1. *Demographic factors* such as age, sex, race, national or geographic origin, social or economic class, profession or vocation.
2. *History and achievements* that have been similar or shared, such as having been victims of prejudice or suppression, having been members of the same or similar organizations, or having worked together on some project.
3. *Beliefs and values*, which may range from taste in music, literature, and life style to the most fundamental principles of human worth, proper form of government, and standards for excellence in achievement.
4. The *same friends* shared by both factions and—perhaps more potent for inducing cooperation—the *same enemies*, especially enemies who might threaten both factions alike.
5. *Motives and goals*, both short term and long-term. This area of commonality is especially important because it works in two ways. First, goals and motives shared by opposing factions, even when not directly relevant to the issue at hand, are a basis for similarity. The speaker should, however, avoid pointing out goals for which the factions must compete with each other. Second, perhaps the strongest appeal to eliminate conflict occurs when the speaker can convince the opposing factions that they can gain more, at least in the long run, by compromise and cooperation than by hostility. To help you discover possible motives and goals review the list of audience motives early in Chapter 10.

Create Understanding   The speaker should aim to create in each faction an understanding of the other's position. Her explanation should be equally sympathetic toward all sides, stating and perhaps comparing the opposing positions and their underlying principles fairly and fully. This does not always bring the sides close to agreement—as with, for example, disputes over legal or federally aided abortion. But it may at least enable the different sides to realize that their opponents are not acting out of pure obstinacy and evil motives. And in some situations two sides may discover that in terms of basic principles they are not really so far apart, or that what is most important to one side has little real importance to the other side.

Reduce Harmful Emotions   It is important to reduce anger, anxiety, or other emotions that obstruct moves toward compromise. This can be done directly by attacking the real causes of the emotion, if the speaker can discover the causes. Why does one faction feel angry or fearful or suspicious toward the other side? Do they feel they have been insulted or treated unfairly or not taken seriously by the other side? Do they fear that if the other side wins this conflict, that side will go on to seize even greater advantages and benefits?

To reduce anger, show that the opponents are not deliberately intending to insult or humiliate your listeners, that their leaders do take your listeners seriously, that some of them apologize for the excesses of others in their faction, or they do genuinely value the good will of your listeners. You can also reduce anger and hostility by showing that the opponents have suffered, have serious problems of their own to solve, and are human just like your listeners.

Fear or anxiety can sometimes be reduced by showing how little the immediate audience will lose by a compromise and how much they stand to gain. The speaker may also be able to show how a concession or compromise now will leave the audience in a better bargaining position on future issues and will create trust among all parties.

Negative emotions can also be reduced indirectly by emphasizing the mutual successes, prosperity, and security of the whole group, and by humor that does not belittle the group. It's difficult for listeners to be deeply angry or fearful when they feel cheerful, comfortable, and secure.

After analyzing the audience she will address, developing an understanding of the opposing factions, and accumulating a stock of points of commonality and other materials, the speaker is ready to organize the speech.

Planning Organization and Presentation

We will consider appropriate structural strategies for three different sorts of situations and purposes: confirming unity against a vague threat, reducing tension between strongly opposed factions, and proposing a compromise to resolve a conflict.

Confirming Unity   For confirming unity in a situation in which potential tension and disunity have not yet surfaced, you would not be likely to state your purpose directly. Such explicit statement of proposition would draw the listeners' attention to the very divisive pressures you want to avoid. Instead, your statement of focus would indicate your purpose as simply to review the accomplishments and qualities of the community, club, political group, corporation, or whatever other organization you want to keep unified. You can then cover the experiences, beliefs, needs and goals, reasons for pride, and other aspects that bind listeners together, using a classification pattern. Or you might cover the group's achievements and ambitions (which depend on continued unity, although this is only implied) in a past-present-future time pattern.

Reducing Tension   For reducing tension in a situation in which the audience is already well aware of divisive tensions, a direct approach is often the most efficient. The statement of focus at the end of the introduction may even be blunt: "Today, I'll explain why we should remain united despite certain pressures to drive us apart." You can then develop your reasons for unity one by one in a clear, straightforward pattern, amplifying each reason by appealing to the listeners' common values and motives.

Achieving Compromise   To achieve compromise between opposing factions, consider using a strategy in which you delay stating your proposition, the compromise, until late in the speech. This enables you to reduce hostile emotions and to lay a groundwork of mutual understanding, common motives, and other points of similarity *before* proposing the compromise. Let's see how this organizational strategy could be used by the speaker attempting to reduce conflict over library hours between angry students and a stubborn administration.

Introduction

	I. This plan to close the library at night is disturbing a lot of students, and I don't imagine the administration is happy with the situation either.
Suggests speaker's objectivity.	II. Although I don't use the library at night, I know from past experience how frustrating it can be to have no good place to study.
Establishes speaker's competence.	III. I've talked to a variety of people involved:
	A. The library director and the business office.
	B. Several people studying in the library late at night.

Statement of focus.

IV. In this dispute over library hours, I'd like to offer what I hope will be some helpful ideas.

Body

Reduces hostility by:

I. Let's not let a difference of opinion make us forget that we are friends, not enemies, in this matter.

reminding of "prosperity" achieved together and

A. The library itself is a part of the quest by both students and administration for a high level of educational opportunity here.
   1. The administration has worked to provide an excellent library facility.
   2. Students have made heavy use of it.

explaining each side's valid reasons to the other.

B. The administration is not out to frustrate students, but they do have to save money.
   1. In late night hours there are few student users and high staff costs.
   2. Quote by library director shows his sympathy for the late night students.
C. We also have to realize that some serious students will be frustrated.
   1. Some are highly motivated students who work days and take evening courses.
   2. Examples of Chris Fox and Mick Weisz show some students have nowhere else to study.

(So it seems we have a clash between the administration's legitimate desire to save money and some students' legitimate need to use the library late at night. Are the administration and the students really that far apart? No.)

Describes common mo-
tives, partly to stress
similarities uniting the
two sides and partly to
set up aims that a com-
promise solution will
meet.

II. Students and administrators have
already shown that they want essentially the same things.
A. We all want the most efficient
uses of financial resources to
benefit the students.
1. Administrators have recently expanded scholarship
aid and free tutoring in the
study skills center.
2. Money to keep the library
open must come from some-
where else.
B. We all want each student to
have the maximum opportunity
for academic development.
C. We all want to keep the library
holdings secure.
1. A library staff spread too
thinly increases chances of
theft and vandalism.
2. Missing items frustrate the
library staff and even more
the students who need to
use the material.

(If both sides have so much in common it seems we should be able to
come to some sort of agreement.)

Statement of proposition.

III. I propose, as at least a place to
start working out a compromise,
this: Keep open late at night some
sections of the library that can be
isolated.

Explains compromise as
being practical.

A. This is a workable solution.
1. The reference room is such
an area, and a reserve book
desk can be put there.
2. See how many students use
this facility to see if the cost
is justified.

Shows how compromise
would meet both sides'
main demands.

B. Both sides would get most of
what they want, although both
sides would also have to give a
little.

1. Students would have a place to study and use of the library's most important facilities late at night.
2. Most of the cost of keeping the entire library operating late at night would be eliminated.

Conclusion

I. All of us would benefit by working toward a solution that is fair to students and realistic for the administration.

Suggests speaker is open-minded.

II. Though I'm certainly willing to listen to other ideas, the compromise I propose seems reasonable.

Visualizes benefits of proposed compromise.

A. We would save money, provide students with a place to study, and keep the library holdings secure.

Final appeal to common values.

B. Perhaps most important, we would show once again that at this school we solve our problems through fair-minded cooperation.

Present a conflict reduction speech with calm, friendly delivery and language. Listeners tend unconsciously to imitate the speaker's apparent emotional state, so it is especially important when attempting to reduce tension that your manner reflects the restraint and reasonableness you hope to induce in the audience.

Summary

Some situations call for special adaptation beyond that covered by the distinction between informative and persuasive speeches. Speeches adapted to such special situations include ceremonial speeches and speeches to reduce conflict.

Ceremonial speeches are given in situations in which topic and task are tightly defined. A ceremonial speaker should be sincere, speak appropriately for the situation, and prepare carefully. Common types of ceremonial speeches include chairpersons' introductions of main speakers, speeches of praise, and speeches of acceptance. Each requires its own special kinds of content.

Conflict reduction speeches are given to confirm unity, to reduce tensions between opposing factions, or to bring about a compromise solution to a conflict. Audience analysis should be careful and objective and should consider the opposing factions to which the speaker must adapt. To be effective, the speaker should seek to emphasize what listeners in the opposing factions have in common, help each faction to understand the other's position, reduce harmful emotions, and use a structural strategy appropriate to purpose and audience attitudes.

Exercises

The following three exercises may be handled as a single round of speeches in which each student selects in advance to give one type of speech (one of the three exercises).

1. Present a five- to eight-minute conflict reduction speech on an issue on which there is a strong difference of opinion. Adapt to your audience as they really are on this issue. For example, if only one faction is represented in your class, try to make the listeners more open to the opposite point of view; but if two factions are represented, try to adapt to both groups. Sources for possible topics include these: strongly opposing reactions in class to someone's earlier persuasive speech; an issue splitting the campus or the local community; a national or international issue concerning which there are strongly opposing opinions locally; or a less intense issue that you see as being potentially divisive. (If two speakers select the same topic, such as an issue between students and administration, this might provide an interesting basis for comparison.)

2. Present a five- to seven-minute speech of praise for some local person, group, or institution. The occasion may be a eulogy for a person living or dead, the giving of a hypothetical award such as for best teacher in the school or best citizen, or a nomination for some award such as outstanding member of the student body. For an organization or institution, the occasion may be an anniversary or the achievement of some goal.

3. Present carefully prepared one- to two-minute speeches of introduction for each of the four or five speakers on a day's panel of speeches of praise and conflict reduction speeches. Adapt each introduction to the particular speaker, topic, and type of speech.

Speaking in Groups

I n this chapter we will look at situations in which a limited number of persons interact specifically to contribute to making a decision. A major distinction in group situations is between *private situations*, in which members are addressing one another, and *public situations*, in which each member is primarily concerned with reaching a listening audience.

In private discussions, a group of people meet to come to a decision on some matter, often a solution for a problem facing the group or some larger organization or society that the members represent. A leader is usually appointed or is elected by the group. Each member of the group is expected to participate actively, and the members usually face one another. (Thus the group discussion is different from an assembly situation, in which most members are not expected to participate beyond perhaps voting. Many of the skills for participation and leadership to be discussed in this chapter, however, also apply to assembly discussion and debate.) Four or five is probably the ideal number of participants for efficient discussion, but groups are often larger in order that a greater variety of viewpoints and subgroups will be represented.

In a typical public group, the participants—usually two to five, plus a neutral moderator—provide a variety of information and viewpoints for an audience. Group members usually interact with one another and often with the audience. Unlike the private group, which usually aims to reach a decision, the public group is typically open-ended, leaving decisions up to the audience members.

Reasons for Group Discussions

Why do so many organizations, from street gangs to executive committees in government and industry, rely on group situations as a way of airing different points of view and making decisions? One reason is that the range of expertise, ideas, and opinions provides a *more complete base for decision making* than any one individual could provide. The assumption here is that decisions become more sound as they are based on a greater range of information and ideas. A second reason is that the dynamic of a group situation is itself a *creative process* in which one person's information can generate another person's ideas, which in turn can be evaluated and amended by a third person, and so forth in an ongoing interactive process. The final product of a private group discussion, or of a public discussion with exchanges among speakers and listeners, may be greater than the sum of the ideas originally brought in by the participants.

Two further reasons apply especially to private discussions in business organizations and other situations in which the discussants have personal interests at stake and must continue to work with one another. People are more likely to understand and actively *support policies or decisions they helped to make* than those that are imposed on them. Finally, in less cooperative situations, discussion can *resolve serious conflicts* in a way that is objective and thoroughly examines the issues.

Merely having people speak in groups does not guarantee these advantages. In fact, groups may waste time, bore participants or listeners, and increase divisive hostility within a group. Productive and enjoyable group sessions are much more likely if those involved understand how efficient discussion operates and if they have technical skills as participants.

Qualities of Good Group Discussions

When people must interact to get a job done, the attitudes and inclinations prevailing in the group may be as important as the format and information they use. A group will probably be successful if it is purposeful, cohesive, and realistic.

Effective Groups Are Purposeful   The executive council of the school band's sponsors has met to determine how to raise funds for the band's next major trip. One member suggests that there must be some way to raise money besides selling candy. The past president of the group responds, "I'd remind you that in the past two years we raised nearly three thousand dollars a year selling candy. And we would have raised even more if the kids had hustled as much as they did in earlier years." One mother defends her child, "Well, the kids have more studies now than they used to. And people are getting tired of buying overpriced band candy. I know that my little Freddie walked our neighborhood day after day." Another mother suggests that Freddie would have been more successful if he had begun door-to-door selling as soon as the candy came in. Freddie's mother responds, "Freddie had a cold that week, and you could hardly expect him to go out in the snow." By now, of course, the issue is rapidly becoming not how to earn money for the band trip but, rather, Freddie's guilt or innocence. Large amounts of time can be wasted in this sort of trivial or irrelevant digression. In a purposeful group, the participants keep clearly in mind the central topic, help the group move from point to point to accomplish its purpose, and resist the temptation to be trapped in time-consuming digressions.

Effective Groups Are Cohesive   In a highly cohesive group, participants tend to build on, modify, and extend one another's ideas, rather than to reject, compete, or tear down. Thus the cohesive group has a much greater potential for developing creative insights and solutions. Participants with opposing viewpoints in a public discussion are likely to provide the audience with a more intelligent and enjoyable presentation if they maintain mutual respect and tact in their disagreements.

Effective Groups Are Realistic   A school board is faced with the problem of balancing academics with worthwhile extracurricular activities. The group quickly decides on a policy of relegating all such activities, including music and athletics, to time after regular school hours. This preserves the academic priority of the school, and it provides several hours after school every day for the other activities. The board members are very pleased with themselves for having solved the problem so well and so quickly . . . until they discover that many of the most active students have to go to jobs or catch school buses when school is out, and that many of the best teachers resent having to spend after-school hours keeping these activities going for students. In the world of practical affairs, decisions have to fit reality, rather than wishful thinking, to be sound. Participants in group discussions can avoid making or advocating decisions on the basis of emotional response to a situation. They can face squarely the problem of how to implement any policy being advocated by trying to predict who will do what and how people will be affected when the policy is in action.

The Problem-Solving Format for Private Group Discussions

The problem-solving format receives detailed treatment in this book because it is an efficient process for groups who must exchange ideas to solve problems and make other decisions.

A Five-Step Framework for Making Decisions on Policy

Private group discussions typically follow a sequence of thought that begins by examining a problem or other need and determining criteria for a solution to meet this problem or need. Several solutions are brought forth and evaluated, and one is selected. Often the process is then continued, to develop plans for implementing and testing the selected solution. Let's see how this process might work for a group of division managers who are concerned with apparent low worker morale in their factory.

I. The managers analyze the problem. The production chief frames the purpose question: What steps, if any, should be taken to increase worker morale? This purpose requires the group to go beyond merely investigating the situation, even if "no action" is the policy they finally decide on. After agreeing to this purpose, which commits them to arrive at a decision on policy, the managers consider the symptoms of the problem. Comparing notes with one another they discover that absenteeism is higher than normal, productivity is lower than usual, the quality control people report a high level of shoddy work, silence and grumbling are prevalent in the company cafeteria, and union stewards are turning in unusual numbers of petty complaints. The problem is widespread and serious. Then the managers search their own minds and respond to one another's suggestions to discover possible causes of the problem. They consider these possible causes: low pay, poor working conditions, lack of worker identity with the company, lack of self-esteem, and feelings of being exploited by management. The managers try to pinpoint the most likely causes of the problem. Pay and working conditions, measured objectively against other factories, are relatively good, so they dismiss those as real causes. Finally they pinpoint as the most likely causes the workers' lack of identity with the company and their feelings of being exploited. How can the managers best solve this problem?

II. The managers' analysis of the problem plus their general management expertise lead them to establish several criteria, or standards, that an ideal solution would meet. It would, of course, solve the problem—at least by increasing productivity and quality of work, and at best by reducing the causes of low worker morale. An ideal solution would also be cost effective, would not risk management's control over the company, would be acceptable to the workers, and would produce both short-term and long-term favorable results.

III. Next the managers brainstorm for possible solutions. Their various suggestions seem to group into three general solutions. First, they could mount an in-plant propaganda campaign, with posters, leaflets, films, and speakers. Second, they could use a more refined system of rewards and punishments for productivity, quality of work, and faithfulness on the job. Third, they could permit worker participation in management—for example, by having workers elect representatives to a labor-management council to consider plant innovation and worker complaints.

IV. The managers consider each solution in relation to the criteria. Past experience in other divisions of the company indicates that although a skillful in-plant propaganda campaign does have positive effects, in the long run it doesn't change worker attitudes enough to be worth the cost. Intensifying the use of rewards and punishments might not be acceptable to the workers and would probably increase their sense of being exploited, thus actually increasing one of the causes of the problem. Finally, the managers decide to try the third solution—greater worker participation in management through a joint labor-management council—despite the fears of some managers that this might pose possible risk to management's control over the company.

V. Because of some managers' misgivings, the joint council is to be instituted only on a trial basis and reevaluated in six months, and a final right of veto will remain with upper-level management. Plans are laid for an initial meeting with union representatives to establish details of the joint council.

Note that the managers' discussion fell into a sequence of five fairly distinct steps. If you can keep this standard five-step framework in mind, your own decision-making discussions are likely to be efficient and productive rather than rambling and indecisive. The framework is especially useful in group discussions aimed at deciding on a policy to solve a problem.

    I. Analyze the problem.
   II. Decide on criteria for an ideal solution.
  III. List the possible solutions.
  IV. Evaluate the solutions against the criteria in order to select the best solution.
   V. Determine how to implement and further test the selected solution.

Suggestions for Applying the Framework

What is done within each step of the framework varies a great deal from situation to situation. The following suggestions for more effectively developing each step will, however, apply to most problem-solving group discussions.

I. Analyze the Problem   If a precise purpose question has not already been framed for the group, arrive at one as early as possible in this step. The phrasing should be objective, and all the participants should agree in their understanding of what it means. Avoid broad, vague phrasing. "What can be done about education at this school?" is both broad and vague. "How can the quality of teaching at this school be improved?" is narrower and more precise. State the question objectively, avoiding bias and premature assumptions. "What should be our government's policy toward the moral crime of abortion?" has already stacked the cards against prochoice proponents. "How can student evaluations be used to get rid of poor teachers?" has already assumed that only one type of student input will be used, and that it will be used for only one purpose.

In analyzing the problem, the group normally wants to determine exactly what is wrong and how serious it is. What are the signs or symptoms that something is wrong? How widespread are the symptoms? Are they likely to be cured or to get worse if nothing is done? Why have current practices failed to solve the problem? What are the underlying causes of the problem? Students don't attend campus-sponsored events because they find them uninteresting. Fine. But why do they find them uninteresting? Is it because the selection board doesn't represent a wide enough range of students? Or is it because publicity about the events doesn't really explain why the events would be interesting to students? The main aim in analysis of the problem is to pinpoint key causes or other points at which solutions can be most effectively directed.

II. Decide on Criteria Some criteria grow directly out of the analysis of the problem. If the problem has three main causes, then an ideal solution would eliminate those three causes. Other criteria are not so obvious or so directly related to the problem. Such criteria might include: Will it be affordable and worth the cost? Will the people involved accept it? Will it avoid harmful side effects or long-term effects? Will it be consistent with the less obvious aims and values of the group? If the problem, for example, is increasing attendance at student union events, it might be solved by strictly limiting events to those with mass appeal, such as popular films and major rock groups; but would such strict limitation be consistent with the overall aims and values of cultural diversity at a college?

Often in a discussion it is useful to brainstorm for a few minutes for criteria, after noting the more obvious ones derived from analysis of the problem. Some of these criteria may be dismissed, by group consensus, as insignificant; others may be combined to produce a manageable number, usually no more than six. The group should also distinguish between those criteria that are "necessary"—that is, that any solution must meet to be at all viable—and those criteria that are in varying degrees "desirable."

III. Develop a List of Possible Solutions Some solutions will probably be obvious from the discussants' general knowledge and research on the topic. But these may not be the most creative and successful solutions in this particular situation. So again, try brainstorming for a few minutes. Don't judge your own or others' ideas, but rather use other people's ideas to trigger your own thinking. Then, when a rough list is down, ideas can be modified, combined, or eliminated to come up with a list of usually no more than three or four serious possibilities.

IV. Select One or More Solutions First decide whether you must make a single choice or whether you can select several of the alternatives. For example, a company trying to decide which model to buy for a uniform fleet of delivery trucks must make a single choice from among the various models available. However, a student programs committee can select several different activities from among all the possibilities available. The group should also realize that no solution is likely to meet all criteria perfectly, so the group is simply trying to seek consensus on which one (or ones), is relatively best.

Perhaps the most important suggestion for this step is that the group should apply the criteria to each solution systematically. In particular, the group should guard against the temptation when considering an emotionally attractive solution to avoid applying significant but "inconvenient" criteria. The best way to be systematic is to take one solution and match it against the list of criteria one by one, then do the same with next solution, and so forth.

V. Plan to Implement and Test the Selected Solution(s)   In a classroom setting, planning to implement and test the selected solution may seem artificial. However, in many real administrative situations this fifth step is necessary if anything is to happen as a result of a group's efforts. Otherwise, great solutions and policies may be decided, but they may be implemented ineffectively, if at all. Or policies put into practice may prove harmful but be continued because no provision was made for reevaluating them. Thus if the topic calls for implementation and testing, plan this as the final step in your practice discussion, if only in a hypothetical way. What are specific individuals to do to put the decision into practice? If people outside the discussion group are involved in implementation, who is to contact those people? Can the cooperation of outsiders be assured? If not, is there a contingency plan? What is the timetable for these contacts and other implementing actions? Is there a plan to see if the policy is working as intended? Is the decision-making group to continue meeting to monitor implementation and results? If the group is to turn over its results to an administrative officer for final evaluation, implementation, and testing, have arrangements been made for writing the report and submitting it to all the group members for final review?

Although a well-prepared group may dispatch its task, from start to finish, in a single session of an hour or two, a group making a major decision on policy may need two or more sessions over a period of several

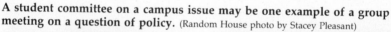

A student committee on a campus issue may be one example of a group meeting on a question of policy. (Random House photo by Stacey Pleasant)

days. In these more extended applications of the process, breaks may occur during which members can do additional research, let emotions cool, or negotiate informally with other members of the committee. Each session can aim at moving a certain distance through the process, and breaks can come between steps. A break between steps III and IV, for example, would permit the members individually to weigh the various solutions against the criteria.

Effective Participation in Private Group Discussions

As in most speaking situations, your confidence and effectiveness will be partly determined by the amount of preparation you do in advance. To a greater extent than with a public speech, however, your effective participation in the group depends on skills beyond your advance preparation. We will consider both advance preparation and the particular skills used in interacting with others during actual discussion.

Preparation for Participation

In some discussions, you will be assigned to research a specific aspect of the topic in advance. Whether or not you are assigned special responsibilities, you should prepare in advance by getting your purpose clearly in mind, by thinking and researching to meet your own needs, and by a final gearing up for the discussion itself.

Analyze the Situation and Determine Your Purpose   Determine the purpose of the group—for example, to make a decision solving a problem for the company, or merely to evaluate existing conditions. Is the prevailing atmosphere likely to be cooperative, or will the group probably have to reconcile conflicting points of view? If you are too far out of step with the group's purpose you will almost certainly be ineffective. Within adaptation to the group's purpose, what is your own purpose? Do you feel some special responsibility to facilitate the group's progress toward a decision? Should you be prepared to contribute some particular area of expertise or to represent some particular viewpoint?

Gather Ideas and Materials   Think through your ideas on the topic and make notes. Preparation may also require research in print material and other sources. Often, interviews with people who have faced situations similar to the one being discussed or who have special knowledge of certain facets of the topic are especially useful sources of information. For example, members of a committee set up to consider how to keep students from dropping out of school might interview financial aid counselors, academic and psychological counselors, people in the study skills division, and instructors and teaching assistants who have some personal contact with students. Why not also interview some students who are dropping out? Or interview students who are satisfied and successful, to find out what causes them to remain. As you begin to accumulate research notes and your own ideas, organize them in different categories: symptoms and scope of the problem, causes of the problem, criteria, possible solutions, and ideas for implementation.

Do Final Preparation   Just as with your last rehearsals for a speech, you can gear yourself for the situation shortly before the discussion. Organize and review your notes so you can quickly find any evidence or other material you might need in the discussion. Size up the other participants. What purposes do they have in the discussion? How do they view the problem or topic? Which of them are likely to help the group toward consensus? Which participants will support your views and which will oppose you, and why? Finally, consider your own characteristics as a participant. Do you tend to be too shy and reticent? Will you have to make a special effort to speak out? If so, prepare now to make such contributions. Or do you tend to talk too often? Should you make a special effort to keep your contributions brief or stick to the topic? Do you have to guard against a tendency to become emotional, hostile, or stubborn?

During the Discussion

Because discussions are directly and informally face-to-face, the participants must be sensitive to one another as well as to the ongoing flow of ideas. Whatever your role in the group effort, you will be more effective if you listen carefully, think clearly, and speak effectively.

Listening   If your contribution is to be intelligently adapted to the flow of the discussion, you need to know accurately what is going on at that point in the discussion. Attentive listening is also one way of showing an open mind and respect for the other participants. Thus it increases your rapport with other members and makes the group more cohesive. As with most other functional listening, that in discussion often takes conscious effort if it is to be fully effective.

1. *Listen fully and fairly* to another person's line of thinking before judging or attacking it. Be fair even to those with whom you expect to disagree. If you are not sure you understand, ask the other person questions to check yourself.
2. *Pay attention to nonverbal cues* sent out by other participants, especially when they are speaking. Facial expressions, level of physical tenseness, and vocal tone can tell you about the emotional feelings of another participant. Such cues may, for example, tell you what points you can safely disagree with and which issues are likely to arouse stubborn hostility.

3. *Take brief notes*—for example, on special aspects of the problem or on criteria. Your purpose is not to keep a running record of the proceedings (unless you are especially assigned to do this) but rather to get down essential points so you won't lose track of them later in the discussion. This is especially important if the discussion is unusually complex or extends over several sessions. Some people also find that jotting a few notes helps them separate the significant from the trivial as the discussion progresses.

Thinking   Although some participants seem to gauge their success by how quickly, frequently, and excitedly they talk, most effective participants tend, at least at times, to back off from such immediate involvement in order to think. Other than planning more carefully what you will say next, what sorts of thinking will increase your effectiveness?

1. *Keep a perspective on main goals*, both the group's and, if they are different, your own. Try to spot the *major* issues and points as they emerge in the discussion, and keep them in mind as the points that should ultimately determine the decision. Avoid getting caught up in trivial subissues, or protecting your ego, or trying to win an argument just for the sake of winning.
2. *Be flexible in your own thinking.* Remember that in a discussion, almost every participant may assume that he or she has the right view or knows the best decision. The realistic participant knows, first, that she along with everyone else will probably have to accept some reasonable compromises and imperfect solutions, and second, that she is quite likely to encounter new points of view, information, or arguments that should cause her genuinely to rethink some of her own opinions.
3. *Evaluate contributions from other participants.* Does the discussant have sound reasoning and reliable evidence supporting his point? What un-stated assumptions do you have to make to accept someone else's line of reasoning? For example, someone gives as a major reason for starting a mass transit system that it will reduce traffic congestion downtown. To accept that reasoning, you have to assume that large numbers of people would switch from private cars to buses or trains if the latter were available. Try to understand why a person who disagrees with you takes the position he does. If there is a strong emotional commitment to the position, you may simply arouse anger by trying directly to refute the point.
4. *Be selective in your own contributions*, not only in what you say but also in how much you say and when you say it. You do have a responsibility to make worthwhile contributions, but they should be made at the point in the discussion at which they are relevant. Don't leap ahead of the group. And it's seldom useful to backtrack to some issue after the group has moved on to other matters. Avoid emotional harangues that merely make you feel better and personal reminiscences that have at best only a dim relevance to the point at hand. Also, know when to stop arguing a point. If you can't concede or compromise gracefully, at least know when the issue has been decided and it's time to stop "beating a dead horse."

Speaking   All your preparation, listening, and thinking pay off in contributions you make to the discussion that will help the group and influence
its decisions in the ways you wish.

1. *Be clear and efficient.* Speak to the issue at hand, usually making only one
   point per contribution. Clarify the relationship of your contribution to the
   flow of the discussion at that point by using transitions such as these: "I'd
   like to give another example of Jones's point that . . ." "I've run across a
   case that seems at odds with Jones's point." "If we apply our second
   criterion to this solution we find that . . ." When appropriate, use examples, comparison, and other detail to clarify your point, as well as evidence to prove it; but keep such detail brief.

2. *Appear reasonable and fair-minded.* The discussant who starts out, "If the
   lousy backbiters in the marketing division would stop sabotaging one
   another's efforts . . ." does not seem to be taking a rational attitude
   toward the point. He is likely to be taken more seriously by the other
   participants if he uses more neutral language: "The people in the marketing division often seem more competitive with each other than cooperative," and then backs up his assertion with some factual information,
   "The supervisor in marketing has recorded four instances in which a
   salesperson used personal contacts to get orders in another person's
   territory." The reasonable participant also states points opposing her own
   fairly and accurately, and is willing to state her own motives and assumptions.

3. *Be pleasant—at least be polite.* People are more likely to agree with their
   friends than with their enemies, so be a friend. Acknowledge the value of
   other people's contributions when those contributions are worthwhile. If
   you concede a point, do so gracefully and with good will. If you disagree,
   even strongly, do so tactfully. A participant can sometimes avoid pointless
   hostility just by phrasing his disagreement so that it is aimed at the idea
   rather than the person: "The solution just offered appears to miss on two
   criteria," rather than, "John, it's obvious you are ignoring our criteria."
   You should be aware of what you are communicating through your own
   vocal inflection, facial expression, and physical tension and gestures—
   especially when you must make a conscious effort to be pleasant. But,
   you are usually better off *being* pleasant in your thinking than trying to
   give a somewhat false impression of being pleasant. Finally, be sure any
   attempts at humor show good will rather than seeming sarcastic.

Effective Leadership in Private Group Discussions

In private group discussions in which decision making occurs, the effectiveness of the leader often largely determines the success of the group in
achieving its goal. The leader may be designated in advance, either because
of his position in the group already—as division head, for example—or
because he is appointed by whoever set up the group. If a leader is not
designated, the group usually should elect one at the beginning of the

proceedings, especially if the group must reach some sort of decision within a fixed time limit. In low-pressure, relaxed situations, in which information exchange and brainstorming are the main aims, the group may just depend on one or more persons to emerge to perform leadership functions as the discussion progresses.

The leader's orientation to the discussion is different from that of a typical participant. While the typical participant may be concerned primarily with his or her own ideas and contributions, the leader is concerned with the overall aim of the group and with guiding the discussion toward consensus on a solution or other decision based on the best input from all participants.

To be an effective leader you should know what to do before as well as during the discussion.

Before the Discussion

Some prediscussion tasks may be done by other people—for example, by whoever requested the discussion. A designated discussion leader, however, has the responsibility of seeing that all prediscussion tasks are done, either by herself or by someone else, so that the discussion can get off to a smooth and efficient start. The following is a list of such tasks:

1. Determine the aims of the discussion   This includes more than just deciding on a purpose question. Is the group merely sharing views and arriving at a theoretical decision, or are the members expected to arrive at a solution that will be implemented? Is the discussion likely to be a cooperative endeavor or mainly an effort to reconcile conflict among opposing factions? Should you, as leader, keep in mind some important, less obvious aims, such as preserving group unity or increasing the confidence and motivation of some members?

2. Select the participants   You are likely to get a better decision if you select people of varied expertise and opinions on the topic. Beyond this, select people who are interested in the topic, cooperative, and energetic, and who have a sense of responsibility.

3. Plan at least a rough agenda   Set up a sequence of main steps or points that must be covered. The five-step process for group discussion, described earlier in this chapter, gives you at least a framework from which to start in working out the agenda. Give some thought to how much time, approximately, you can spend on each step in the discussion, given the total amount of time available for the session(s). You may want to provide your participants in advance with copies of this tentative agenda and possibly with a fact sheet of background information on the topic. You may also ask each participant to research a particular area of the topic.

4. Arrange physical facilities   This means more than just securing a room. Participants should be able to sit facing one another and should have a surface on which to write. A round table is ideal. Classroom desk-chairs in a circle are workable. If you sit at an oblong table, try to avoid yourself (or anyone else) sitting at the head of the table, unless you intend to run the meeting in a rather authoritarian way. You may also want to make sure pads of paper and pencils are available, so the less prepared will be able to take notes.

5. Prepare yourself on the topic   A good background on the topic, gained through reading and interviewing, gives you the ethos to lead the meeting and gain the confidence of the other participants. You are also better able to judge when each step in the process has been adequately investigated—for example, when all the important criteria or all the important solutions have been brought out. Avoid, however, forming your own conclusions.

During the Discussion

The leader's responsibilities are to be open-minded and objective, to help the group move efficiently toward the best possible decision, and to help other discussants feel comfortable while doing so.

1. Start the discussion in a friendly and purposeful mood   Introduce each member, mentioning any special area of expertise, or let the members introduce themselves. A bit of small talk, preferably related to the task at hand, may help create a friendly and cooperative atmosphere before the group gets down to serious business. State briefly the topic and aim of the discussion, any necessary background information, the agenda, and any ground rules. See if there are any major objections to your view of the aims and plan for the discussion, so you can modify these if necessary. Then the group can at least start with consensus about its purpose and method.

2. Keep the discussion moving toward its goal   Keep your overall time frame in mind, and try to pace the discussion so that you allow sufficient time for each step on your agenda. And stick to your agenda to reduce the chance of, for example, deciding on criteria to solve a problem before the problem is understood, or of deciding on a solution before everyone has had a chance to suggest possible criteria. Summarize the main points at each step—for example, "We seem to have agreed that our three main criteria are . . ." These summaries should state the consensus of the group at each step in the discussion. If there is a significant difference of opinion among the discussants and it isn't feasible to include all points of view as you move into the next part of the discussion, at least record the minority point of view fairly and then proceed with the majority view. In most cases, however, the minority viewpoints can be included right until the final decision. For example, even if only one or two people consider a criterion important whereas all the rest of the discussants consider it trivial, the criterion can still be included.

3. Draw useful contributions from all participants A successful leader gets each participant to provide the best information and ideas that she or he is capable of providing. Useful contributions from discussants include remarks that make other participants more actively cooperative, that reduce tension, and that help to focus the group's thinking on its purpose, so the successful leader will also encourage some of these supportive remarks as well as information and ideas.

People's inclinations to talk are not always in direct ratio to the value of what they have to say. Thus the leader often has to encourage some participants and restrain others.

You encourage a participant by respecting his ideas or knowledge. Be especially aware of those who are not participating because of a lack of confidence. Ask them to comment on a point at issue. "What would you add to our analysis of the problem?" "Which of these criteria seem most important to you?" If you know the group member has done some special research, ask him for information at that point in the discussion. You may discover that some of the quieter members have a great deal to contribute as they become more involved and confident. (You may also discover that some are better left undisturbed because they are apathetic and unprepared.) As you are about to conclude each main block in the agenda, give the group a final chance to comment: "I think we have our criteria pretty well in mind, as I've listed them. Are there any final additions or other comments?"

As leader, you may have to exercise some control over participants who become domineering, irrelevant, repetitious, or hostile. Such participants can waste time, discourage other participants, and lead the group to faulty decisions. For the domineering participant, try to draw out others in response: "Let's hear what some of the rest of you think about Mary's point. How about you, Fred?" Especially, try to draw out other participants who may have information or opinions at odds with the dominant participant. To reduce inefficient and irrelevant discussion, you can remind participants of the need to keep moving toward the group's goal. You can discourage digressive discussion: "That line of thought is interesting, but I think it is getting us off the point." Hostility and tension may be reduced by reminding participants of the larger perspective of the group's goals: Some of us understandably feel strongly about that point, but we will all lose if we can't come to some kind of agreement here."

If the group needs to arrive at a decision but has serious differences of opinion and exchanges are tending to become heated, or if some discussants tend to go off on tangents, your control has to be tighter. You exercise tighter control when each person has to be recognized by you as chairperson so you can control who talks and who doesn't, and when you more frequently direct questions to specific members of the group. Unless such tight control is necessary to keep the group moving cohesively toward a necessary goal, it should probably be avoided. Less formality tends to encourage friendly, open, spontaneous exchanges. However, even the firmest leader can be objective and courteous and can convey the sense that whatever she does is done to help the group achieve its aims: "We aren't going to finish our job today unless we stick to the point and speak one at a time. You have the floor first, Tom."

4. End the discussion with a sense of your task completed.   End each discussion session with a summary of main points decided on and with a sense of positive accomplishment. If this session is your group's final connection with the topic, emphasize the goals achieved and thank the participants. Be sure your summary of the main points of decision accurately reflects the group's thinking.

Your group may still have some connection with the topic. If your group is responsible for seeing some action taken on the decision, be sure the necessary tasks have been clearly and specifically assigned and accepted by the discussants and some plan for follow-up has been made. If you are to discuss the topic further in another session, focus on where you are now in your agenda and what is to be done in the next session.

Discussion leaders in businesses and other organizations often have to write up a report: a summary of the problem, the criteria, perhaps the alternate solutions considered, the final decision and justification for that decision, and possibly plans for implementing the decision. This report may be circulated to the participants for their final comments or for them to keep as a record of the proceedings, and a final version of the report will often be required by a higher-level administrator. For training, your instructor may expect you to write such a final report.

Public Group Discussions

We now turn to speaking in groups primarily for an audience. The first sort tends to be a discussion with an audience looking on. The second sort, a symposium, is more explicitly addressed to the audience.

Panel Discussions

A panel discussion resembles a private group discussion except that it is held before a radio, television, or physically present audience. A participant in a panel discussion, although he or she responds directly to other participants, is actually trying to inform or persuade the listening audience;

Each participant in a panel discussion is speaking to the audience as well as the other members of the panel. (Gale Zucker)

thus the effective panelist keeps in mind that her target audience is "out there" rather than across the table from her. An audience question period, if used at all, is usually a minor part of the proceedings.

The panel may be primarily cooperative, in the sense that the members are experts sharing various sorts of information with listeners who have a special interest in the topic. More commonly, panels are at least mildly adversarial, and it is the pointed but tactful interplay of opposing points of view that makes the panel interesting fun as well as informative for the listeners.

The panel is usually managed by a moderator who is genuinely neutral on the topic. The moderator's job is to introduce the topic and the panelists, maintain some degree of order, and see that the time is divided fairly among the panelists. A skillful moderator can also do much to avoid the chaotic, rambling, sometimes redundant structure that is perhaps the chief drawback in panel discussions. By adapting the five-step process described earlier, the moderator can provide at least a basic sequence of separate points through which the panel can progress. For a panel on air pollution, for example, the moderator might guide the participants through the following three general questions (and he might also let the panelists know in advance of his plan, so they could prepare accordingly):

1. How serious is air pollution in this community?
2. What criteria seem most important in coping with air pollution?
3. What are some possible solutions for local air pollution?

Symposiums

In a typical symposium, each of the two to four speakers presents a short speech to the audience, and after the short speeches the speakers answer questions from the audience and may also comment on one another's remarks. The initial round of set speeches gets the proceedings off to a more coherent start than is usually the case with a panel discussion, and the audience question period involves the listeners actively rather than as merely passive spectators. With a diversified group of effective speakers and ample time for interaction among audience and speakers, a symposium before a live audience can be an exciting event. Long-winded opening speeches, however, can make it boring, so each speaker should present his or her position crisply and within the agreed time limit. This requires careful advance preparation, just as for any other speech.

As with a panel discussion, the symposium is presided over by a neutral moderator who introduces the topic and speakers. (See Chapter 11 for suggestions on making such introductions.) In addition, the moderator tries to preserve a friendly atmosphere, often is responsible for directing audience questions to particular speakers, may involve less active speakers by asking them to comment on replies by other speakers, and tactfully interrupts excessively long-winded questions from the audience or replies from the speakers. A well-prepared moderator will have ready a few questions to get the ball rolling if the audience doesn't immediately have questions for the speakers.

Cooperative symposiums may provide background information on a controversial topic or may simply provide useful information to the audience. Each speaker should be responsible for a separate aspect of the topic, and the moderator or other organizer of the symposium should make that division of labor clear when the event is organized days or weeks before it takes place. For example, four speakers might be brought together to explain to a parent-teacher association the implications of a bill in the state legislature to change the required high school curriculum: a member of the state education board would explain the conditions that had brought about pressure to change the curriculum; a state legislative aide would explain the provisions in the bill; two local school administrators would explain likely effects of the bill on academics and on extracurricular activities. A symposium orienting new college students to extracurricular opportunities on campus might have separate speakers on intramural sports, student government, publications, and speech and drama competitions.

Adversarial symposiums are intended to contrast two or more opposing viewpoints on a controversial topic. In a symposium on how to increase state revenues, for example, one speaker might advocate a state income tax, another an increase in sales tax, and a third raising fees on various licenses and permits. Normally, speakers for the symposium are selected on the basis of their known varied positions on the topic. In more artificial situations, such as a classroom exercise, the symposium organizer may have to assign each speaker a position.

Summary

People deliberate together in groups to profit from and build on each other's thinking, to resolve conflicting viewpoints, and to increase acceptance of final decisions. Groups may confer privately to reach decisions, or they may present material publicly to help audiences be better informed in decision making. Effective group discussions are usually purposeful, cohesive, and realistic.

The process of deciding on a policy to solve a problem can be divided into five steps: (1) analyzing the problem; (2) deciding on criteria; (3) setting forth possible solutions; (4) selecting one solution as the best policy; (5) planning to implement and test the solution.

An effective participant in a private group discussion prepares by analyzing the situation and determining his purpose, by gathering ideas and materials, and by considering his own characteristics and the characteristics of the other participants to which he should adapt. During the discussion he listens fully and fairly to other participants, thinks about the goals of the group as well as the contributions made by others and himself, and speaks efficiently and reasonably when making contributions to the discussion.

An effective leader of a private group discussion prepares by determining the aims of the discussion, selecting participants, planning an agenda, arranging physical facilities, and gaining some knowledge of the topic. During the discussion she starts the group in a friendly and purposeful mood, keeps the discussion moving toward its goal, draws useful contributions from all participants, and ends the discussion with a sense of completion and with arrangements made for any necessary follow-up matters.

Public discussions may be in the form of a panel of experts simply discussing a topic among themselves in front of an audience. More coherent presentation of alternative viewpoints and greater audience involvement is, however, likely with a symposium: set speeches followed by audience questioning and interaction among participants. Public presentations may merely provide information on various aspects of the topic, or they may have a more adversarial tone emphasizing differing viewpoints on the topic.

Exercises

1. Bring to class a specific purpose question that would be suitable for a policy-making discussion in class. Areas in which to locate purpose questions include these: issues of personal attitudes and behavior, campus issues, local and state issues, and national and international issues. The purpose questions may be simply listed; or if time permits, some may be evaluated and modified. They provide a bank of topics for exercises 2 and 3.

2. As a class, carry a cooperative group discussion through the five-step process described in this chapter.

3. As a class, divide into four groups, each of which will discuss a different purpose question selected by the group in advance. Each group may use a private discussion or a symposium format which may be predominantly cooperative or adversarial.

Sources for Further Reading

The purpose of the following annotated bibliography is to introduce a cross section of major works by people who have contributed significantly to the body of theory on which textbooks such as *Speaking Effectively* are based.

These eleven sources are placed in three fairly distinct groups. The first three are from the classical period in Greece and Rome during which persuasive public speaking was a subject of great interest. The next five are modern sources that continue the classical emphasis on persuasion but usually extend it to media and modes in addition to public speaking. The final three sources reject the emphasis on persuasion in favor of an emphasis on understanding how language can be used to improve accuracy in communication and decision making.

1. Aristotle, *The Rhetoric of Aristotle*. Translated and edited by Lane Cooper. Englewood Cliffs, N.J.: Prentice-Hall, 1960. Aristotle's *Rhetoric*, written about 330 B.C., was intended as a complete, systematic, and psychologically valid theory of persuasive public speaking. It is probably the most influential single work in the history of communication theory: its various concepts and sets of categories can still be found in modern books on composition, persuasion, and public speaking.

2. *Rhetorica ad Herennium* (ascribed, probably erroneously, to Cicero). Translated by Harry Caplan. Cambridge, Mass.: Harvard University Press, 1954. This tightly organized handbook for the persuader, primarily in the law courts, was written about 80 B.C. Though lacking the theoretical or ethical perspective of other major classical works, it provides detailed, often useful advice on each skill and step involved in putting a persuasive speech together.

3. Cicero, *De Oratore* (in *Cicero on Oratory and Orators*). Translated and edited by J. S. Watson. Carbondale: Southern Illinois University Press, 1970. Although drawing considerably on Aristotelian theory, *De Oratore*, written in 55 B.C., is thoroughly infused with practical insight gained from Cicero's great knowledge of other orators and his own experience as one of the most successful speakers of all time. Cicero's themes of qualities of an orator and preparation for a speaking career are interwoven with more direct blocks of theory in a dialogue format.

4. Burke, Kenneth, *A Rhetoric of Motives*. New York: Prentice-Hall, 1952. (Reissued by The University of California Press, 1969.) Burke brings an almost overwhelming range of ideas, materials, and unusual perspectives to bear on how a person influences others—or himself. His concerns extend to all forms of verbal communication, and sometimes even beyond language as a medium.

5. Toulmin, Stephen, *The Uses of Argument*. London and New York: The Cambridge University Press, 1958. Although best known for the "Toulmin model" for schematizing deductive argument, Toulmin covers a broader range of matters on the use of logical reasoning in decision making. Because his focus is on the reasoning process itself, his book is relevant for both the persuader and the evaluator of persuasion.

6. Perelman, Chaim, and Olbrechts-Tyteca, L., *The New Rhetoric: A Treatise on Argumentation*. Translated by John Wilkinson and Purcell Weaver. Notre Dame, Ind. and London: University of Notre Dame Press, 1969. (Originally published in France in 1958.) These authors provide a thorough and carefully structured treatment of the means, primarily through logical appeals, for gaining a listener's or reader's agreement to proffered propositions. Their insights frequently go beyond the sources in classical rhetoric on which the book is largely based.

7. Weaver, Richard M., "Language is Sermonic." *Language Is Sermonic: Richard M. Weaver on the Nature of Rhetoric*, 201–225. Edited by Richard L. Johannesen, Rennard Strickland, and Ralph T. Ewbanks. Baton Rouge: Louisiana State University Press, 1970. (Originally given as a public lecture at the University of Oklahoma in 1962.) Weaver established an ethical basis for persuasive speaking which stimulates the emotions as well as the reason, and he provides an overview of techniques for such appeals to the whole person.

8. Bitzer, Lloyd, "The Rhetorical Situation." *Philosophy & Rhetoric* I (January 1968), 1–14. Bitzer defined the rhetorically effective speech as a "fitting response" to the situation which called it forth. His analysis of situation primarily in terms of occasion, rather than audience or speaker, encouraged an expanded view of adaptation of speech to situation.

9. Richards, I. A., *The Philosophy of Rhetoric*. New York: Oxford University Press, 1965. (Originally given as a series of six lectures at Bryn Mawr College in 1936.) Richards urged that rhetoric "should be a study of misunderstanding and its remedies." His focus is on how words acquire meaning for each person and how they operate in various sorts of verbal and psychological contexts to convey multidimensional meaning from mind to mind.

10. Berlo, David K., *The Process of Communication*. New York: Holt, Rinehart, & Winston, 1960. Berlo provides a practical description of the communication process and extends this explanation into several related matters, such as the ways in which social systems operate as communication networks.

11. Hayakawa, S. I., *Language in Thought and Action*, 4th ed. San Diego: Harcourt Brace Jovanovich, 1978. This book deals with ways in which the use, or misuse, of words influences our communication, primarily as receivers, and our thinking. Hayakawa's book is practical, readable, and often entertaining.

Aristotle's *Rhetoric* and Cicero's *De Oratore* are also printed in various other translations and editions. The *Rhetoric*, for example, is in the Random House Modern Library series. *De Oratore* is in the Harvard University Press Loeb Classical Library series. The essays by Bitzer and Weaver are also each reprinted in other collections. Both, for example, are in *Contemporary Theories of Rhetoric: Selected Readings*, edited by Richard L. Johannesen; New York: Harper & Row, 1971.

Sample Speeches

Individual Rights and the American Revolution
Robert Webking

For many informative speeches, the most important qualities are clarity and adaptation to the immediate audience. Credibility of the speaker is largely assumed, and interest, while important, is secondary. The following speech by Dr. Robert Webking, associate professor of Political Science and director of the Academic Advising Center at the University of Texas at El Paso, is such an informative speech. For his audience Professor Webking's credibility was established by his extensive writings on the founding of the American government and by his having received the student award for teacher of the year three consecutive times and in 1985 the faculty Award for Distinguished Achievement in Teaching. This version of a lecture to a freshman class in American government is used as an exercise for note taking in the University Study Skills Center.

Structure, supporting material, and a direct oral style are used to increase clarity to the immediate audience. Note, in structure, the distinct introduction and statement of focus, partition of the body into four main sections, use of transitions, and summary conclusion. Note also the efficient, informal use of a range of supporting materials from definition to hypothetical examples. Personal pronouns, short key sentences, parallelism, rhetorical questions, and restatement create a sense of direct contact with the audience. The speech is reprinted with permission from Robert Webking.

1 To understand the founding principles of American politics, we begin with the document most closely associated with the creation of the United States' political regime. That's the Declaration of Independence, the document which, in 1776, the Americans used to separate themselves from Great Britain and to establish themselves as a separate political community.

2 The Declaration, to be sure, is primarily a revolutionary document.

That is, it is explaining why the Americans believed it just for them to revolt from the British Government and to set up their own government. It is not a document like the Constitution that actually creates a new government, but what it does do in explaining the justice of revolution is to explain the principles that would have to lie behind any good political regime.

3   The Declaration of Independence is divided into three more or less distinct parts. First there is a relatively short part, the statement of political principles. The second and longest part is the list of grievances against King George III. The third part is the part for which the Declaration was actually written at that time. It is the final and formal statement that the United States are and ought to be separate from Great Britain.

4   What interests us today is that first part, the theoretical part. We want to know about the principles that justify revolution, and therefore the principles that any good government will have to live up to. This part is very well known. In it Jefferson speaks of something he calls self-evident truths. A self-evident truth is not exactly something that is obvious; it is not exactly something that everybody automatically agrees to. It is something that any reasonable person who is not biased and who understands the language will see as valid.

5   Jefferson says that politics and political practice need to be based upon four self-evident truths. First he says that "all men are created equal." The first self-evident truth is equality. We need to pause and consider in what sense it is, in fact, self-evidently true that human beings are equal.

6   If you look around at a bunch of human beings, what are obvious are differences—differences in height, differences in weight, differences in intellectual ability, in wealth, in gender, in coloring. Some of those differences are important. Some are less important. But what is clear, at least what seems to be clear at first, is that there are differences among human beings. Yet Jefferson is saying that there is an important sense in which all human beings are equal, not "ought to be" equal but "are."

7   Well, what is that sense? If you think about it, there is only one way in which you can say it is self-evident that all human beings are the same, that they are all equal. That one way is very basic and very simple. Human beings are equal in the simple fact that they are all human beings.

8   Why is that important? Because of the fact that all human beings are fundamentally the same, it is not at all obvious that any human being has the right to rule another human being or that any human being is obliged to obey another human being. No one can just assume, for example, that there is such a thing as a legitimate king or that anyone would have to obey a king.

9   So this first self-evident truth, that all human beings are equal, establishes the fact that it is not obvious that any human being has the right to rule another. Indeed this equality becomes apparent in the second

self-evident truth as well. Jefferson writes, secondly, that all people are "endowed by their creator with certain unalienable rights and that among these are life, liberty, and the pursuit of happiness."

10   Now we are getting some specific information about the ways in which human beings are equal. They are equal in the possession of certain unalienable rights. We have to understand this concept of rights. We talk about our rights, we assert our rights, we criticize other people for violating our rights, but it's worthwhile to pause for a minute and to think about just what it is we mean when we say that human beings have rights. The concept of individual rights is a moral concept. It has to do with what is correct and incorrect, what is just and unjust, what is allowable and what is not allowable in human conduct. A related concept, and yet in some ways an opposite concept, is the moral concept of duty. If you have a duty to obey your parents it means it is right for you to obey your parents and that it is wrong if you don't obey your parents. The concept of rights is similar in the sense that it is a moral concept having to do with what it is human beings ought to do and ought not to do. But it is different in the sense that it does not constrain human beings to do certain things as duties do, instead it frees human beings.

11   To be more specific, when I say that someone has a right to life, what it means is this, that someone may do whatever he or she thinks necessary to secure his or her life. There are no limits here. You are the judge of what it takes to secure and defend your right, and you may do absolutely whatever you think essential to do that. That's what a right is. It is moral permission to act in any way whatever for whatever it is that you have the right to.

12   An unalienable right, which is what Jefferson speaks of in the Declaration, cannot be taken away from a human being. It cannot be given away by a human being. Jefferson is saying everywhere you see a human being you are seeing a creature with a right to life, a right to liberty, and a right to pursue happiness. These rights can be violated, and frequently are violated by governments. That's part of the point in the Declaration of Independence. But these rights can't be taken away and can't be given away.

13   So, human beings have these rights to life, to liberty, and to pursue happiness. And concepts of rights say quite simply that human beings may do whatever they think necessary to reach these goals.

14   If we were still in a state where there were no government, and no laws governing our behavior, only this concept of rights, and if I believed that in order to pursue happiness what I needed was a Porsche and you had a Porsche, it would be absolutely morally permissible for me to kill you, steal your keys, and take your Porsche, because in doing so I would be satisfying my right to pursue happiness. I would be violating your right to life but there is nothing that says I can't do that until we establish a law that says I can't do that. So to say that human beings have rights is

not at all to say that human beings' rights are secure. Indeed the mere concept of rights leads to a circumstance where human life would be very unpleasant. All human beings trying to secure their lives and their liberty, trying to pursue happiness, would desire the same thing, would get in one another's way, and would be likely to harm or kill each other. So that without government, human beings' rights, while they exist, would be constantly violated, continually insecure.

15 That's why governments are created. Indeed Jefferson says in the next phrase of the Declaration of Independence, "to secure these rights governments are instituted among men." Perhaps for our purposes this is the key concept because in this phrase Jefferson says in very plain language what it is that government is all about. Government exists to secure individual rights. There is no other reason, no more sophisticated reason. How do people create government?

16 He indicates that in the next self-evident truth. He says "to secure these rights, governments are instituted among men, deriving their just powers from the consent of the govern."

17 Consent is a third self-evident truth for Jefferson. All just governments, all legitimate governments, all governments that individuals are actually obliged to obey, are created by consent. If you think about it, it makes sense. If it is true that all human beings have the right to liberty, then it follows that no one can be morally obliged to obey another person unless he or she first agrees to obey that other person. So the only way that a government can justly demand obedience of people is if those people have in the first place agreed to obey the government. That is why governments must derive their just power from consent. Now why would people consent to be governed when according to nature they don't have to?

18 We have already seen that people consent to be governed because without government, without the power of government and law, individual rights are insecure. Everyone pursuing his or her own rights leads us to a circumstance where no one's rights are secure unless there are some rules that everyone is obeying. Those rules are created by government. People consent to be governed in order to be able to secure their rights more effectively then they would be able to without government. It's a calculation people make. The idea is something like this: I agree not to murder other people so long as other people agree not to murder me. Now without making that agreement, I have the perfect right to murder other people if I think it will help me secure my life or my liberty or pursue happiness. But the fact of the matter is, I'm going to realize that my life will be more secure with this agreement and with the government enforcing it than my life would be without this agreement and without the government enforcing it. Look at it as a bargain that one makes with fellow citizens and with the law. You say to the laws, "look I'll agree to abide by your rules; I'll obey the law, so long as you secure my rights."

It's a contract. This contract leads to security of individuals' rights, and it also requires that governments at times begin to violate individual rights.

19   A government violates individual rights when it arrests people who commit crimes and puts them in jail. That's violating people's right to liberty. Government violates individual rights certainly when it executes people for crimes such as murder. That's violating people's right to life. Yet government may do that when individuals have violated the contract. Government is obligated to protect my rights only so long as I keep my side of the agreement, which is to obey the law. When I stop obeying the law, government is perfectly free to stop securing my rights. Indeed if someone out there disobeys the law, government is obliged, in order to secure everybody else's rights, to arrest and punish that person. That is how government secures my rights from invasion by that criminal. So people consent to be governed in order to secure their rights. The government is there in order to enforce the contract that people make with one another to limit their behavior so as to allow everyone's rights to be more secure.

20   The Declaration of Independence has a certain reputation, one we learned of in grade school, of being a great statement in favor of democratic government. The democratic part is when Jefferson says that legitimate governments derive their authority from consent. But it's important to realize just what this democratic part is saying. It says that governments must be created in a democratic way, it does not say that they must operate in a democratic way. The Declaration of Independence is very interesting on this point. It does not have much to say about how governments should go about doing what they do in order to be good. It's much more concerned with purposes. It does not say that in order to be good a government must be a democracy in form. What it does say is that in order to be good, a government must secure individual rights and it must be created by consent.

21   Thus, logically according to the Declaration of Independence, it is entirely possible to have a just and good monarchy. This would be a monarchy that was created by consent and one that operated to secure individual rights. Indeed, the Americans believed that until about ten years before the Declaration of Independence was written they had lived under a just monarchy, one that had been created by consent. They understood that consent to have happened in Great Britain in 1688. What they had to prove in the Declaration of Independence then was not simply that they were revolting because they lived under a monarchy and monarchies are bad, they had to prove that they could revolt because they were living under an unjust monarchy, one that was failing to secure individual rights. That's why there is that long middle section in which Jefferson lists particular grievances against King George III. He has to show the various ways in which this monarch is failing to secure individual rights and is in fact violating individual rights. So the Declaration of

Independence leaves open the possibility that there could be a just monarchy.

22   It's also important to note that the Declaration of Independence leaves open the possibility that there could be an unjust democracy. Governments are not to be judged on the basis of whether they are democratic or not, they are to be judged on the basis of whether they secure individual rights or not. There's nothing magical about majority rule. Indeed it's very likely that fifty-one percent of the people could rule in such a way as to secure their own interests at the expense of minority rights, and Jefferson's logic in the Declaration of Independence would say that is an unjust government. So the Declaration of Independence is a democratic document in the sense that it says government must secure everyone's rights, but it is not a democratic document in the sense that it would say that all just governments are democracies.

23   That brings us to the fourth self-evident truth. This one simply says that if a government fails to secure people's rights, if it is not created by consent, then obviously people don't have to obey it. People may disobey, people may revolt, people may create new governments for themselves. That is the legal point being made in the Declaration of Independence.

24   Here are the principles of government that we have: equality as humans, inalienable rights, government established by consent of the governed to secure those rights, and the right to overthrow a government which fails to secure the rights of the governed. In 1776 Jefferson is saying that King George III of Great Britain is failing to secure individual rights effectively. Therefore we, as formally citizens of the British government, may rebel against that government because it is failing to live up to proper principles.

The Resources War
Harry M. Conger

This speech was delivered to the Town Hall of California, Los Angeles, California, on September 5, 1985. Mr. Conger is chairman, president, and chief executive officer of the Homestake Mining Company. The speaker faced two significant challenges if this persuasive speech was to be effective. First, he had to arouse concern for his topic in an audience that was probably unconcerned and neutral. Second, he had to overcome likely listeners' obstacles to him as a biased source. To meet these challenges, the speaker skillfully used a problem-solution pattern, delaying his four-part proposition until he had shown how a serious problem threatened his listeners' interests. Note also how, when moving from the general nature of the problem to those aspects with which he could be personally identified (paragraphs 17 through 19), the speaker explicitly develops his personal credibility: "I am not a lobbyist. . . . But as a miner, . . ."

In addition to analyzing the speech as a model of problem-solution structural

strategy, you might consider how Mr. Conger develops threats to listeners'
interests, provides evidence and other supporting materials, and uses a recurring
metaphor to make his central idea memorable. The speech is reprinted with
permission from Vital Speeches of the Day *(December 1, 1985).*

1 I'm here today to talk on the subject of the resources war. It is a
"war" that cannot be won unless it is waged. It must be waged if our
nation is to remain a first-rate economic and military power. Unfortunately,
the stakes are high and yet most Americans are not tuned into the problem.

2 I would like to discuss the problems we face as well as some
solutions.

3 Throughout our nation's two hundred year history, we Americans
have optimistically viewed our spacious territory as the "land of plenty."
Indeed, America possesses lands of awesome beauty and splendor.
Generation after generation of Americans have come to believe that the
land would give forth endless resources on a road of endless prosperity.

4 Only in the 1970s, however, did we suddenly come face to face with
the realization that our natural bounty is finite. The Arab oil embargoes
made this painfully clear. As a nation, we struggled to cope with the first
days of our dependence on others for vital resources. Riding in a taxi
yesterday, I heard a good ol' country song that reminded me of this
problem. The fellow sang, "Have we seen the best of the free life? Are
the good times really over for good?"

5 Of course, I don't believe they are and neither do you. But the
problem of our dependence on foreign imports of resources may be
reaching a crisis point. Oil is only the surface of our increasing minerals
dependence.

6 The economic handicaps of such dependence on foreign imports
have had a telling impact on our daily lives. But what does it bode for our
nation's security? Is our nation's destiny falling into hands other than our
own? How safe is America as she enters the eighties?

7 The salient truth is that she may not be safe for long. More and
more we rely on foreign sources of supply for strategic raw materials vital
to our defense industries. In response to this growing crisis, I wish to
urge upon you the need for a "new realism." No American should ignore
the importance of mining and minerals to our nation's security.

8 Since the end of World War II, we have been locked in fierce
competition with the Soviet Union for sources of strategic minerals. This
competition is often referred to as the "resources war." It is waged by
proxy in the jungles of South America, the deserts of Africa and the
Middle East, and now in the cold of the Arctic poles. In the future it may
even be waged on the moon.

9 In terms of minerals self-sufficiency, the U.S. and the Soviet Union
are poles apart, no pun intended. Halfway through the eighties, we find

that we are more than 50 percent dependent on foreign sources for at least 19 strategic minerals. In contrast, the Soviet Union is only dependent on imports for two commodities: fluorspar and barite.

10 This minerals imbalance gives the resources war a peculiar and certainly dangerous twist: not only do the Soviets want to keep us at a disadvantage, but they also want to disrupt or even block our sources of raw materials. We hold no such leverage over them.

11 The resources war is a war that is joined everyday. It is waged even as we gather here. If for instance, the central African nation of Zaire were to suddenly fall into the hands of a Soviet backed communist government, what would come of our heavy dependence on her for supplies of cobalt and chromium, to name a few?

12 Our reliance on Zaire for these two minerals provides a vivid example of what is at stake in the resources war. Cobalt and chromium may not be the best-known minerals, but it may surprise you to learn that without them, we couldn't fly an F-16 or F-15. They are vital to the production of jet-fighter engines.

13 Given the strategic importance of cobalt and chromium, I doubt that many Americans would question the importance of a friendly Zaire to our nation's security. The Soviets have certainly understood this. That explains why they have attempted time and again, through the use of neighboring surrogates, to undermine the stability of Zaire. It is a dangerous ploy, for everybody involved.

14 This is but one example of how the resources war is waged. It amply reveals the stakes involved. In almost every case, the players and situation are similar. We find ourselves at the severe disadvantage of being dependent on unstable, lesser-developed nations for much of our supplies of vital resources.

15 The resources war is the "stuff" of survival in a world that is still not safe for democracy and freedom-loving peoples. With each loss of a valuable trading partner and ally to Soviet or unfriendly control, our nation's security and economic well-being are dealt a tremendous blow. That goes for the entire free world as well.

16 This is a struggle that simply cannot go ignored by opinion leaders such as you.

17 Perhaps by now you may be wondering what my purpose is for telling you about the resources war. Let me assure you that I am not a lobbyist blowing a siren because our industry profits are down. No, the resources war is something that concerns us all.

18 Admittedly, I am not a defense expert. I cannot pretend to know everything about how America can best secure her foreign supplies of strategic raw materials.

19 But as a miner, I can tell you that we have been fighting the resources war with one hand tied behind our back. Despite the stakes

involved, we have seriously neglected our domestic mining industry over the years. The mining industry is on the edge of crisis and ruin. It's almost as if we have brought the resources war on ourselves.

20 The serious nature of this struggle requires that we take a more conscious, comprehensive look at the importance of mining. How much longer can we ignore the strategic and economic penalties in not having a healthy mining industry at home?

21 What are the problems facing mining? How and why did one of our hands get tied behind our back? How can we free that hand and bring mining back in this country? What can we do to ease our dependence on imports and thus lower the stakes of the resources war?

22 First, let me cover the problems we face:

23 Problem number one: over-regulation. Over the years mining has acquired the image of being dirty, environmentally destructive and a nuisance. To correct the excesses of mining, conservationists sought more and more government regulation of the industry. This has led to a situation in which mining is now suffocated by excess regulation. We went from one extreme to the other. The regulatory regime is so burdensome that minerals extraction and production have become anything but cost effective.

24 Problem number two: land use restrictions. Astounding as it may seem, two-thirds of our public lands are off limits to mining. Talk about handicaps! It's like the NFL telling the 49ers they can only use Joe Montana in four games a year. The U.S. mining industry is dying off because accessible ore deposits are running out and mines are closing down. Just a few weeks ago Kennecott closed its Utah copper mines. Few took notice of this event, despite the fact that it is the industry equivalent of GM shutting down its Chevrolet division!

25 Problem number three: production costs. When mineral-rich, near-the-surface ore deposits are used up, extractive mining companies must dig deeper. This requires technology-intensive extraction methods, which in turn require huge capital outlays. Thus production costs have risen in conjunction with the steady depletion of our richest known ore deposits.

26 Problem number four: foreign competition. Extraction and processing of resources is shifting to lesser-developed nations. In these countries, production costs are much lower. Ore deposits are "younger," closer to the surface and thus richer in mineral content. They are more easily extracted and processed. When these natural advantages are added to lower labor costs and governmental export subsidies, the cards become even more stacked against the U.S. mining industry. We also cannot overlook the negative effects of a strong dollar. How can we compete with cheap imports caused by an artificially high U.S. dollar? Despite the generally strong recovery, many mining companies are reeling from losses due to shrinking markets and depressed prices. Both conditions are aggravated by unfair foreign competition.

27   Obviously, I wasn't kidding when I said we are fighting the resources war with one hand tied behind our back. But there are solutions to the problems we now face. We must get down to the business of restoring proper strength to our mining industry, before it's too late. As part of a comprehensive effort toward revitalizing this all-important industry, we suggest the following four-point program.

28   First, we urge comprehensive and thoughtful implementation of the Mineral Policy Act of 1970 and the National Materials Mineral Policy, Research and Development Act of 1980. These administrative policies set forth the fundamental goals of mineral strength and reliability for America. They recognize the importance of mining to all other industrial production, particularly in defense.

29   Second, we seek more cost efficient tax policies. In the past couple of decades, fiscal policies have put a stranglehold on mining. The opposite should be happening. I, for one, could never understand why Uncle Sam would want to render American industries helpless in an increasingly competitive world market. We need to explore ways in which domestic tax policies could be used to help, not hurt, our industry compete more effectively with overseas producers. Depletion allowances should not be tampered with, so that domestic companies will have the extra capital needed for research and development of more cost-effective extraction methods. The goal should be removal of all handicaps.

30   Third, we urge that more public lands be released for exploration. Mining is not what it was. Today, multiple use of land is appropriate and can be conducted with proper regard for the environment. Where long-term use of a site is required, land reclamation and restoration will follow. So, I say, let's don't close off 66 percent of our land until we know what's beneath it. Who knows, there may be reserves of cobalt and chromium out there! In any case, what we need are policies that will bring about a proper balance between environmental concerns and minerals production.

31   Finally, more attention needs to be given to the national stockpile. The U.S. Congress recognized the importance of minerals to our national security when it authorized creation of a stockpile. That was in 1939. But since then, the effort to meet acceptable stockpile levels for certain strategic minerals has been half-hearted at best. Many people wrongly believe that minerals are like tap water. They think minerals can be turned on at random and in seemingly endless supplies. The reality is harsh. It takes years to find and get at most of our remaining ore deposits. In a crunch, our capacity for minerals production would not meet needs. The national stockpile, if correctly used, would alleviate the potential for shortages during a crisis period.

32   My friends, we simply cannot win the resources war unless we wage it. We cannot achieve realistic minerals self-sufficiency unless we untie the bonds that have handicapped mining in America for too long.

33   Our increasing dependence on foreign sources for strategic minerals

imperils our national security and threatens our prosperity at home. The resources war pits our survival as a free nation against the insatiable appetite of the Soviet Union for world domination through elimination of the U.S. as economic and military leader of the free world.

34   We can overcome our minerals malnutrition and win this war. But first, we must understand what the stakes are. We must realize that America cannot remain a first rate economic and military power if we have a second rate mining industry. And most important of all, we must never forget one elemental truth: "Our horn of plenty begins with a hole in the ground."

Keynote Address:
Democratic National Convention, 1976
Barbara Jordan

Just before midnight on July 12, 1976, U.S. Representative from Texas Barbara Jordan faced a weary convention audience in Madison Square Garden in New York City. This ten-minute speech electrified her audience, and she received a memorable ovation from delegates and media reporters. The speech gained greatly from the speaker's manifest sincerity and commanding presence in delivery and from her elevated ethical tone. Rather than attacking the Republican party, she appealed positively to the values and motives of all Americans, beginning with her interpretation of her important role at the national convention (as a woman and a black) as a positive sign for America.

Keynote speeches may be regarded as ceremonial speeches of praise. Often, however, it is more perceptive to regard such speeches, including this one, as the type of conflict reduction speech given to confirm unity. Note, for example, Ms. Jordan's emphasis of such common values as equality and national unity. What other appeals does she make to those areas of commonality discussed on page 249 of this book? Note also how the speaker personalizes and invigorates the political principles explained in Professor Webking's informative speech; see, for example, the last two paragraphs of her speech. The organization is subtle, appropriately so for the speech as ceremonial or confirming unity, but the structural strategy is discernible on close examination. The speech also abounds in those stylistic devices—ellipsis, parallelism, rhetorical questions, short climax sentences—that gain most from dramatically effective delivery. The speech is reprinted with permission from Barbara Jordan.

1   One hundred and forty-four years ago, members of the Democratic party first met in convention to select a presidential candidate. Since that time, Democrats have continued to convene once every four years and draft a party platform and nominate a presidential candidate. And our meeting this week is a continuation of that tradition.

2 But there is something different about tonight. There is something special about tonight. What is different? What is special? I, Barbara Jordan, am a keynote speaker.

3 A lot of years passed since 1832, and during that time it would have been most unusual for any national political party to ask that a Barbara Jordan deliver a keynote address . . . but tonight here I am. And I feel that notwithstanding the past that my presence here is one additional bit of evidence that the American Dream need not forever be deferred.

4 Now that I have this grand distinction what in the world am I supposed to say?

5 I could easily spend this time praising the accomplishments of this party and attacking the Republicans but I don't choose to do that.

6 I could list the many problems which Americans have. I could list the problems which cause people to feel cynical, angry, frustrated: problems which include lack of integrity in government; the feeling that the individual no longer counts; the reality of material and spiritual poverty; the feeling that the grand American experiment is failing or has failed. I could recite these problems and then I could sit down and offer no solutions. But I don't choose to do that either.

7 The citizens of America expect more. They deserve and they want more than a recital of problems.

8 We are a people in a quandary about the present. We are a people in search of our future. We are a people in search of a national community.

9 We are a people trying not only to solve the problems of the present: unemployment, inflation . . . but we are attempting on a larger scale to fulfill the promise of America. We are attempting to fulfill our national purpose: to create and sustain a society in which all of us are equal.

10 Throughout our history, when people have looked for new ways to solve their problems, and to uphold the principles of this nation, many times they have turned to political parties. They have often turned to the Democratic party.

11 What is it, what is it about the Democratic party that makes it the instrument that people use when they search for ways to shape their future? Well I believe the answer to that question lies in our concepts of governing. Our concept of government is derived from our view of people. It is a concept deeply rooted in a set of beliefs firmly etched in the national conscience of all of us.

12 Now what are these beliefs?

13 First, we believe in equality for all and privileges for none. This is a belief that each American regardless of background has equal standing in the public forum, all of us. Because we believe this idea so firmly, we are an inclusive rather than an exclusive party. Let everybody come.

14 I think it is no accident that most of those emigrating to America in the nineteenth century identified with the Democratic party. We are a heterogeneous party made up of Americans of diverse backgrounds.

15 We believe that the people are the source of all governmental power; that the authority of the people is to be extended, not restricted. This can be accomplished only by providing each citizen with every opportunity to participate in the management of the government. They must have that.

16 We believe that the government which represents the authority of all the people, not just one interest group, but all the people, has an obligation to actively underscore, actively seek to remove those obstacles which would block individual achievement . . . obstacles emanating from race, sex, economic condition. The government must seek to remove them.

17 We are a party of innovation. We do not reject our traditions, but we are willing to adapt to changing circumstances, when change we must. We are willing to suffer the discomfort of change in order to achieve a better future.

18 We have a positive vision of the future founded on the belief that the gap between the promise and reality of America can one day be finally closed. We believe that.

19 This, my friends, is the bedrock of our concept of government. This is a part of the reason why Americans have turned to the Democratic party. These are the foundations upon which a national community can be built.

20 Let's all understand that these guiding principles cannot be discarded for short-term political gains. They represent what this country is all about. They are indigenous to the American idea. And these are principles which are not negotiable.

21 In other times, I could stand here and give this kind of exposition on the beliefs of the Democratic party and that would be enough. But today that is not enough. People want more. That is not sufficient reason for the majority of the people of this country to vote Democratic. We have made mistakes. In our haste to do all things for all people, we did not foresee the full consequences of our actions. And when the people raised their voices, we didn't hear. But our deafness was only a temporary condition, and not an irreversible condition.

22 Even as I stand here and admit that we have made mistakes I still believe that as the people of America sit in judgment on each party, they will recognize that our mistakes were mistakes of the heart. They'll recognize that.

23 And now we must look to the future. Let us heed the voice of the people and recognize their common sense. If we do not, we not only blaspheme our political heritage, we ignore the common ties that bind all Americans.

24 Many fear the future. Many are distrustful of their leaders, and believe that their voices are never heard. Many seek only to satisfy their private work wants. To satisfy private interests.

25 But this is the great danger America faces. That we will cease to be

one nation and become instead a collection of interest groups; city against suburb, region against region, individual against individual. Each seeking to satisfy private wants.

26   If that happens, who then will speak for America?

27   Who then will speak for the common good?

28   This is the question which must be answered in 1976.

29   Are we to be one people bound together by common spirit sharing in a common endeavor or will we become a divided nation?

30   For all of its uncertainty, we cannot flee the future. We must not become the new puritans and reject our society. We must address and master the future together. It can be done if we restore the belief that we share a sense of national community, that we share a common national endeavor. It can be done.

31   There is no executive order; there is no law that can require the American people to form a national community. This we must do as individuals and if we do it as individuals, there is no President of the United States who can veto that decision.

32   As a first step, we must restore our belief in ourselves. We are a generous people so why can't we be generous with each other? We need to take to heart the words spoken by Thomas Jefferson: "Let us restore to social intercourse that harmony and that affection without which liberty and even life are but dreary things."

33   A nation is formed by the willingness of each of us to share in the responsibility for upholding the common good.

34   A government is invigorated when each of us is willing to participate in shaping the future of this nation.

35   In this election year we must define the common good and begin again to shape a common good and begin again to shape a common future. Let each person do his or her part. If one citizen is unwilling to participate, all of us are going to suffer. For the American idea, though it is shared by all of us, is realized in each one of us.

36   And now, what are those of us who are elected public officials supposed to do? We call ourselves public servants but I'll tell you this: we as public servants must set an example for the rest of the nation. It is hypocritical for the public officials to admonish and exhort the people to uphold the common good if we are derelict in upholding the common good. More is required of public officials than slogans and handshakes and press releases. More is required. We must hold ourselves strictly accountable. We must provide the people with a vision of the future.

37   If we promise as public officials, we must deliver. If we as public officials propose, we must produce. If we say to the American people it is time for you to be sacrificial, sacrifice. If the public official says that, we (public officials) must be the first to give. We must be. And again, if we make mistakes, we must be willing to admit them. We have to do that. What we have to do is strike a balance between the idea that government

should do everything and the idea, the belief, that government ought to do nothing. Strike a balance.

38 Let there be no illusions about the difficulty of forming this kind of national community. It's tough, difficult, not easy. But a spirit of harmony will survive in America only if each of us remembers that we share a common destiny. If each of us remembers when self-interest and bitterness seem to prevail, that we share a common destiny.

39 I have confidence that we can form this kind of national community.

40 I have confidence that the Democratic party can lead the way. I have that confidence. We cannot improve on the system of government handed down to us by the founders of the Republic, there is no way to improve upon that. But what we can do is to find new ways to implement that system and realize our destiny.

41 Now, I began this speech by commenting to you on the uniqueness of a Barbara Jordan making the keynote address. Well I am going to close my speech by quoting a Republican president and I ask you that as you listen to these words of Abraham Lincoln, relate them to the concept of a national community in which every last one of us participates: "As I would not be a slave, so I would not be a master."

42 This expresses my idea of democracy. Whatever differs from this, to the extent of the difference is no democracy.

Index